CHOOSING AN ELECTORAL SYSTEM

Copublished with the Eagleton Institute of Politics,
Rutgers University

CHOOSING AN ELECTORAL SYSTEM

Issues and Alternatives

Arend Lijphart
Bernard Grofman

American Political Parties and Elections

general editor:
Gerald M. Pomper

PRAEGER SPECIAL STUDIES • PRAEGER SCIENTIFIC

New York • Philadelphia • Eastbourne, UK
Toronto • Hong Kong • Tokyo • Sydney

Library of Congress Cataloging in Publication Data
Choosing an electoral system.

Bibliography: p.
Includes index.
1. Representative government and representation—
Addresses, essays, lectures. 2. Proportional repre-
sentation—Addresses, essays, lectures. 3. Elections—
Addresses, essays, lectures. I. Lijphart, Arend.
II. Grofman, Bernard. III. Title.
JF1051.C545 1984   324.6'3   84-18283
ISBN 0-03-069546-5   (alk. paper)

Published in 1984 by Praeger Publishers
CBS Educational and Professional Publishing,
a Division of CBS Inc.
521 Fifth Avenue, New York, NY 10175 USA

©1984 by Praeger Publishers

56789 052 98765432

Printed in the United States of America
on acid-free paper

Acknowledgments

The editors gratefully acknowledge the support that they have received from the German Marshall Fund of the United States and the National Science Foundation. The book was completed while Arend Lijphart was a German Marshall Fund Fellow (grant # 3-53531), and portions of the research were funded by the National Science Foundation NSF #SES 81-07554 to Bernard Grofman. All statements of fact and opinion in this volume are the exclusive responsibility of the editors and authors.

Contents

PART IV THE SINGLE TRANSFERABLE VOTE

PART V ADDITIONAL-MEMBER SYSTEMS

PART VI OTHER ALTERNATIVES

PART VII PROSPECTS FOR ELECTORAL REFORM

List of Tables and Figures

Tables

Figures

PART I
INTRODUCTION

1

Choosing an Electoral System

Arend Lijphart and Bernard Grofman

After several decades of indifference to electoral reform, the electoral system has again become a controversial question in many countries. Electoral laws are no longer regarded as unalterable facts, and there has been a renewed scholarly attention to the study of electoral systems. The aim of this book is to bring together in one volume, and in nontechnical form, all of the basic issues and all of the key alternatives for electoral choice, presented by scholars with widely varying electoral system preferences. We believe that *Choosing an Electoral System* is unique in that respect. The volume is not slanted for or against any particular system. The authors explore the factors that should be taken into consideration when political entities—from supranational organizations to local governments—choose their electoral systems, and the various alternatives from which choices can be made.

We sought out scholars from different countries—the United States, Canada, Great Britain, France, Italy, and Australia—who represent a great variety of perspectives and interpretations. We are expecially pleased that this volume includes new contributions by the four eminent scholars who were the main protagonists in the electoral systems debate of an earlier era: George H. Hallett, Jr., whose book *Proportional Representation* (coauthored with Clarence G. Hoag) was first published in 1926; Ferdinand A. Hermens, whose *Democracy or Anarchy?* appeared in 1941; Maurice Duverger, whose book *Political Parties* in its original French edition was published in 1951; and Enid Lakeman, whose book *Voting in Democracies* (coauthored with James D. Lambert), retitled *How Democracies Vote* in later editions, was first published in 1955. We have also tried to bridge a number of harmful gaps that have heretofore characterized the study of electoral systems: the almost complete divorce between students of comparative politics and social choice theorists, between political scientists and political

3

geographers, and between comparativists and students of American politics. William H. Riker, Steven J. Brams, and Peter C. Fishburn represent the axiomatic treatment of election systems typical of social choice theory (Chapters 10, 14, and 17); R. J. Johnston and Peter J. Taylor are political geographers rather than political scientists (Chapters 5 and 6); and Leon Weaver shows, in Chapter 19, that the United States is a rich mine of data which is too rarely tapped in the literature on comparative election systems.

CHOICES AND ALTERNATIVES

Plurality and list proportional representation (PR) systems account for most of the national electoral systems that are currently used. For instance, they are used for the national legislative elections (of the lower or only houses) in 17 of the 21 democracies that have been continuously democratic since approximately the end of the Second World War: the West European democracies plus the United States, Canada, Israel, Japan, Australia, and New Zealand. The four exceptions—countries that use neither list PR nor plurality systems—are France, Australia, Ireland, and Japan.

We believe that the debate over electoral choice has often been too narrowly and improperly defined—as a choice between plurality on the one hand and list PR on the other. Thus, in Part II of our book, we begin with a general discussion of competing values, including stability and proportionality—values which may be differentially satisfied by different electoral systems—and we devote Part III to the question of whether plurality and PR should be regarded as completely different and incompatible systems. Part IV deals with the single transferable vote (STV) as an alternative to both plurality and party list systems, and Part V is devoted to a survey of systems which aim at proportionality but use single-member district elections as one component of the electoral process. Part VI surveys methods, such as the limited vote, which are neither plurality nor strict PR. Finally, Part VII deals with the question of whether the recent electoral reforms in the United States and abroad, as well as the many proposals for reform, are the harbingers of major changes in electoral systems.

We have come to regard the dichotomy between PR and plurality as misleading for several reasons. First of all, the dividing line between majoritarian systems and nonmajoritarian systems (see Chapters 8 and 21 by Dieter Nohlen, Grofman 1975, and Grofman and Lijphart 1984) is more fundamental than that between plurality and PR. The plurality rule—also often referred to as the first-past-the-post or relative majority method—is only one of these majoritarian systems. The others are the double-ballot majority system, exemplified by contemporary France and discussed by Domenico Fisichella in Chapter 18, and the alternative vote or majority-preferential system, used in Australia and analyzed by J. F. H. Wright in Chapter 12.

Second, PR is not one electoral system but a general category that includes a great variety of systems. The two most important subtypes are list PR and the single transferable vote (STV), but these two methods differ fundamentally in their treatment of political party slates and in other aspects of their probable effect upon political competition.

Third, another legitimate dichotomous classification of electoral systems is to contrast the two basic methods of PR with all other systems. Richard Rose uses this dichotomy in Chapter 7. His non-PR category includes not only the plurality and majority systems but also the so-called semiproportional systems—the cumulative vote, limited vote, and the Japanese single nontransferable vote (SNTV)—methods which are discussed in Chapter 19 by Leon Weaver and in Chapter 20 by Arend Lijphart.

Fourth, there are substantial variations within the two basic subtypes of PR methods, and modifications (for instance, in district size and in threshold requirements for representation) can affect the extent to which any PR *method* satisfies the PR *principle* of providing proportionality between a group's vote share and its share of seats in the legislature. In general, the extent to which any election method, as embodied in practice, satisfies the PR *principle* is a matter of empirical investigation. For example, some plurality systems may, in practice, come closer to aggregate proportionality of result than some PR systems (see Chapter 5 by Peter J. Taylor and Chapter 7 by Richard Rose).

Fifth, plurality versus PR can be regarded as the principal contrast only with regard to legislative elections, or, more generally, elections of bodies with two or more members. When a single office, typically an executive office, has to be filled, all PR and semiproportional methods become irrelevant. The principal alternatives are now restricted to plurality, the double-ballot system, and the alternative vote—as well as the method of "approval voting" proposed by Steven J. Brams and Peter C. Fishburn (1983b) but not yet used for any significant election.

PLURALITY AND PROPORTIONAL REPRESENTATION: AN OVERVIEW

In the debate on election methods, two arguments predominate. The proponents of the plurality rule argue that its great advantage is that it produces firm government, or, in any case, that it is much more likely to do so than PR. Their line of reasoning is that the plurality method, by discriminating against small parties, encourages a two-party system, which in turn makes stable one-party government possible. Hermens and Duverger state this case forcefully and in detail in Chapters 2 and 3. The main argument of the PR advocates is that a democratic legislature should be representative of all of the interests and viewpoints of the electorate, and hence that the only proper form of representation is proportional representation. Enid Lakeman cogently presents this rationale in Chapter 4. She does not, of course, favor all forms of PR equally: she prefers PR to plurality, but within PR she prefers STV to list PR. This is also the basic conviction of Hallett and Wright who specifically address the issue of STV in Part IV. In general, strong PR advocates tend to be strongly in favor of the STV form of PR. It is ironic that list PR, which is the most common electoral system in Western democracies, does not have any enthusiastic champions. STV may be the theoretically optimal form of PR in the opinion of the academics, but, in practice, list PR is more attractive to established political parties and hence much more widely used.

It is important to note that the PR and plurality advocates are not in complete disagreement. In fact, they tend to concur on two points. First, with regard to the empirical consequences of PR methods and plurality, the two sides agree that PR methods are likely to lead to greater proportionality and plurality to stable one-party rule. Second, they do not dispute that both proportionality and firm government are desirable goals. Their disagreement concerns the *priority* of these values. To the partisans of the PR principle, strong government based on disproportional representation is illegitimate, just as a dictatorial government, however effective and benevolent, would be unacceptable. For those favoring plurality, effective government has the highest priority; after that, they are not opposed to proportionality per se. For instance, Hermens is willing to accept a number of adjustments to plurality in order to achieve greater proportionality—or, at least, to limit the degree of disproportionality—such as supplementary seats to make sure that the party with the most votes will also get the most seats and that the winning party will not be too much over-represented (Chapter 2). For Duverger, PR is a threat to stable government only when the executive is dependent on a legislative vote of confidence in a parliamentary system. This logic leads him to accept, and even favor, PR for the election of the U.S. House of Representatives and American state legislatures (Chapter 3). In Chapter 6, R. J. Johnston reaches a similar conclusion.

In recent years, the debate on whether strong one-party government or proportionality should be accorded a higher priority has become more complicated: the intrinsic merits of each of these goals are now under serious and increasing challenge. Especially in Britain, as Enid Lakeman observes in Chapter 4, there is growing concern that alternating one-party governments cause too many and too sharp reversals in policy—and hence result in weak instead of strong government when the effects of governmental actions are taken into consideration (see also Finer 1975). Conversely, as both Peter J. Taylor and Johnston argue in Chapters 5 and 6, while PR systems do provide a roughly proportional share of legislative seats for large and small parties alike, they often fail to provide a proportional share of governmental power. Small parties may be fairly represented in a parliament under PR, but they may be completely irrelevant and powerless when government coalitions are formed. On the other hand, they may be so fortunate as to hold the balance of power between much stronger parties—as is the case of the German Free Democrats—and, as a result, exert influence to a disproportionally high degree compared with their electoral support. PR clearly does not mean proportional power as measured by tenure in executive office, whereas the British plurality system, as Taylor shows in Chapter 5, has actually succeeded in achieving a high degree of proportional tenure over time.

Many other advantages and disadvantages of PR and plurality may be cited (see Mackenzie 1958, pp. 69–71). To the supporters of the plurality system, two further considerations are especially important: the close and clear contact that is established between the representative and his or her geographically defined constituency, and the unsurpassed simplicity of the voting method. Both of these advantages require that the plurality rule be applied in single-member districts, but this is almost universally the case in national-level elections. An additional advantage of PR is that it permits minority representation, not only for small parties but also, as the empirical evidence shows, of women as well as ethnic and cultural minorities. Moreover, PR can largely avoid the problem of gerrymandering, which is unavoidable under plurality. As Johnston points out, impartiality in the drawing of district boundaries is impossible (Chapter 6). The problem becomes less serious in multimember PR districts as the number of representatives per district increases; when there are about five or more members in a district, PR can be regarded as completely immune to gerrymandering.

A BRIDGEABLE GAP?

PR and plurality may be the main alternatives in choosing an electoral system, but the four chapters in Part III show that they are not clear and unambiguous alternatives. In Chapter 7, Rose shows that, when the actual degree of proportionality achieved by different electoral systems is examined, the difference between PR and non-PR systems is one of degree, not of kind. For instance, the most proportional plurality system, the United States, is even considerably more proportional than the least proportional PR system, Spain. Nohlen explains this discrepancy in Chapter 8 by drawing a distinction—which we believe to be a critical one—between the principles and the methods of proportionality and majority rule. In particular, in designing an electoral system, one may start out with a PR formula but then add several other rules—such as a relatively small district magnitude (the number of members elected in each district) and a high minimum threshold that parties have to surmount in order to gain any representation—that will yield a far from proportional result. Such a system follows PR methods but not the PR principle.

A specific example of the application of PR methods in order to achieve the principle of plurality is Rein Taagepera's original proposal to substitute two-member PR districts for single-member plurality districts (Chapter 9). His premise is the empirical proposition that PR formulas will yield less and less proportional results as the district magnitude decreases. A two-member district PR system could achieve the functional purpose of plurality even better than the plurality method itself. And it would avoid some of the disadvantages of the plurality method, such as its strong incentive to gerrymander and its strong disincentive to the emergence of a major new party even when the electorate is dissatisfied with both parties in a two-party system. In a similar vein, Hermens proposes three-member districts as an acceptable alternative to the usual plurality method in single-member districts (Chapter 2).

Rose's chapter also argues that the type of electoral system is relatively unimportant with regard to the formation and composition of governments. William H. Riker agrees with this conclusion and further maintains that there is not much difference between PR and plurality in two other respects: they both represent minorities fairly well, but neither can pass a rigorous test according to various other important democratic criteria (Chapter 10). Since both systems are equally unfair and inadequate, the crucial consideration for Riker is how to prevent necessarily unrepresentative governments from doing too much harm by means of constitutional and political restraints like separation of powers, decentralization, and multipartism.

STV AND ADDITIONAL-MEMBER SYSTEMS

When the choice of an electoral system is considered in the abstract, there is a virtually infinite number of possibilities from which electoral reformers can choose. However, when we look at concrete situations, the choice is much more limited in two respects. First, the pressures for electoral reform are much stronger in plurality than in PR systems. Changes from plurality to PR are therefore considerably more likely than changes from PR to plurality. As Hermens observes, "any national adoption of PR tends to be irreversible" (Chapter 2). Second, if current plurality systems will shift to PR, they are likely to adopt either STV or the additional-member system instead of other forms of PR. For this reason, Parts IV and V of this book pay special attention to these two systems.

The attractiveness of STV and the additional-member system as models for electoral reform is rather paradoxical, because they are both rare phenomena. The vast majority of the countries that use PR have list PR systems. STV is used at the national level only in Ireland, Malta, and Australia—and, in Australia, only for the less important upper house. The additional-member system was devised for the *Bundestag* elections in the Federal Republic of Germany, and has not been adopted by any other country so far. The explanation of the paradox is that STV and the additional-member system are PR methods with special features that make them attractive in countries with plurality traditions: they entail voting for individual candidates instead of, or—in the case of additional-member systems—in addition to party lists, and voting in relatively small districts. Wherever PR has been adopted at the subnational level in English-speaking countries—Northern Ireland, the Australian state of Tasmania, and local governments in the United States—it has invariably taken the form of STV (see Chapters 12, 19, and 22 by Wright, Weaver, and David E. Butler).

Part IV contains two chapters that are favorable to STV and two that are more critical of STV. Hallett has been a strong STV advocate since the 1920s, and he presents its case in detail in Chapter 11, starting with the controversial argument that the proportionality principle is clearly supported, if not mandated, by the United States Constitution as well as basic Supreme Court decisions. A special advantage of STV in the context of American politics is that it eliminates the need for party primaries. Wright evaluates the operation of STV in Australia in Chapter 12. Australia has been an especially interesting and active laboratory for experiments with preferential systems, both the alternative vote and STV—usually referred to in Australia as the majority-preferential and quota-preferential systems. According to Wright's analysis, the alternative vote has not been much of an improvement over plurality, but STV has performed well.

Richard S. Katz, and Brams and Fishburn subject STV to a critical examination in Chapters 13 and 14. Largely because STV is impractical in districts that elect many representatives, it cannot be as proportional as list PR with large district magnitudes or national supplementary seats. It would be an exaggeration, however, to deny that STV is a PR system. The fact that STV allows completely free intraparty choice to the voters is usually regarded as one of its main advantages, but it can also be considered a disadvantage because it weakens party cohesion and party responsibility just as direct primaries do. Moreover, STV can be shown to have a number of curious logical defects. Especially the fact that STV is not monotonic—i.e. that a candidate can be hurt instead of helped by receiving more higher preferences from the voters—is regarded as a fatal defect by its critics. The crucial question here, in our view, is how often such situations are likely to occur—a question to which we do not, as yet, have an answer.

Additional-member systems are examined in Part V. The German political scientist Max Kaase appraises its operation in his own country in Chapter 15. There is little doubt that the system has worked very well in most respects in West Germany, but, as Kaase cautions, this is due to several other factors in addition to the intrinsic merits of the additional-member system. One of its features that is sometimes praised—the voters' right to split their first and second votes—can actually be shown to be deceptive, since the second vote marks the decisive choice; it also contains the potential for serious abuse by two parties acting in collusion.

The additional-member model has attracted a great deal of interest, especially in Britain and Canada. William P. Irvine favors the application of the model to Canadian parliamentary elections, and he scrutinizes its probable effects, as well as the different forms that it could take, in Chapter 16. One of the objections that may be raised against the system is that it does not provide much incentive to parties to win the district seats since a proportional share of the seats is guaranteed by the additional seats. Brams and Fishburn focus on this problem in Chapter 17. They show that there may be circumstances under which it would be better for a party's overall representation if it deliberately fails to win any district seats. It is possible to draft a rule to prevent such a manipulative strategy, but this would necessarily have a negative effect on the proportionality of the election result.

OTHER ALTERNATIVES

In Part VI, several other alternatives to both PR and plurality are discussed. In the category of majoritarian systems, the alternative vote and the double-ballot system are the principal alternatives to plurality. The alternative vote, mainly used in Australia, has already been treated in Wright's analysis of the different Australian preferential systems (Chapter 12). The double-ballot majority system is examined by Fisichella in Chapter 18. It may be preferable to plurality in two respects. First, from the perspective of the democratic principle, it makes it more likely that an elected representative has the support of a clear majority instead of a mere plurality of his or her constituents. Second, from a practical point of view, it may be a potent weapon against antisystem parties; whereas the disproportionality of the plurality rule mainly hurts the smaller parties that are not regionally concentrated, the double-ballot system's disproportionality discriminates against extremist parties even when they are relatively large. As Fisichella cautions, however, a number of important conditions have to be fulfilled in order to achieve this result. Moreover, the double-ballot system (under the name majority runoff) has been used in the American South and Southwest as a tool to reduce the representation of racial and linguistic minorities.

The remaining alternatives to PR and plurality fall in the category of semi-proportional and "mixed" PR-plurality systems. The most important of these is the limited vote (including, as a special case of the limited vote, the single nontransferable vote or SNTV). In Chapter 19, Weaver examines the operation of the limited vote in American local government, and in Chapter 20 Lijphart examines its use in Japanese and Spanish national elections. Compared with the very limited American experience with STV and the cumulative vote, the limited vote has been used much more widely, although it has not attracted as much attention and has not been adequately studied. Its greater capacity for survival in American politics, as Weaver points out, should recommend it to American electoral reformers. Lijphart evaluates the limited vote as well as plurality systems with special provisions for minority representation as possible compromises between PR and plurality. The SNTV form of the limited vote has been used in Japan for a long time, and has a number of definite advantages such as minority representation and simplicity. The same advantages can also be cited for New Zealand's system of plurality in single-member districts including a few special ethnic minority districts. But neither can be regarded as an ideal combination of plurality and PR.

HOW LIKELY IS ELECTORAL REFORM?

Since the beginning of the 1970s, there have been several major changes in electoral systems. STV replaced plurality for Northern Ireland elections in 1973. France introduced PR for the election of its representatives in the European Parliament in 1979 and for the regional elections in Corsica in 1982. And Japan adopted list PR instead of SNTV for the election of two-fifths of its upper house in 1982. In the United States, at the state and local level, Illinois abolished the cumulative vote for its lower house elections in 1980 as the result of a referendum, while multimember plurality districts have been replaced with single-member districts in a number of Southern and Southwestern states as a result of action by federal courts and the U.S. Department of Justice under special provisions of the Voting Rights Act of 1965. The entire presidential nominating process in the United States has also undergone a drastic transformation, in the direction of greater proportionality.

In addition, the electoral system has become a highly controversial issue in the other three Western democracies that use the plurality method for national legislative elections: Great Britain, Canada, and New Zealand. One strong stimulus has been the occurrence of the electoral anomaly that the second largest party, in terms of votes, has won a plurality of parliamentary seats, as in Britain in 1974, or even an outright majority, as in New Zealand in 1978 and 1981. The debate in Britain has also been stimulated by the first direct election of the European Parliament in 1979 and by the commitment by all of the member states to adopt a uniform electoral system for future elections of this supranational parliament (see Chapter 22 by Karlheinz Reif). For the 1979 election, the British government recommended—but Parliament rejected—the list PR system as used in Finland for the election of Britain's representatives.

Finally, we should not overlook the major actual and proposed changes in earlier decades. Most of the countries that use PR now originally used majority or plurality systems. In Britain, plurality was almost abolished on two occasions, in 1918 and 1930, and the Irish parliament voted twice to abolish STV, but the voters decided to retain it in referendums in 1959, although by only a very narrow margin, and again in 1968.

Do these examples show that important electoral system changes are a realistic possibility and hence that crucial choices with regard to electoral systems will have to be made? This book is obviously predicated on the assumption that electoral systems are at least potentially variable and are not complete constants, but it would be unrealistic to suggest that they are easily malleable and manipulable. It should be noted that the examples of recent electoral reform cited above do not include any changes in national lower-house election systems.

In Chapter 21, Nohlen argues forcefully that minor changes may be made with relative ease, but that major changes—especially shifts from plurality to PR and vice versa—are extremely unlikely. This means that the element of choice in electoral systems is narrowly circumscribed. In the chapter that follows, however, Butler surveys all of the pressures for, as well as the resistance to, reform of the British plurality system of elections, and he concludes that it is unlikely that it will *not* be reformed in the near future.

The slow and painful pace of electoral system change is also demonstrated in the final chapter by Karlheinz Reif. Even though the ten members of the European Community are formally and firmly committed to the adoption of a common electoral system for the European Parliament, they have been very reluctant to abandon their national electoral system traditions, not only with regard to the crucial choice of whether or not to use PR methods, but also with regard to a host of minor details of electoral procedure. On the other hand, Reif also shows that there has been considerable convergence. By embracing PR, France obviously took the biggest step in this direction. On the whole, the systems of electing the ten national delegations to the European Parliament are much more similar to each other than the systems of electing the ten national parliaments. Changes and choices in electoral systems may not be highly probable, but they are certainly possible.

PART II
COMPETING VALUES:
PROPORTIONALITY AND
STABILITY

2
Representation and Proportional Representation
Ferdinand A. Hermens

THEORETICAL PREMISES

Serious difficulties often arise from a failure to ask the right questions. The proponents of proportional representation (PR) consider it obvious that, in the words of the Royal Commission on Systems of Election (1910, p. 28): "The object of a representative body is to represent." Victor Considérant (1842), to whom, together with John Stuart Mill, we owe the classical formulation of the theory of PR (and who strongly favored that system) went so far as to say: "Should the Chamber of Representatives represent the electorate? That is the whole question. If such is the case, every opinion, however absurd, even monstrous it may appear, must have its representatives in proportion to its strength in the electorate."*

Yet, a century ago, Benjamin Disraeli made his hero, Coningsby, remark: "Do you know that the more I think the more I am perplexed by what is meant by Representation." We may, indeed, ask whether the members of a modern parliament can be representatives in the sense that their predemocratic predecessors were, and then, whether the "opinions" to be represented exist by themselves, unaffected by the impact of whatever system of elections is applied.

As to the first point, the term representation, as used in everyday language, presupposes three factors: The people to be represented, the representative, and those before whom representation takes place. In the field of law, a client is represented by his lawyer before a court. Similarly, a country is represented by a diplomat before the government of another country (Leibholz 1929).

---

*Translations from foreign languages are the author's.

In the beginning of parliamentary assemblies the three factors existed. The prince, the addressee of representation, asked local units of the country's "estates" to send "representatives" to a common meeting place. He wanted new taxes, or support in an impending war, or both. The representatives had been charged by their constituents (mostly few in number and known to them personally) to give the required consent only after the prince had listened to their "wishes and grievances" and promised redress. The prince, of course, had both the initiative and the final say. In exercising his prerogatives he fulfilled a vital function: he assured unity and continuity in the country's affairs.

When the decisive step toward establishing a democracy was taken the independent princely executive ceased to exist. It had to be replaced; the task was to form an effective government. This meant that the time was past in which a mere representation of parts would do. There had to be enough unity in a parliament to form and support a government. Logic demanded that the voters themselves be confronted with the clear request to group themselves in such a way that there would be a majority capable of governing and an opposition capable of controlling and eventually replacing it. The old predemocratic and passive type of representation had to be replaced by one that was both democratic and dynamic.

It is interesting to note that James Madison, in the frequently misunderstood *Federalist* No. 10, was fully aware of what was needed. There was a positive side to his discussion, treated very briefly, and a negative one, treated fully. As to the former, Madison expressed the hope that elected representatives would "refine and enlarge the public view." That statement has earned him the charge of being an "elitist," but what we call "public opinion" at least has to be *defined*. It does not exist as a Kantian *Ding an sich*—"thing in itself." There are all the impulses and tentative views which millions of individuals have on common affairs, and then there is the interaction of small and large groups. Individuals make their direct input into the groups nearest to them, and the process spreads, in an ever-widening circle, into larger groups. A great deal of shaping and directing takes place before something emerges which is accepted as *the* opinion (or even *the* interest) of a group, and eventually, of the country at large.

As to the negative aspects of the problems involved, Madison was fully cognizant of the "propensity of mankind to fall into mutual animosities," caused by noneconomic as well as by economic elements of division, and by "speculation" as well as by practice. In listing these elements he was not, as the younger Beard (1913) assumed, a determinist. Walter Lippmann (1940), in one of his most vigorous columns, has reminded us that the very first sentence of No. 10 indicated the opposite: "Among the numerous advantages promised by a well constructed Union, none deserves to be more accurately developed than its tendency to *break and control* the violence of faction" (italics supplied). Madison was not yet aware of the positive functions of parties and interest groups in the democratic process, but what he really meant to "break and control" was the propensity to violence. That makes him very modern, since the willingness to use violence is the decisive characteristic of totalitarian parties (Hermens, 1933; 1959b).

Madison wanted to stop such groups without interfering with liberty. We cannot try to destroy the *causes* of "the mischief of faction"; we must do the job "by controlling its effects." One political institution is central to this process: "If a faction consists of less than a majority, relief is supplied by the republican principle which enables the majority to defeat it by regular vote." That might not be possible in every single constituency, but for the political life of a large country, Madison pointed to the equivalent of what John Kenneth Galbraith, speaking in economic terms, called the interplay of "countervailing powers": where so many groups and interests coexist, the building of a majority is not compatible with the domination of a true "faction."

Close to two hundred years have verified Madison's theory. From the Anti-Masons of the 1830s to the Know-Nothings of the 1840s and 1850s, to the Klan of the post-Civil War days and of the 1920s, to the radical groups of the 1930s and to the segregationists of the post-World War II period, "factions" with a substantial following have been brought to book by majority voting (Hermens 1962). The need to appeal to a wide electorate induced them, in some cases, to compromise their views by sponsoring comparatively moderate candidates. Thus, the Anti-Masons, in order to win votes, nominated the widely respected William Wirt for the presidency, who was a Mason. The latter circumstance contributed to the fact that they were roundly defeated. Their party simply vanished after the election.

The same basic game was played with variations during the latest racial crisis. Then Governor Strom Thurmond lost out in his presidential bid of 1948 but, moderating his views, he was elected senator, and when running for reelection in 1980 he secured a significant number of black votes. So did George Wallace in 1982. The erstwhile advocate of "segregation forever" captured enough black votes to win the Democratic primary. He was supported by most blacks in the final contest with his Republican opponent, and after his victory he appointed two blacks to his cabinet. Generally speaking, it can be said that majority voting contains a combination of stick and carrot. Any truly "factional" group is defeated, and the rank and file of their followers are absorbed by the major and moderate parties. Individual leaders who come to accept the rules of the system have a chance to win a part in it. The result has made it possible for us to "keep" our republic for close to two centuries, in spite of the fact that an unusual degree of violence is said by some to be a part of our political culture.

It could be said that the United States has had a "militant democracy" from the start. It has managed to operate it as part and parcel of the democratic process, without any need to infringe on the liberty of the citizen. This was possible because plurality voting does not simply mean lining up a large block of voters against a smaller one. A generation ago, Thomas Woodlock was able to say

"Democracy is the protection of minorities by the rule of the majority." The reason is that government by majority is government by persuasion. Members of a variety of ethnic, religious, economic, and other groups must be brought together. The result is civic education of the most effective kind. Members of minority groups, by cooperating, learn first of all to tolerate and then to appreciate each other. Their leaders must pursue policies acceptable to all.

Nor is this process of integration limited to intraparty relations. At least two major groups will try to win a majority, and the contest between them will be settled by the undecided voters in the center. This group of "marginal voters" will determine their country's politics, just as "marginal utility" is said to determine the price. As a result, majority elections are, in the formulation of Harry D. Gideonse (1940) more than a "census"; they aim at a consensus in the community. That consensus is dynamic, changing in response to the challenges of the times, but always real (Hermens 1958; 1959a, pp. 175–210).

ELECTORAL SYSTEMS IN PRACTICE

When we consider the practical effects of electoral systems in some detail, we must begin with what Aldous Huxley at one time said about the difference between the natural sciences, which can isolate their objects, quantify them and, finally, freely experiment with a combination of factors, and the social sciences, which can follow such procedures only approximately.

Let us refer to a simple example, used by the Bonn professors, Werner Schoellgen and Helmut Unkelbach. A student sits at his desk on an autumn day, and watches three events. First, a tile falls from a roof and hits the ground fast and in a straight line. A leaf falls from a tree, drifts off a little in a gentle breeze, but reaches the ground with some delay. Finally, a bird drops a feather, a wind blows and carries it out of sight. For the untutored observer no common regularity underlies these three events. We may, however, remember a day in a physics high school class when the teacher demonstrated that, in a vacuum, the feather falls just as straight and just as fast as a piece of lead. Gravity is the common force behind the observed events and has the same effect on every object, which becomes visible if we isolate it. A competing force, such as the air resistance and wind, may always enter the picture, compensate for some of the effects of gravity, and overcompensate for them in a case like that of the feather.

When this writer was dealing, for the first time, with the problems arising out of the multiplicity of variables which confronts us every step of the way in the social sciences, he suggested an approximation of the procedure used to solve simultaneous equations (Hermens 1933), which consists in trying to attribute a value to the crucial independent variable, or variables, to be considered.

In the case of electoral systems, there are three types of variables which have to be identified, the first being the "purity" of the system. Maurice Duverger (1954; 1982) has drawn attention to the effect of the different versions of majority voting. Differences resulting from various types of PR have also been noted. They became more significant after the Second World War when a "pure" PR, aiming at complete and nationwide proportionality between votes cast and seats obtained was, in some cases, deliberately abandoned in favor of limiting devices. The best known is the German requirement that a party, unless it wins at least three seats in single-member constituencies, must have secured five percent of the votes in order to obtain seats from the list.

The second set of variables concerns the other ingredients of the political structure. For example, under a parliamentary system it may make a difference whether the government has the right to dissolve parliament, or whether the other prerogatives of the government are enhanced or reduced.

The third group of modifying factors arises from the environment, in particular in the areas of foreign affairs and of the economy. These factors can compensate for some (or even all) of the effects inherent in an electoral system. It might be added in passing that in referring to these effects it seems preferable to speak of "tendencies" rather than of "laws" (Riker 1982b). The latter term implies a stringency which is alien to the social world, and it is interesting to note that already James Madison (in the above quoted first sentence of *The Federalist* No. 10) used the word "tendency." In that case full allowance is made for possible compensating factors, but it is also implied that once these are removed (or sufficiently weakened) the original force will assert itself. To rely on compensating factors means giving hostages to fortune.

PR AND FRAGMENTATION

It is now time to turn to the changes operated by the dynamics of electoral systems. As Rudolf Wildenmann (1965) has stated repeatedly, electoral systems are so important because they confront all of the "deeper realities" of the social structure, of a political culture, or of ethnic and ideological divisions, with the channels through which they must move. Voters develop a rather good perception as to what these channels will let pass and what they will block, and campaign managers adjust their tactics to the options with which they are presented.

Since proponents of PR have insisted, even in recent discussions, that all they want to do is to give expression to the orientations already existing in the electorate, reference may be made to earlier "Freudian slips" from within their ranks. The list begins with Thomas Hare, the coinventor of the single-transferable system (STV) of PR, which is frequently associated with his name. Hare (1873, pp. xv, 26–27) wanted full proportionality on a national scale. The voter would be given "a freedom of choice not only of the two or three [candidates likely to offer themselves under plurality voting] but of the candidates for all the other constituencies of the kingdom.'' Probably "two or three thousand candidates" would be in the running. As a result: "Many more candidates will be everywhere put in nomination. . . . Minorities . . . [will, under the single-transferable vote] far exceed the entire number of any minorities now existing, by the operation of numberless affinities and compulsions, which, in a state of liberation, *will dissolve the present majorities*'' (italics supplied).

More carefully worded views as to the dynamics of PR were expressed by Clarence Gilbert Hoag and George H. Hallett, Jr. (1926, pp. 433–34). Writing in the middle 1920s, when the Progressives were still strong, they said:

> Suppose we had in the American Congress—as we have had in reality already and might have under PR—a Republican, a Democratic and a Progressive party, no one with an absolute majority in itself. Suppose further, that under the influence of proportional representation, each had a definite platform on a few major issues and each member was elected on a supplementary platform of his own, so that all important elements within each party were represented. Under these circumstances we should have some questions decided by Republicans and Democrats against Progressives, some by Republicans and Progressives against Democrats, some by Democrats and Progressives against Republicans. . . . The House of Representatives would become representative in fact as in name.

In evaluating this statement we may disregard the fact that PR parties, with their tendency to doctrinal rigidity, are something different from the minor parties which develop under majority voting. We may also overlook the fact that any consistent system of PR would permit new parties other than the Progressives to gain a foothold in Congress, and expand it when conditions favor them. Suffice it to concentrate on the last sentence, according to which the House of Representatives would be "representative in fact as well as in name" only if the seats were shared by more than two parties. Representation, then, is assumed to call for a measure, at least, of fragmentation.

The actual results achieved under the Hare system in recent elections, as held in various countries, have been characterized by small constituencies, the practical aspects of the STV excluding the national voting which Thomas Hare had in mind. The largest STV constituencies ever used were constituted by the boroughs of the city of New York, which had a PR Council between 1937 and 1947, and used borough-wide constituencies. For the first attempt, made in 1937, there were ninety-nine candidates in the borough of Brooklyn, and the ballot was over four feet long. Some voters panicked and failed to mark even one valid choice, making the ballot "invalid." Others struggled on valiantly, but the then city editor of the *New York Times* told the author that he had seen ballots with twenty or so choices marked and yet, in the end, cast aside as "exhausted" because all designated candidates were either already elected or already eliminated.

Others had clearly voted "alphabetically," marking one or two candidates whose views they felt they knew and then giving preferences to those listed next to them. Altogether thirty-one percent of the Brooklyn ballots were either invalid or became "exhausted" because not enough preferences had been marked.[1] Matters were less bizarre in the other boroughs but still, on the same day on which Mayor LaGuardia and his city-wide running mates obtained, under the majority system, close to sixty percent of the votes, Fusion won just half of the Council seats. It failed to get control of that body when one of its members was absent during the organizing session. The Tammany members voted for a set-up giving them control and the courts let the result stand for the rest of the term. The Fusion vote slipped during the following elections and the reform group never controlled the Council.

The *New York Times*, which had favored the adoption of PR, turned against it on November 14, 1941, in an editorial entitled "PR and the Council." Before the final vote to abolish it was taken in 1947 it published a series of four editorials (issues of October 27, 28, 29 and 30) under the title "The Record on PR" in which it examined one election after the other. The repeal was followed by an editorial of November 5, "PR Is Repealed," and another on "The Results of PR" which reconfirmed the paper's stand. This unusual series of fact-packed analyses should be taken into account before any attempt is made to rewrite the history of New York's PR experience. Let us quote briefly from the first editorial:

> We favor repeal of PR for these reasons, and others:
> 1. It has failed to produce a City Council that fairly represented the sentiments of the people, notably so in the LaGuardia regime when Fusion was in control of the city administration, but Tammany continued to dominate the Council.
> 2. It has fostered the growth of splinter parties, seating Communists and other radicals who could not, by normal majority and district voting methods, have hoped to become members and giving them an official sounding-board for views shared by only a meager fraction in the electorate.

Some of the drawbacks mentioned by the *New York Times* were due to the technical difficulties which the STV presents in comparatively large constituencies; they are the reason why Harold Gosnell (1939) advocated "A List System with Single Candidate Preference" as an alternative. When STV is applied in smaller constituencies, the number of candidates is reduced. The voter has a better chance to mark his preferences effectively, though his task is never as simple as under majority voting or, for that matter, with a list system of PR.

We shall return to the fact that small constituencies mean reduced proportionality and create some danger of gerrymandering. In any event, no system of PR simply leaves the "opinions" to be represented as they are. The dynamics of channeling make their appearance immediately and the results will always somewhat, and under certain conditions dramatically, differ from what the proponents of PR had hoped to "represent."

Changes in the Nature of Parties and of the Political System.

The dynamics of electoral systems are not limited to changes in the number of parties, but extend to their nature and to that of the political system. Under plurality voting there is a tendency for a two-party system to develop in the sense that, out of an unlimited number of parties, only two can expect either to win a majority of the seats, or to be the strongest opposition, with a chance to win an absolute majority in the next election. The result means "people's parties," which appeal to voters with a wide range of views, the decision between them being made by the "floating" vote in the center. Such parties do have different tendencies within them, but if these tendencies are organized (which, as a rule, they are not), their influence is limited and the entire line-up is characterized by fluidity and flexibility. The upshot is pragmatism and practicality in government. Political leaders worth their salt, if they assume power, will have, of course, certain policies in mind, they will have communicated them to their followers before the election, and they will keep in constant touch with the electorate afterwards. But if unexpected circumstances warrant a reordering of priorities, this can be done without undue difficulty.

Matters are more difficult when there exists a second ballot with a tendency indicating that more than one party will be needed to form a government. The most liberal arrangement existed during the France of the Third Republic, when anyone could compete in the second ballot, even if he had not been a candidate in the first. Some of the integrating effects of majority voting remain. Extremists are always under pressure, and may be trounced in the second ballot, as the Rightist "Leagues" were in the 1936 elections and the Communists in every case when they refused to cooperate with more moderate groups on terms acceptable to the latter. Furthermore, the various parties right of center and left of center tend to support each other in the second ballot (sometimes even in the first), with the result that there will be a system of "two blocs" which, as René Capitant (1934, p. 23) pointed out, may not be entirely dissimilar to a two-party system. The whole system would have been more workable had the government possessed an effective right of parliamentary dissolution.

On the other hand, a reasonably consistent system of PR means, in the first place, the dethronement of the marginal voter in the center. There is no longer any one group which extends its influence over the entire political spectrum. Parties settle anywhere on the political map, and they enter campaigns (as their leaders, in the German case, used to say in the days of the Weimar Republic) "frei nach allen Seiten"—"free in all directions." As to the results, Sidney Sonnino said, in the case of Italy, when he was one of those who warned vigorously against the adoption of PR in 1919: "The necessity of having lists in an election where several deputies are elected, makes the parties rigid. . . . It becomes their major preoccupation to prevent contacts between groups representing various tendencies, though these tendencies are related, and to differentiate themselves from the other parties. . ." (Camera dei Deputati 1919, pp. 19989–90).

PR parties, then, do not just represent differences as they are. They escalate them, making it hard to find the way to a "politics of accommodation" when the time comes to form a coalition. Helmut Unkelbach (1956) emphasized that this tendency is particularly strong with parties close to each other.

PR means not only a difference in the general characteristics of parties and party systems; it also makes success easier for extremists, as well as for parties representing a particular economic interest. All details depend so much, however, on the combination of variables which occur in a particular country at a particular time that the author may be permitted to refer to earlier publications.[2]

PROBLEMS OF THE RECENT PAST

The postwar period is characterized, in the first place, by a new industrial revolution: the world's production tripled between 1948 and 1973. Instead of the widely expected postwar depression there was an economic upward movement which, until the oil crisis changed the picture, was interrupted only by short and mild "recessions" rather than by long and deep "depressions." Second, it became an accepted practice to reduce the proportionality of PR and thereby reduce its effects, though we shall see that the measures taken did not uniformly attain their purpose. Third, the nature and the consequences of totalitarian government were firmly impressed on the people's minds. The German "Basic Law" contained a provision outlawing totalitarian parties, which came to be paralleled by somewhat weaker provisions in other countries.

Problems in France

France exemplifies, on account of the kaleidoscopic changes in the political scene which followed upon modifications of the constitutional structure, so much of what has to be said about the "representative" character of PR that it will be given most of our remaining space. First, municipal and provincial (cantonal) elections were held, in 1945, under the old majority system with an unlimited second ballot. The traditional parties, discredited by their collaboration with Marshal Pétain and the Nazis, all but collapsed. The beneficiaries were the Christian Democrats (the MRP), the Communists, and particularly the Socialists. The latter had about the same number of votes as the Communists, but outdistanced them so decisively in terms of seats that Léon Blum could write "We have the wind in the sails.'' All was to change when General de Gaulle yielded to the demand for PR made by the "mass parties," the Communists, the Socialists, and the MRP. PR was introduced by decree for the elections to the Constituent Assembly.

The result was a political revolution. After the municipal and cantonal elections, a French journalist (Leduc 1945) writing in an American weekly had expressed a widely held view when he said: "In the light of the recent cantonal elections, France seems likely to be the next big country in Europe where a conspicuous trend to democratic socialism will triumph.'' When the results for the PR elections were announced the Communists and their "progressive" allies had been able to collect votes all over the country and to turn them into seats, outscoring the Socialists in both. In November 1946 the Communists became, for a time, "France's premier party" with 28.6 percent of the votes against 17.9 percent for the Socialists, who were later to decline to 15 percent.

Eventually, this came to mean what it had meant in other countries before (in the Weimar Republic in particular): The Socialists had to form government coalitions with parties to their Right, thus losing credit with their supporters. The "bourgeois" parties of the Center suffered for the same reason, and when the Gaullist Rally for the Republic (R.P.R.) attracted millions, the centrist parties had to conduct a two-front war against the Communists and their opponents from the Right. Under the law as it then stood, the 1951 elections would have given the R.P.R. and the Communists a parliamentary majority that, one way or the other, would have meant the end of the Fourth Republic (Campbell 1951). This result was averted by changing the election law: A party with an absolute majority of the votes in an electoral district (usually a *département*) was to take all of the seats. When a coalition of parties had more than fifty percent of the vote, the seats were to be divided among its members according to the d'Hondt system of PR. In 1951, enough arrangements between the parties of the "Third Force" were concluded to provide a leeway in terms of seats and to make it possible for the relatively successful governments of Antoine Pinay and Pierre Mendès-France to be formed. For the January 1956 elections, not enough "apparentements" between the moderate parties could be concluded and the outcome of the elections was almost what the old PR law would have produced. In a little more than two years, the leaders of the Fourth Republic were glad that General de Gaulle rescued them from the threat of a military takeover. The country was tired of the political paralysis which had become the hallmark of the Fourth Republic.

Meanwhile, a few more lessons had been taught. First, reducing the proportionality of PR can be counter-productive. General de Gaulle had resisted "integral" PR because he wanted to eliminate splinter parties. The d'Hondt system was applied in constituencies electing, on an average, five to six deputies. By that time, the "Radicals" (France's traditional Republican party) were the principal sufferers, as were other small but moderate groups. The Communists were among the beneficiaries.

Second, France's "political culture" had changed overnight. The individualism of the Third Republic had been replaced by the ironclad political discipline of the "mass parties." The pattern changed somewhat when the Gaullist R.P.R. split, but basically PR France was different from its predecessor, as if to confirm Aristotle (Modern Library edition, 1943, p. 130), who said that when a country's constitution changes, it becomes a different country. Only at a time when the thinking of so many political scientists seems to have been completely submerged by the categories of a sociology which is no longer (as it was in the case of Max Weber) aware of the dynamics of the political structure could this fundamental fact be so totally ignored.

Finally, any national adoption of PR tends to be irreversible. A parliament elected by PR will contain small parties which may not survive a return to majority voting. There are also actual and imaginary beneficiaries within the major parties: leaders who do not want to forego the virtual certainty of reelection under PR, party machines which arrange the party lists, and interest groups which can penetrate a party more easily under PR than under majority voting.

The Fifth Republic was once again to confirm Aristotle's dictum that when a country's political structure changes, so does the country. De Gaulle accepted the office of prime minister only after having made certain that the new constitution would not be subject to the veto of the vested interests. It was drawn up under the guidance of Michel Debré, who was given the chance to have his country follow the advice which he and his associates had given it in 1944, and the final draft was to be ratified by a referendum.

The system of voting constitutes a "sanitized" version of the two-ballot system used during most of the Third Republic: Candidates can run in a second ballot only if they had participated in the first and obtained votes equal to at least 12.5 percent of the registered voters. This came to mean that practically only the two top candidates from the first ballot could compete in the second.

The most significant result of French majority voting is rarely noticed: There is little chance for the extreme Right. Its strength was obvious when the Secret Army Organization (OAS) attempted to take revenge for de Gaulle's Algerian policy by acts of terrorism, proving that a defeated faction may, indeed, in Madison's words, "clog the administration, it may convulse the society." Madison, however, took satisfaction from the fact that "It will be unable to execute and mask its violence under the forms of the Constitution." In Gaullist France, majority voting pushed the extremists into a kind of isolation in which they could not survive for long.

The Communists, whose strong trade union support provided them with local strongholds in which they were hard to beat, were under great pressure everywhere else. In 1958, when they were isolated, their percentage of the popular vote fell to 18.9, and the number of their seats to ten. They did better when they allied themselves with the Socialists and other leftists, but after Mitterrand took control of the Socialist party, he set himself the goals of first winning back the votes which the Socialists had lost to the Communists after 1945, and then to make his party the leader of the Left, and ultimately win for it an absolute parliamentary majority. He could have done none of that under PR. Mitterrand also managed to cooperate with the Communists in such a way that they had to support him in the second ballot of the 1981 presidential elections, and trade support with his party in the second ballot of the ensuing parliamentary elections. In this process the dynamism of majority voting carried Mitterrand from 25.8 percent in the first ballot of the presidential elections to 51.8 percent in the second; the Socialist candidates in the following parliamentary elections secured 37.1 percent of the vote in the first ballot, and the trend in their favor continued in the second. The Socialists and those affiliated with them won 269 of the 491 seats, while the Communists had to be satisfied with 44.

Problems in Germany

There is only one point to make in regard to Germany: In spite of PR, a "two-and-a-half party system" developed, but it is accident prone. The neo-Nazi Socialist Reich Party (SRP) peaked in the *Land* elections of 1951 and caused serious national and international problems until it was declared unconstitutional in 1952. Its successor, the National Democratic Party (NDP) entered a succession of *Land* legislatures between 1966 and 1969. In that year's Bundestag elections a shift of one percent of the total vote from the Free Democratic Party (FDP) to the NDP would have put the former out and the latter in.

Now it is the Greens (the new ecological party) who, at the time of this writing, have entered six of the ten *Land* legislatures. In Hamburg, the June 1982 elections eliminated the FDP and admitted the Greens. No government could be formed until, in December, new elections returned the SPD with an absolute majority. In Hesse, the September 1982 elections eliminated the FDP, put in the Greens and failed to give the CDU the expected majority. The state remained ungovernable when the new elections in September 1983 again failed to produce a majority.

For a while it seemed that the Bundestag elections of March 6, 1983 might reproduce the Hamburg result of June 1982, or the Hesse result. Some foreign correspondents were nominating Germany as the future "sick man of Europe." But as luck would have it, both the FDP and the Greens got in, and the Christian Democratic–Christian Social Union (CDU/CSU) and the FDP had a comfortable majority.

The Greens may ultimately succumb to their own contradictions, but in the meantime they can exploit every fear and every anxiety in regard to environmental, nuclear, and foreign policy issues. In the country they compete with all parties for votes, in particular with the SPD and the FDP. They have eliminated the Social Democrats, for some time to come, as a credible alternative to the

Christian Democrats. The Greens' influence on actual and potential Free Democratic voters is smaller, and is all but negligible on the Christian Democrats. Still, somehow, with an electorate barely exceeding five percent, they have affected Germany's entire political spectrum. The outcome hardly represents the wishes of the great majority of the Germans.

Problems in Italy

Italy provides another illustration of how difficult it is to repeal PR (or to remedy its most serious consequences) once a thoroughly proportional system has taken hold. In 1981 and 1982, the forty-third postwar government, a five-party coalition headed by the Republican, Giovanni Spadolini, managed to do some useful work, but tension between the partners kept mounting. When Spadolini was defeated in September, President Pertini persuaded him to stay, but by December he had no alternative but to go, and the succeeding government of the veteran Amintore Fanfani was forced out in April. Bettino Craxi, the able and aggressive leader of the Socialists, had a share in these events. His opponents saw him motivated only by a desire to strengthen his party in the new elections, but he is one of the few Italian leaders who is aware that his country's troubles have deep institutional roots.

The road leading from this realization to remedial action, however, is longer and thornier in Italy than anywhere else. For example: Craxi is an admirer of Mitterrand and would like to duplicate his success, but the political situation of the two countries, which was reasonably comparable at the end of the war, is now entirely different. This concerns particularly the political structure of the Left. In 1946, the Italian Socialists polled 20.7 percent of the votes and the Communists 19.0 percent. As in France, PR permitted the Communists to gain on the Socialists. In 1976 the spread was greatest, with the Communists receiving 34.4 percent of the vote, the Socialists 9.6 percent, and the Social Democrats (who were still united with the Socialists in 1946) 3.4 percent. When such shifts occur, there comes a time when old remedies no longer work. As of now, majority elections in single-member constituencies would create all but unsolvable problems. If space permitted, it could be shown that other solutions *are* conceivable, but they presuppose a joint attempt of the moderate parties to find a way back to a workable democratic system and this is no easy task.

Craxi has been indefatigable in proposing partial remedies. Some minor reforms could prove incremental, opening the road to more serious measures. Evidently, however, nothing on the model of the German five percent clause would do, as that might simply wipe out the smaller parties, such as the Liberals, the Republicans, and the Social Democrats.

A way out presupposes a change in the intellectual atmosphere within which the pertinent discussions take place. The starting point might well be a realism inspired by what happened after the second PR Chamber had been elected in 1921. Prime Minister Giovanni Giolitti had succeeded with some of the measures needed to end what Gaetano Salvemini (1927, pp. 19–22) had termed the "post-war neurasthenia"; he had pardoned the hundreds of thousands of deserters and initiated measures to bring inflation under control. But, Salvemini concludes, the new Chamber was worse than its predecessor; there was "parliamentary paralysis." Giolitti, realizing what that meant, thought of a law abolishing PR and restoring the old type of majority voting with run-off elections which, at that time, was likely to produce a Chamber capable of functioning. But, as two French jurists (Esmein and Nézard 1927, vol. 1, p. 373) reported: "He found in this disorderly Chamber such a systematic opposition to this project that he resigned at the first occasion." The deputy Alessio, who in 1919 had expressly predicted that PR would lead to "paralysis," suggested a different approach: "In my view the new ministry ought to dissolve the Chamber, abolish PR by royal decree, and proceed at once to general elections in order to have its acts ratified by the new Chamber. Only in this way can the country be saved."[3]

In present-day Italy nothing that simple is possible. Nor is the situation quite that urgent; there is no Mussolini at the gates. What Alessio proposed in 1921 has, however, one important implication: there comes a time when normal procedures do not work. Thus, when the Spadolini cabinet fell, Craxi insisted on a special parliamentary committee to consider reforms. It came to an end when the Chamber was dissolved, and it is questionable whether, if reconstituted, it will produce agreement on even minor changes and, if so, whether these will be implemented. A special group will be needed, on the model of the one which was instituted in the United States in 1786 and 1787. In Italy, the sanction of a special referendum might be useful. Needless to say, the group could *not* be constituted on the basis of the present party line-up. Final success does, of course, presuppose agreement by the major democratic groups, in particular the Christian Democrats and the Socialists. Minor parties can make valuable suggestions *if* they can be steered away from simply proposing measures to perpetuate their existence, for which all manner of rationalizations can be mobilized.

Italy does have men and women fully equal intellectually to the work to be done, and also has institutions and organizations which have taken an intelligent interest in such matters for some time. The task is to bring them together in the special group mentioned above, and to present their findings to the political powers in such a manner that they cannot be ignored.

CONCLUSIONS

The above discussion may seem to imply an uncompromising stand in opposition even to those who feel that the plurality system of voting should be subject to periodic examination for the purpose of making adjustments to the specific needs of time and place. This would be a misunderstanding. We must, to be sure, always accept John Jay's insistence in *The Federalist* (No. 64) on the "absolute necessity of system." With regard to the political structure, this requires that we be aware of our priorities. The need for integration, culminating in the quest for majorities, stands at the top. But we might as well make sure that the party with the most votes also has the most seats. Supplementary seats for the parties with the highest percentage of the votes are the simplest solution. Such an arrangement will also rule out the possibility of creating a majority by gerrymandering. Furthermore, the incentive to vote, even in constituencies in which a preferred party has little chance, will be increased.

Second, a majority needs to be checked by an opposition of adequate strength, which the plurality system in single-member constituencies (let alone in multiple-member constituencies) does not always provide. Sixty percent of the seats is enough for any majority to do its job. Again, supplementary seats may be provided. Or there may be a small national list, for which there are also other reasons, such as making sure that a few national leaders are not left to the hazards of a particular constituency, or that women, or minority representatives, have better chances.

Third, three-member constituencies can be arranged, with two seats going to the strongest party and one to the runner-up, preferably only if the latter wins at least half as many votes as the former. Such a system also increases the chances for women and the representatives of minorities. Still, it weakens the integrating effects of the single-member constituency, as it encourages a major party to align itself with a minor one. Proponents of the English type of one-party majority system of voting will object, but those who look for a way out of situations like those in contemporary Germany, or perhaps even Italy, might welcome it. Presumably, a major party would team up with a minor one only if the latter is willing to join it in a government.

Lastly, the d'Hondt system of PR in three-member constituencies has been recommended in Germany during both the Weimar and the Bonn Republics. Given current German voting behavior, and assuming that it does not change with the electoral system, such an arrangement could prove functional. This is less likely in England, however, where the minor parties are stronger, and even less in France or Italy. Simulations such as those undertaken by Rudolf Wildenmann and Werner Kaltefleiter would be a *conditio sine qua non* for a rational choice (for details, see Hermens 1968c; 1972b; 1976).

There is, finally, what the Spanish have called, in recent years, *el fin de los automatismos institucionales*—"the end of institutional automatisms." There are tendencies in modern society, largely resulting from the intensification of interest group activities, but also from a new hardening of ideological barriers, which cannot be controlled by an "invisible hand" in either political or economic life. This does not mean that the old tendencies no longer exist, but only that the compensatory factors standing in the way of its operation should be examined from case to case and from country to country. There can be no objection to adjustments which are likely to effectively correct these new developments.

NOTES

1. More incongruities are listed in New York State Constitutional Convention Committee 1938. The Committee was appointed by Governor Herbert H. Lehman to collate factual data for the use of the delegates to the Constitutional Convention of 1938.

2. The second edition of Hermens (1941) contains a supplement dealing with developments from 1941 until 1972 (Hermens 1972a, pp. 443–87). Various countries are treated in Hermens (1958), chapters 11–19. Additional material may be found in the second German edition (Hermens 1968a) and in the Italian edition (Hermens 1968b). The 1966–1978 volumes of the yearbook *Verfassung und Verfassungswirklichkeit* contain material on various countries by a number of authors.

3. Quoted in a speech by the Fascist deputy Giunta in the Chamber on July 14, 1923, who mentions this fact in order to discredit Signor Alessio (Camera dei Deputati 1923, p. 10615).

3

Which Is the Best Electoral System?*

Maurice Duverger

Every political party obviously prefers the electoral system that favors it. In Great Britain, the Liberals have long demanded proportional representation (PR), which would prevent them from being crushed by the plurality method. In France, the Radicals, Centrists, and very small parties dream of obtaining an independent representation in the National Assembly by means of PR. The Communists demand it in order to escape the domination by the Socialists in an alliance in which they are reduced to a mere supporting role. Beyond these special interests, the national interest may lead to a change in the established electoral system. In Italy, for instance, some people hope to institute a two-ballot majority system in order to put an end to the weakness and instability of the governments.

The problem is often stated on the level of abstract principles instead of practical efficacy. PR has always had proponents who try to demonstrate its fairness in contrast with plurality or majority methods, which are said to be unjust. That question must first be examined. The answer will not resolve the problem completely, but it will help to pose it clearly by removing the false pretenses and illusions that hide its true meaning. Before I describe the factors that guide the choice of an electoral system, I must first outline a theory of political representation.[1]

WHAT SHOULD BE REPRESENTED?

According to democratic theory, an election allows the citizens to designate "representatives" in the legal sense of the term: the former are supposed to give to the latter a mandate to speak and act in their name. This institution, derived

*Translated by Arend Lijphart.

from private law, has been transposed into public law. The personal mandate with which a person entrusts another person has been converted into a collective mandate that a nation assigns to the deputies, sometimes interpreted as an "imperative" mandate and sometimes as a "representative" mandate. At the end of the nineteenth century, the invention of PR changed the meaning of the term "representation" from a legal to a factual relationship. Parliament came to be thought of as a portrait of the nation, as a small-scale reproduction of the collectivity of the voters: it represents the nation as a portrait represents its model, and no longer as the trustee represents his mandator.

The fidelity of this representation may be checked since public opinion polls have made it possible to ascertain the opinion of a mass of people by other methods. After all, isn't the sample that is interviewed, like parliament, a small-scale reproduction of the whole country, a microcosm in the image of the macrocosm? Doesn't the usual randomness of the sampling method restore, in a new form, the old procedures of the ancient democracies?

Representation of Opinions and Representation of Wills

The doctrinaire PR advocates and the poll-takers have made us accustomed to thinking of an election as a means of obtaining a more or less accurate image of all of the opinions in a country—or even as a means of "photographing" these opinions. But democracy does not consist of assembling a parliament which is a small-sized model of the distribution of a nation's different spiritual families in all their diversity and nuances. Voters should not choose their doubles who must resemble them as closely as possible. They should choose governments with the capacity to make decisions.

By dispersing the voters among numerous independent parties, PR prevents the citizens from expressing a clear choice for a governmental team. It transfers this choice to the party leaders. For instance, after legislative elections in Italy, Belgium, the Netherlands, and Denmark, several types of majority are possible, most of them fragile and divided. Which one is preferred by the citizens? It is impossible to know this. Only the new deputies can choose between the different potential combinations, with the freedom to make a different choice later without reference to the voters.

PR properly expresses the citizens' diverse preferences, but it does not allow them to choose a concrete set of policies and a team to execute them. In contrast with this representation of opinions, what may be called the representation of wills enables the voters to choose those who will lead them during the entire life of the legislature. The citizens cannot govern themselves, but the delegation of power may be reduced to one step (citizens–government) instead of being stretched out to two steps (citizens–deputies–government) in which the second step becomes predominant. Above all, the decisive act of choosing the governing team may be accomplished by the voters themselves instead of being left to the deputies. The old distinction between active and passive citizens may be legitimately invoked here.

A comparative analysis of Western democracies highlights an unresolvable contradiction between these two representations of opinions and of wills. The former requires that many parties present themselves to the citizens in order that each citizen can choose a candidate who is very close to his preferences. It also implies that the seats won should be exactly proportional to the votes received. The latter needs completely opposite mechanisms. In order to enable the voters to impose the government of their choice and to give this government the means to act during the entire life of the legislature, a small number of parties is needed; each of these parties should be strongly disciplined and should fit into a bipolar pattern, based either on two exclusive large organizations or on two alliances that firmly unite disciplined partners.

When one speaks of the exactness or the sincerity of representation, one should always specify the level that one has in mind. Which is the most exact and the most sincere electoral system? The system that permits the English to choose the prime minister whom they prefer and that gives him or her the means to govern the nation for five years? Or the system that prevents the Italians, the Belgians, and the Dutch from designating their government and that forces them to transfer to the party notables the responsibility to form a cabinet condemned to impotence and subject to several changes during the legislature's life? What is the point of guaranteeing that each party's number of deputies will be exactly proportional to that of its voters, if it remains free to ally itself with whomever, whenever, and for whatever purpose it wishes, and to change partners at any moment?

When do the voters have the greatest freedom? When they select the supreme leader themselves, a leader who cannot be changed except by their will and who has the means to carry out the program approved by them? Or when they are imprisoned by the party machines between two general elections, which are like permissions to vote restricted to the expression of states of mind and excluding the choice of the government? Where is equality better secured? In countries which base the percentage of seats on that of the votes but which allow the parties to freely play the cards thus distributed, permitting dozens of different combinations whose only shared trait is their incapacity to govern? Or in countries less faithful to mathematical vigor, but certain of giving power to the Left after an electoral victory of the Left and to the Right after a rightist victory and of not letting this power change hands without a new popular consultation?

Where do we find true democracy? In nations that treat the voters as real possessors of sovereignty, who effectively decide the delegation of governmental power? Or in those which transform them into passive citizens as soon as they have cast their votes and which reserve the choice of the leaders to a small circle, a political class, of active citizens? It is tempting to interpret the responses to these questions in the form of a law that approximates both Condorcet's theorem and Heisenberg's uncertainty principle: the more accurate the representation of opinions, the less accurate the representation of wills, and vice versa.

Photograph or Projection?

The basic argument of the PR advocates is that it gives a photographic image of public opinion that is as faithful a likeness as possible. That is true if we compare the vote percentages received by the different parties and their seat percentages. But the distribution of the votes is itself dependent on the country's party system, which in turn depends on the type of electoral system. PR projects as much as it records. Electoral mechanisms are strange devices—simultaneously cameras and projectors. They register images which they have partly created themselves. The comparison of electoral trends before and after an electoral reform can be very revealing in this respect. This has already been done for the Scandinavian countries (Duverger 1954, p. 379). Similarly, the last elections in the French Fourth Republic in 1956 could be compared with the first elections of the Fifth Republic in 1958.

One cannot equate an election with a portrait of which public opinion is the model. Blaming certain types of electoral systems for distorting opinions, praising the merits of others more faithful to public opinion—this just does not make sense. One can only determine the accuracy of a portrait by comparing it with its model if the model is directly ascertainable. Here our model is not. The many nuances of the political rainbow recorded by multipartism and the electoral systems that develop it are no more consistent with the truth than the sharp dichotomous cut of the two-party system and the plurality and majority electoral methods. Fragmenting the fundamental oppositions among the many secondary oppositions or cutting them in two along the line marking the essential opposition—these are different interpretations of public opinion, but interpretations just the same. Seurat's pointillism interprets reality in a different sense from Cézanne's architectonic style, but they are both still interpretations.

Moreover, an election is more than a simple interpretation of the citizens' opinions. It also takes part in their formation. The model does not exist independently of the portrait, or rather, of the total of the processes that go into the development of the portrait. The technique used for the portrait affects the physiognomy of the model; it helps to shape the model to some extent. Parties are not the projection of pre-existing political opinions, or, at most, they are only partly so.

At any given moment, a country's opinion expresses itself through a party system born earlier, which necessarily distorts it. It is true that this gap between opinions and parties may be filled by campaign propaganda; but, more precisely, the campaign tends to bring the voters' opinions in line with the party programs instead of allowing their free expression. These programs must undoubtedly take current opinions into consideration, but there is a margin of freedom in their formulation. In any case, the relationship between opinions and parties is not a one-way street; it is characterized by a series of actions and reciprocal reactions.

As a result, there may be, and indeed there often is, a very big gap between the voters' opinions and the policies advocated by the parties representing them. A 1952 survey by the French Institute of Public Opinion provides a revealing example. Although it was conducted in the middle of the Cold War and although the Communist party centered all of its propaganda on the idea that the United States followed an aggressive policy, only thirty percent of the Communist voters (less than one in three) thought that the United States had such a policy.

Political representation is the result of a complex combination of the expression of opinions existing in the period and country under consideration, the implantation of these opinions in the organizations and mentalities formed by historical evolution, and the pressure of institutional mechanisms. Among the latter, electoral systems have a considerable influence. Party systems depend closely on electoral systems in a relationship illuminated by the analytical model which American authors have called Duverger's law, although I share its paternity with many other scholars (see Riker 1982b), and although I certainly do not want to exaggerate the scope of a formula that is limited to only one of the causal factors. Its most recent formulation is as follows:

"(1) the plurality method tends to lead to a two-party system; (2) proportional representation tends to lead to a system of many mutually independent parties; (3) the two-ballot majority system tends to lead to multipartism moderated by alliances" (Duverger 1980, p. 144).[2]

Here I shall examine only a few consequences of these tendencies in conjunction with other elements of the political regimes under consideration.

FACTORS FOR CHOOSING AN ELECTORAL SYSTEM

The above theoretical analysis was necessary in order to state the problem of choosing an electoral system properly. The ethical arguments about the authenticity of representation and the fairness of the distribution of seats compared with that of the votes are largely, if not completely, specious. One cannot seriously present PR as a moral and fair system, and the plurality and majority systems as immoral techniques, because they are alleged to be unfair. On the contrary, one must clearly state that PR generally weakens democracy and that plurality and majority systems strengthen it, which, in the final analysis, makes the latter more moral and just: The first duty in the development of morality and justice in political relationships consists of reinforcing democracy and weakening dictatorship.

The choice of an electoral system is therefore governed by concrete factors. It depends, above all else, on the function that the elected representatives must exercise. In order to form a consultative assembly which expresses all of a country's nuances, PR is clearly preferable. In order to form stable and strong governments, capable of making decisions throughout the legislature's term, plurality is the best method. The extent and diversity of social antagonisms are another element of the problem, as well as the parties' discipline and their acceptance of pluralism. The choice of a particular type of electoral system depends on the society that has to use it, on the nature of its institutions and on the relationships among its political forces. I shall limit myself to a few observations within the framework thus sketched.

Choosing Proportional Representation

The advantage of PR is that it permits a delicately differentiated representation which expresses all of a country's diversity. When the life and the actions of governments are not at stake, it is obviously preferable to open the gates to fifteen parliamentary groups as in the Weimar Reichstag, to the eleven parties of the Italian chamber and the Danish Folketing, to the ten to fourteen of the Dutch States-General, and to the ten of the French Fourth Republic's National Assembly, instead of restricting the system to the two large parties of the British House of Commons, where the majoritarian bulldozer crushes all small parties.

A young constitutional expert has recently suggested the adoption of PR for the election of the French Senate, currently elected by an indirect method that favors the very small communes with a conservative outlook (Duhamel 1983). Because this second chamber lacks any power over the investiture and maintenance of the prime minister and his cabinet, and because it cannot prevent the National Assembly from making the final decision on the adoption of the laws, it would gain a great deal from election by PR which would enable numerous small parties to make their voices heard without hurting either the stability or the effectiveness of the executive.

One might ask whether such a solution would not be equally advantageous for the United States House of Representatives. The American two-party system, produced by the plurality method of election, is only compatible with presidential government because of the fluidity of each of the two large parties and the consequent absence of voting discipline. With the British type of two-party system, the American government would find itself completely deadlocked if the president were a Democrat and the congressional majority Republican, or vice versa. But the two American parties are mere receptacles containing too haphazard a mixture of different elected members to properly represent the diverse tendencies of public opinion. PR could lead to a real renewal of political life. It would undoubtedly be even more beneficial for the state legislatures. While I make these suggestions, I have no illusions about their chances of being accepted, of course.

Choosing a Plurality or Majority System

The plurality and majority methods are certainly preferable to PR in all regimes in which the investiture and maintenance of the government depend on the majority of the deputies. This is the case in British-style parliamentary regimes and in French-style semipresidential regimes. To be sure, it can happen that PR does not prevent the formation of a two-party system, as in Austria and the German Federal Republic. But these cases are exceptions and depend on special circumstances. The two large Austrian parties are huge organizations, firmly structured and deeply rooted in the national tradition. In West Germany, the Second World War, military defeat, and the division of the country were needed to destroy the Nazi and Communist movements that paralyzed the Weimar Republic. The mixed nature of the Bundestag elections helps to promote a bipolar system: the dualism of the plurality vote in the single-member districts influences the second vote which is counted according to PR.

The plurality and two-ballot majority systems can only produce stable and strong majorities if the parties practice voting discipline in parliament, which is not the automatic result of the electoral method. A comparison of the American and British parties illustrates this as far as the plurality method is concerned. A comparison of the French parties in the Third and Fifth Republics shows it to be the case for the two-ballot majority method used by both regimes. Between 1875 and 1940 the tendency was toward a dualism of electoral alliances as predicted by Duverger's law, but these broke up quickly in parliament because most of the parties remained flexible, like their American counterparts. Since 1962, the two-ballot system has given rise to the same dualism of electoral alliances, but this dualism is maintained in the National Assembly because all parties have become disciplined.

The choice between the plurality method (one ballot) and the majority method (two ballots) depends on the number and nature of the parties of the country concerned. In West Germany and Austria, the adoption of plurality voting would certainly be a very good reform, protecting the two-party system from the whims of the small Liberal party and from the hazards that can always arise from extremist movements like today's Greens. In France, the adoption of plurality instead of the two-ballot system would undoubtedly be pernicious, because the plurality method does not work well when there are more than two large parties; the risk would be that it would yield anomalous results, such as Great Britain experienced from 1920 to 1935, and that France would not be able to get out of this situation as rapidly, for want of a dualist tradition.

Likewise, the adoption of the plurality system is inconceivable in a country where one of the two parties that it would tend to leave in the political arena would not give absolute guarantees to behave democratically in case of an electoral victory that would put it in power by itself. In contemporary Italy, it is unthinkable that the Communist party should assume exclusive power in spite of its more liberal appearance than that of Communists elsewhere. Its strength, compared with the much smaller Socialist party, also makes it more difficult to replace PR by a two-ballot majority system. Such a reform would entail the danger of perpetuating the Right in the government, because an alliance of the Left could not assume power if the Communist party would be stronger than its partner. The victory of the Left in France in 1981 was the result of the weakening of the Communist party, which fell to fifteen percent of the votes in the presidential election and to sixteen percent in the legislative elections, whereas the Socialists received almost thirty-eight percent.

Nevertheless, replacing PR by a two-ballot majority system serves to weaken the extremist party in each coalition. As in a two-party system, the bipolarization of alliances directs the political struggle to the center where the votes that spell victory for the Left or for the Right can be found. On the second ballot, the shifting votes in each alliance move more from the extremist to the moderate partner than the other way around. Do these phenomena explain the decline of the French Communists? Upon the establishment of the majority system in 1958, they suffered a considerable loss, falling from 25.7 percent of the votes to 18.9 percent. The popularity of General de Gaulle cannot sufficiently account for this decline from which the party was unable to raise itself. After a growth to 21.8 percent in 1962 and 22.5 percent in 1968, it began to decline again and reached its lowest point in 1981. This is all the more serious as the weaker party is always penalized on the second ballot, since the banner of the coalition is usually carried by its stronger candidate.

The Theory of Frequent Changes of the Electoral System

It is sometimes argued that every electoral reform is beneficial after a certain period of time, because it introduces an element of renewal in the political game, which otherwise has a tendency to become frozen. It is true that both PR and the plurality and majority methods stabilize representation once the political system is established in accordance with their mechanisms. However, PR deserves the accusation of political sclerosis more than the plurality and majority systems. In the latter, the possibility of alternation introduces a very important element of mobility. The triumphs of Margaret Thatcher in Great Britain in 1979 and of François Mitterrand in France in 1981 have greatly stirred their two nations. The overall fluctuations in PR systems are much weaker. Renovating changes affect only the margins of the party system, which are deprived of representation by the plurality and majority methods. But the agitation of the small parties usually remains superficial and inconsequential. In any case, we have to point out that the majority of Western democracies hardly ever change their electoral systems.

NOTES

1. The theory of representation outlined here was first presented in Duverger (1956), pp. 211–220.

2. Riker (1982b) only counts the first formula as Duverger's law, regarding the others as "hypotheses" that are further removed from verification. This difference is a difference of degree, not of kind: sociological laws, too, are working hypotheses (see Duverger 1984).

4

The Case for
Proportional Representation
Enid Lakeman

In order to discuss which electoral system is best, we must first agree on what an election is for. Elections are held for a wide variety of bodies, from the legislature or president of a powerful state to the officers and committee of a little local society, but all have one object in common: to consult the wishes of the people the elected body is to serve. There is no point in consulting them if no notice is to be taken of their answer. So an election must involve giving the electors a choice and causing that choice to have an effect on which persons are elected.

All elections involve both, but in very different degrees. Behind the iron curtain the choice may be simply yes or no to a single candidate; in a British parliamentary election there is a choice of several candidates but each is preselected by a party; in Israel the choice is among several parties but not among individual candidates; some other countries have a choice among candidates as well as parties. As for affecting the result, in Israel about ninety-five percent of those who vote elect a member of the party they voted for; in Britain about half the votes elect nobody, and many others are cast for candidates who would have been elected without their help. Other countries fall between these extremes.

Should we set limits, either to freedom of choice or to its effectiveness? Ought we, for example, to exclude from parliament people of extreme views, or to ensure that one party is in a position to govern? If there is to be any such overriding of the voters' wishes, it should be for a reason clearly stated and accepted by at least the majority of the nation. If most Germans think it desirable to exclude from the Bundestag parties with less than five percent support of the electorate, they are entitled to frame their electoral law accordingly, but when British Liberals with thirteen percent support are excluded from the European parliament, although nobody has been asked to agree to such a limit, there is something wrong.

Is a working majority for one party so desirable as to justify giving one party a majority of seats even if only a minority of the electorate has voted for it? If so, Mussolini's law awarding two-thirds of the seats to the party with the most votes is logical. It is not logical to rely, for so important a matter, on a system that may give such a result by chance. The British system is extremely chancy. It did, in 1945, give nearly two-thirds of the seats to the party with the most votes (forty-eight percent), but six years later turned that same party out of office, although its support had slightly *increased* and exceeded, by some two hundred thousand votes, that of the next largest party.

The uncertainty of any relation between a party's popular support and the seats it wins is inevitable if only one person is elected from each constituency, whether by a clear majority, as for the Australian House of Representatives, or by a plurality, as in Britan, the United States, Canada, or New Zealand. This is because of the large number of votes that have no effect on the result. Even without such complications as more than two parties or unequal electorates, the result can be anything between the winning of every seat by a party with only just over half the votes and defeat of a party with far more support.

Constituency	I	II	III	Total Votes	Seats
1. Party A	*20,001*	*20,001*	*20,001*	60,003	3
Party B	20,000	20,000	20,000	60,000	0
2. Party A	*20,001*	*20,001*	10,001	50,003	2
Party B	20,000	20,000	*30,000*	70,000	1

Further uncertainty is introduced by any change in the voters' behavior or in constituency boundaries. In example 1 of the above table, just three people changing from Party A to Party B could completely reverse the result. In the actual elections of October 1974 and May 1979 in the county of Hertfordshire, the Labour party's share of the votes declined from 38.5 percent to 34.5 percent, but its seats crashed from four out of nine to zero out of nine. On the other hand, in example 2, over nine thousand voters in constituency III could switch from Party B to Party A without affecting the result. In County Durham in the same two elections, the Labour vote declined from 59.5 to 57.6 percent but the party still held all sixteen seats. It would have lost one if just over one thousand voters had stayed at home in Darlington, but would not lose any if twenty thousand in Houghton le Spring did.

The recent rise of the Liberal/Social Democrat alliance, producing three parties not far from equal in strength, has drawn attention to another feature of the British gamble: the existence of a threshold amounting to about one-third of the total votes. If the third party rises above that level it may nearly annihilate the other two; with only a slightly smaller share of the votes, it may win very few seats. In the 1983 election, the Alliance polled twenty-six percent of the total vote, but it won only twenty-three seats (3.5 percent), while Labour, with only two percent more votes, won nine times as many seats.

Attempts to produce a closer relation between the voters' expressed wishes and the result in terms of seats won have taken two forms. One concentrates on the organized political parties, counts votes for them and awards each party seats in proportion to its votes. The other disregards parties and aims to make, as nearly as possible, every vote contribute to the election of a candidate whom that voter supports. These are two fundamentally different approaches, and arguments for or against one do not necessarily apply to the other. In some ways, they can have opposite effects. Practically all critics of PR seriously weaken their case by treating the two as if they were one system.

What both do have in common is the pooling of votes to elect more than one representative at a time. This is inevitable if we are to avoid the huge waste of votes and consequent distortions inherent in a single-member system. It is indeed possible for *voting* to take place in single-member constituencies (in additional-member systems), but to achieve anything like proportional representation of parties, those votes must be pooled over a much larger area.

PARTY LIST SYSTEMS

Systems based on voting for a party are used to elect the parliaments of all of the continental European democracies except France. Israel goes to the limit of accuracy in party representation (except that it excludes parties with less than one percent of the votes): the whole country is one constituency, each party presents a list of candidates in an order decided by the party, and votes are cast for those lists. The European countries modify this to a greater or lesser extent by dividing their territory into smaller multimember constituences and/or giving the voter some power (large or small) to discriminate between individual candidates. The method of calculating proportionality also varies. There may be some deliberate weighting in favor of large parties or of smaller ones, but in all cases the seats won by a party are proportional to its votes within narrow limits. Two list systems differ markedly from the rest: the Swiss and the West German.

The Swiss voter has as many votes as there are seats to be won in his canton and may distribute them among candidates of one party or of several; he may cumulate two votes on one candidate. A party's seats are decided by the total votes for its candidates and are filled by the candidates with the most votes. An important feature of this system is that, unlike list systems in general, it permits a voter to support candidates who are united for a particular cause although standing in different parties.

In Germany, the Weimar Republic used a system almost identical with the Israeli. After the Second World War, this was changed with the object of introducing a personal element: half the Bundestag is elected in the same manner as the British House of Commons, but a second vote is cast for a party list in the voter's Land and additional seats are awarded to each party so as to make its total seats proportional to these second votes. Excluded from this distribution is any party that has not polled at least five percent of the second votes or won three seats in the single-member constituencies. This system is appreciably more personal than the British, because a voter who personally admires a candidate in his constituency can support that candidate with his first vote while not necessarily helping that candidate's party. This advantage does not extend to the "AMS" (additional member) variant of the system produced by a committee of the Hansard Society (1976), which uses only one vote and awards the additional seats to those unelected candidates who have polled the highest percentages of votes. Since a candidate's votes depend overwhelmingly on his party's strength in that constituency, and very little on the voters' opinion of him personally, any impression that the voters have a say in choosing the person who is to represent them is an illusion.

THE SINGLE TRANSFERABLE VOTE

In the English-speaking world, "PR" has always meant the single transferable vote, invented in England and simultaneously in Denmark early in the nineteenth century. The voter numbers candidates in the order of his preference, thus instructing the returning officer to give the vote to candidate 1, but if it cannot help to elect that candidate (either because he has enough votes without it or because he has so few as to be without hope of election) to give it instead to candidate 2. If it cannot help candidate 2 either, it goes to the voter's third choice, and so on if necessary. To be sure of election a candidate needs a quota of the total votes, worked out by the Droop formula:

$$\frac{\text{total valid votes}}{\text{seats} + 1} + 1$$

For example, if there are five seats to be filled, six candidates could each get one-sixth of the votes but only five could get more, so anyone with more than one-sixth of the votes cannot fail to be among the five elected.

In a parliamentary election, it is likely that most voters will vote 1, 2, 3, etc. for all candidates of their preferred party. If the party's supporters are equal in number to one quota, this will cause their votes to accumulate on the party's one most favored candidate and elect him; twice as many will elect two, and so on. Hence, there will be proportional representation of parties, with an accuracy depending (as in list systems) on how many members are elected from each constituency.

Thus, the proportional representation of parties is not something for which the system is designed, but is a consequence of voters choosing to support a party. The same effects follow if the voters choose in the same way to support some other group—such as their own race, religion, sex, etc. For instance, in elections within a professional association the "parties" are likely to be different branches of the same profession, seniors and juniors, men and women, or different parts of the country. Moreover, the vote is likely to reflect, at the same time, the voter's opinion on more than one such matter. In an X-vote election, as for the British House of Commons, a voter has to decide which one of his many interests shall decide his vote. He may, for instance, wish to promote the interests of his ethnic group but finds that the only candidate of the group stands for a party he dislikes; which is he to choose? When several people are to be elected together, he is much less likely to be faced with this either/or choice. A party large enough to have hope of winning more than one seat must select more than one candidate and will be wise to choose them so as to appeal to a wide range of voters. Moreover, if the vote is transferable there is no longer any risk to a party in splitting its vote among a number of candidates, so if it does not spontaneously include, say, a woman or a black candidate, those who want one can insist on nominating such a candidate. The voters' preferences then decide who is elected and who is not. The voter will start his numbering with a candidate who both belongs to his preferred party and shares his interest in some question the voter thinks important; he can then go on either to candidates of the same party with rather less acceptable views on the special question or to candidates of other parties who share his special interest.

EFFECTS OF DIFFERENT SYSTEMS

Reckless statements are often made to the effect that such and such an electoral system "always" or "never" produces certain effects. Such assertions are unlikely to be true, since there are too many other factors involved, but we should be able to determine whether any given system has a tendency to encourage or discourage certain developments.

To do so, it is necessary to examine all, or at least a large and representative sample, of the actual applications of each system. Opponents of PR condemn themselves if they continue to rely on a few selected examples of ill-governed, unstable countries (the current favorite is Italy) without attempting to explain why Switzerland is so exceedingly stable or to mention that Austria has returned the same party with an overall majority in three elections running. It won't do to condemn PR in the Weimar Republic for producing Hitler while not considering why in the postwar Federal Republic no such tendency has appeared. It won't do to hold up Ireland's three elections in 1981–82 as proof of instability without mentioning the preceding four-year governments or suggesting why Britain's two elections in eight months in 1974 are not to be regarded as showing instability. Factual errors are too common. The assertion that France elected her parliament by PR from 1946 to 1958 can be made only by someone who has not looked at the highly unproportional result of the 1951 election. The commonest mistake is to raise against PR in general, objections that apply, if at all, only to party list systems.

Multiplicity of Parties

If, in order to put a particular point of view to the electorate, it is necessary to submit a separate party list, this must have some tendency to encourage a large number of parties. But this does not, in practice, happen to anything like the extent that is often imagined. European countries changing from a single-member system to a proportional one have usually experienced some increase in the number of parties represented, but not a large one. To take an oft-quoted example, the Netherlands already had ten parties in the last parliament elected by a single-member system and under PR has had between seven and fifteen; the present number is twelve, as in the British House of Commons in 1979. The Weimar Republic certainly suffered from many splinter parties, but their number never exceeded that in the last pre-1919 Reichstag, elected from single-member constituencies. In France, when party list PR was introduced in 1945, the number of parties in the Chamber acually decreased, from fourteen to ten.

The single transferable vote should, in theory, and does, in practice, have the opposite tendency. The Greens have now won seats in the Bundestag and ecology parties are springing up in other countries, but their members could probably serve their cause more effectively if they were able to give preference to ecology-minded candidates within the established parties. In the Dublin municipal elections of 1979, a major issue was the development or preservation of a prehistoric site. The voters produced a preservationist majority on the new council, simply by giving preference, within each of the existing parties, to those candidates who supported preservation. No new party was required. New parties have, indeed, sprung up from time to time and have disappeared when the occasion for them has passed. The present Dáil contains three major parties, one with only two members, and three Independents. The oldest user of STV, Tasmania, is unique among the Australian states in having only two parties (and the occasional Independent); it needs no Country party, since anyone wanting the farming interests represented needs only to give preference to candidates who are farmers.

Stable Government

It is not the number of parties which is seen as a threat so much as the absence of a parliamentary majority for any one of them. Opponents of PR believe it will produce that situation, with the result that a large party cannot govern without undue dependence on support from a small one. Of course it is true that there could no longer be anything like the present situation in the United Kingdom, where a party supported by only forty-four percent of those who voted in the 1979 election already had a comfortable majority of fifty-three percent of the seats. The 1983 election produced a *decrease* in the government party's support from forty-four to forty-two percent but a large *increase* in its parliamentary seats to sixty-one percent—144 seats more than all other parties combined.

If we are not to allow that forty-two percent to impose their will on the other fifty-eight percent, we must admit some limit on the largest party's power. When a British general election has given no one party a working majority in parliament (which has happened this century in about one election in every three), the resulting government has generally been unsatisfactory and short-lived—because the party in power has tried to continue with methods that work only if the government has an assured majority. The essential condition for success is for the leading party to admit that it has not got a mandate for everything it wants to do but has the right and the power to carry out those parts of its program which have support in other parties also. It can either govern alone, limiting its actions to those commanding sufficient support from other parties (a common solution in Denmark) or form a coalition with one or more other parties with whom it can agree on a common program.

The success of such a government must depend a great deal on the psychology of those involved. Italy, whose parties have not long since evolved from warring personal factions, is far less stable than Switzerland, with her firmly rooted democracy and a belief that it is wrong for one section of the nation to impose its will on another. But the electoral system will also play a part.

Any proportional system will increase the pressure to make a coalition work, since there is not the temptation which exists in the United Kingdom to resort to a new election in the hope of a radically different result. The small shift of public opinion likely over a short time can produce only a small change in the parliament, not the upheaval possible under a single-member system.

However, some proportional systems will be more helpful than others. It is said that in an election unlikely to produce a parliamentary majority for any one party, the voters do not know what they are voting for. A coalition will be engineered between party leaders in the proverbial smoke-filled room, without reference to the voters' wishes. That is true with a pure party list system (including the British party list of one name); it is less true if the voters have a choice within the list (e.g. between a candidate known to favor a coalition with Party A and one known to prefer Party B), as in Belgium, for instance. It is still less true if the voter himself can indicate which of the other parties he would prefer his own to associate with. That is the position in Switzerland and to a minor extent for the third party in West Germany. An FDP supporter has no hope that his first vote may elect an FDP candidate, so he may use it for SPD or CDU, as the case may be, giving his own party only his second vote—the only one that affects the number of seats it wins. By far, the greatest power to decide what coalition shall emerge is given by the single transferable vote. In the Irish election of 1973, the Fine Gael and Labour parties announced that if, together, they achieved a majority in the Dáil, they would form a coalition government, and each asked its supporters to promote this by voting 1, 2, 3 . . . for candidates of the one party and then going on to those of the other. This the majority of voters did, and thus gave the coalition a majority of the seats. They were perfectly free to accept or reject this advice, and had they rejected it there would have been no coalition majority.

Voters by STV can also give an indication of which major policies they would prefer the coalition to pursue, choosing, for instance, right- or left-wing candidates of a party, as the case may be; the coalition partners can therefore frame their common program with a knowledge of what will command the most support.

This is an important factor in stability. A government that comes to power with a majority of seats but not of votes may be extremely stable for the duration of one parliament, but if it is defeated in the next election, the country may be rendered very unstable. To take a concrete instance, postwar Labour governments in Britain have nationalized certain industries, some of which subsequent Conservative governments have denationalized; Labour proclaims its intention, when it regains power, of renationalizing these without compensation. This has led worried industrialists to seek a remedy for such repeated reversals which make it impossible for them to plan ahead beyond the next election. With coalition governments, whose policies are necessarily a compromise, a wholesale reversal of policy on a change of government is less likely. In the Federal Republic of Germany, the small Free Democrat party, by allying itself with the Christian Democrats instead of the Social Democrats, has changed the government, but there is no expectation of any drastic change of policy such as will occur in Britain if Labour replaces the Conservative government in the next election. In all of the Scandinavian countries, it is taken for granted that the general pattern will remain; policies have originated in different parties, but if found successful are continued by the others. With STV, continuity is even more likely, since the voters will give preference to those candidates with whom they agree on important questions, thus producing a parliamentary majority for or against (for instance) nationalization which will not be changed unless and until the majority of the voters change their minds.

Adversary Politics

There is growing dislike of the unpleasant atmosphere of British politics, of the tendency to think in terms of party warfare rather than of government in the interests of the whole nation. That again is encouraged by the majority system of election. In each constituency, only one candidate can win; he must strive to "kill" his opponents. Where he has only to take his fair share of several seats, hostility is likely to be less. The British elector has to vote as if he thought candidate X was perfect and all others abominable; STV will force him to recognize that there are degrees of excellence among the candidates of his preferred party and will further invite him to consider candidates of other parties and indicate any with whom he has a measure of agreement. This change of atmosphere must help a coalition to work. When STV was restored in Northern Ireland it did produce a noticeable improvement, particularly in local government. The Derry council, which had been notorious for bad temper and violence, began to cooperate immediately in 1973 for the general good of the town and this improvement has been maintained; ten years later a report from Omagh draws attention to the same thing.

Large Constituencies

As pointed out at the beginning of this chapter, multimember constituencies are unavoidable if we want to make sure that the party with the most votes wins the most seats. However, it is right to consider the drawbacks they are alleged to have.

It is said that they will destroy the personal link between an MP and his constituents. That might well be so in the case of an impersonal party list system, but can it be true if the elector is enabled to choose the *person* he wants to represent him, instead of just accepting a party nominee? There is, in any case, much evidence that the link is weak. Many electors do not even know the name of their MP, and while he can truly represent all of them in such matters as seeing that they get all of the social benefits to which they are entitled, he cannot do anything for the constituent who wants action contrary to the policy of the MP's party. Can a Socialist "represented" by a right-wing Conservative or a Conservative by a left-wing Labour MP really look on that person as *his* MP? With STV, practically every voter gets an MP who is at least of his preferred party and in most cases also a man or woman preferred by him to other candidates of the same party—and whom, at the next election, he can either return again or replace by a different person, according to whether he considers the MP to have served him well or ill.

Any proportional system will also give more people an MP who knows their local circumstances and is well-known to them before he even becomes a candidate. With single-member constituencies, the Conservative in an industrial city, a Labour man in the "stockbroker belt" has no chance of ever representing his own home in parliament, but has a safe seat if he can get himself adopted for the other's home. When any large minority can win a seat as well as the majority, each can stay among the people he knows and represent the minority there. The

Member's connection with his constituents is likely also to be far more lasting. A good MP is much less likely to lose his seat when there is a swing against his party (with STV, the Members the party loses will be those whom the voters think can best be spared), and he is far less likely to be separated from his constituents by a boundary revision. The current redistribution in Britain is causing endless trouble of that kind, while if there were multimember constituencies covering such natural units as the city of Leeds or the county of Somerset, they could remain unchanged for the foreseeable future, while any increase or decrease in their electorate could be met by awarding them one seat more or fewer.

Multimember constituencies as such (even with a defective voting system) have an additional advantage: they give a fair chance of election to categories of people who now, under a single-member system, find great difficulty in becoming candidates for a winnable seat. The most conspicuous of such groups are the female majority and ethnic minorities. A party that has to select only one candidate in a constituency probably agrees that there ought to be some black faces in the House of Commons and more than our present 3.5 percent of women, but believes that to select such a candidate would reduce its chance of winning. But if it has to select several candidates, it is in the party's interest to choose them so as to make a wide appeal—including both men and women, white and black.

It is for this reason that all countries with single-member systems have about the same low percentage of women MPs as Britain has, while, with the solitary exception of Malta, all countries with proportional systems have more—usually far more. The half of the Bundestag elected like the House of Commons has a similar percentage of women; the half elected from Land lists always has several times as many. In Ireland, under STV, it is of course not only inclusion in a party's team that matters but also the voters' preferences. If the electors want more women TDs, they can insist on nominating them and giving them preference over men. Irish women have traditionally taken very much a back seat, but they have recently begun to assert themselves, and in the last election, the percentage of women elected rose from 4.8 to 8.4 percent. Similarly, New York, feeling that it was imperative for Puerto Ricans and blacks to have representation on its school boards, introduced STV for that purpose, with entirely satisfactory results. Such groups get their due voice on elected bodies, without any need for the formation of racial parties.

ELECTIONS EXIST FOR THE ELECTORS

If we really want elections to reflect the wishes of the electors, the single transferable vote is by far the most effective means of doing this, whether those wishes relate to political parties or to anything else. The party list systems used in continental Europe do accurately reflect the voters' wishes concerning each party, but not on other matters. They count votes for each party against every other party, emphasizing their divisions and offering no means for the voters to express agreements. The more flexible Swiss system does allow voters to cross the party lines and it has an excellent record of contributing to the unity of that country's diverse population. However, it is less effective than STV as a mirror of opinion, largely because a vote for an individual counts also for that individual's party (whether the voter wishes it to or not) and also counts against every other vote, including those given by the same voter. This involves the danger that a candidate may be defeated by the second, etc. votes of his own supporters. The single transferable vote is free from these defects. It gives the voter maximum freedom to express his opinions and assurance that this will affect the election result in the way he wishes. It has proved its value as what a member of the religious minority in Ireland called "a healing and unifying force."

5

The Case for
Proportional Tenure: A Defense of
the British Electoral System

Peter J. Taylor

Electoral reform is a complicated issue involving many interlocking themes. The ethical, or moral, arguments in this debate are one such theme. These arguments are of particular interest because of their one-sided nature: proponents of reform tend to use "fairness" as a major element of their case; opponents of reform do not. For instance Lakeman's (1974, p. 7) treatise on electoral systems is dedicated to the reformer John H. Humphreys who had "a deep faith in the moral basis of democracy" and a sincere belief in "fair play." In a similar manner, the essays on electoral reform collected by Finer make frequent references to the unfairness of the present system:

> The obvious argument for electoral reform is that it would ensure greater justice or fairness in the representative process. This is pretty self-evident and is rarely challenged in principle (Finer 1975, p. 77).

Moreover, the Hansard Society (1976, p. 2) report on electoral reform comes to an identical conclusion:

> there can be no doubt that the first-past-the-post system does not produce a fair representation of the views of the people in Parliament. Indeed supporters of the present system do not attempt to defend it on grounds of fairness.

It seems that we have the strange situation of a debate where both sides agree that all the "good guys" (in a moral sense) are concentrated on one side of the argument. Certainly the moral argument against reform seems largely to have gone by default.[1] Perhaps this is because there can be no moral basis to the arguments against electoral reform. In this chapter I hope to demonstrate that this is not the case. A logically consistent argument can be constructed which shows the present British system to operate in a just and fair manner. The development of this argument is the theoretical purpose of the chapter; illustration of the argument using British elections from 1945 to 1979 constitutes the empirical purpose of the chapter.

In any logical argument, a change in conclusion presupposes a change in assumptions. This brings us to the consideration of the purpose of an election. The current debate emphasizes the view that democratic elections are a means of translating public opinion, in the form of votes, into a legislative body, in the form of parliamentary seats. It is but a short step from this assumption to the assertion that seats should be proportional to votes for political parties and hence to a conclusion favoring proportional representation systems of voting. An alternative view of an election is that it is a means for producing governments, for endorsing or changing the government in power. In some countries, notably the United States and France, these two purposes of an election are to some extent separated as the electorate is asked to vote for the executive and legislature separately. In a parliamentary democracy, however, the two "types" of election are combined into a single general election. There is, therefore, a confusion of purpose to some degree in parliamentary elections which is reflected in the electoral reform debate. In the ensuing argument I will emphasize the "government producing" purpose of elections.

The change in assumption from a proportional legislature to a concern for government may be justified in terms of voter perceptions. It can be clearly shown that people in Britain vote for parties much more than for constituency candidates—a change of candidate has little effect on a constituency result in party voting terms. In fact, it is not stretching the case to suggest that most voters think in terms of support or rejection of the current government when they go to the ballot box. In this sense, general elections are perceived almost as referenda on the government. Without taking this argument any further, it will be clear that the assumption that general elections are primarily about the executive role of government—which party rules—can be justified as a reasonable assumption.

Opponents of electoral reform normally emphasize this second role of elections and go on to argue that the present system gives us strong and stable one-party government. It is at this point that the "moral" basis of proportional representation is conceded; mathematical fairness, it is argued, must be set aside for practical reasons of good firm government. However, this position is not a very sound one, suggesting, as it does, that "fair" electoral procedures conflict with "good" government! The argument is particularly weak when viewed in the light of the February 1974 election where six million Liberal votes produced only fourteen MPs and this "sacrifice" of the third party did *not* produce firm government but rather a minority government plus another election within eight months. The 1974 elections clearly bolstered the unfairness argument for change while diminishing the strong government argument against change. It is clear that the search for a moral argument against reform will be unsuccessful if general elections are looked at individually. If the purpose of elections is to produce a government, however, then we need to take a longer-term view of the alternating governments.

Governments need time to carry out the policies they put before the electorate. Thus, we can view general elections as a means of allocating time in government to the most popular party in order to carry out its program. A maximum period of five years is available to the winning party, but usually they choose to remain in office for some period less than five years. Although there is no convention for a specific period of office to be allocated to a party which wins an election, the size of its majority in parliament clearly affects its length of office. In Table 5.1, government majorities over both the official opposition and all parties are shown alongside the length of the respective parliaments for the ten general elections from 1945 to 1974.

Clearly, there are pressures on a party with a small majority to go to the polls fairly quickly in order to obtain a bigger majority. Hence, even though the timing of a general election is the sole prerogative of the prime minister, this decision-making is relatively predictable. Empirically, there exists a simple relationship between government tenure, and a party's majority over the official opposition which can be described by the following equation:

$$y = 14.8 \log X - 14.9$$

where y is the length of the parliament and X is the majority. The strength of this relationship is shown by the correlation of $+0.95$. (This can be interpreted as indicating that ninety percent of the variation in length of parliaments from 1945 to 1979 can be accounted for solely by the size of majority over the opposition, without directly concerning ourselves with such particular features as local government elections, by-elections, and opinion polls which usually figure in discussion of prime ministerial decisions on election timing.) What this very clear-cut relationship means is that, in effect, elections can be viewed as an allocation of government time to a party. Parties with a majority of over seventy-five are basically "given" between four years and the five-year maximum term of office. On the other hand, a party with a majority of only forty has a period of approximately forty months to carry out its program. This latter example is of interest, since Labour had a majority of forty-two over Conservatives in October 1974. Despite a low overall majority which disappeared in 1977, the Labour Government was able to survive for just over forty months, albeit with Liberal support.

By viewing elections as allocating time to a party, we can begin to make a new assessment of the present system. The period from 1945 to 1979 can be divided up between the two main parties. In this period the Conservatives governed for 197 months and Labour 190 months. This even balance of tenure,

Table 5.1 Governments, Tenures, and Majorities in Parliaments of the United Kingdom, 1945–1979

General Election	Party Elected to Form Government	Tenure: Length of Parliament (months)	Majority* over Official Opposition	Overall Majority*
1945	Labour	55	180	146
1950	Labour	19	16	5
1951	Conservative	42	27	18
1955	Conservative	52	68	60
1959	Conservative	60	107	100
1964	Labour	17	13	4
1966	Labour	49	90	76
1970	Conservative	43	42	30
1974 (Feb)	Labour	8	4	-33
1974 (Oct)	Labour	42	42	3

*These are majorities resulting from the General Election and will change during a parliament due to by-election results. This is particularly important after the October 1974 election when the Government lost its overall majority in 1977.

Conservatives having fifty-one percent and Labour forty-nine percent of government time, closely reflects the party's balance in their respective support since 1945. In the ten general elections covered by this period, the Conservatives have gained 122 million votes to Labour's 124 million. This indicates a slight bias to the Conservatives but a high level of proportionality does exist—the even balance of the electorate is reflected by the even allocation of Conservative and Labour months in office. We may term this "proportionate tenure."

Two outstanding problems remain. First, what of the underrepresentation of minor parties which is clearly illustrated for individual elections? In the ten elections from 1945 to 1974 the Liberals have accumulated a total of only 27 million votes, far fewer than the two major parties. However, they are clearly underrepresented in government over our longer perspective since this 9½ percent of all general election votes cast has provided them with zero months of office. However, I think we can view voting for the Liberals as a rather different case than voting for the Labour and Conservative parties. Liberal supporters can have had little hope, since 1945, of producing a Liberal government. Their main hope of office is obviously in coalition with one of the two major parties. Since 1945, there have been three close elections where the Liberals nearly held a balance of power between the major parties (1951, 1964, and October 1974), while on one occasion they did hold potential power when they turned down the Conservative offer of a coalition after the February 1974 election. Such a coalition would have had a majority of twenty over Labour and could have expected about twenty months in office, thus substantially redressing the Liberal's lack of office. The refusal of the Liberal Party to accept office on this occasion is a part of the cause of the lack of exact proportionality in votes and office for the third party. It cannot be used as an indictment of the present electoral system. Furthermore, a Lib–Lab pact was set up for eighteen months in 1977 and 1978 in which the third party was consulted on the government's program. This does not constitute tenure of office, but is in keeping with the general level of Liberal popular support.

The second outstanding problem relating to the .British system is that, occasionally, the party polling most votes does *not* win a plurality of seats in parliament. This direct reversal of the electorate's wishes occurred in 1951 and February 1974. Such a result is difficult to justify. However, it must be seen in proper time perspective. Such results will only occur in close general elections thus producing relatively small parliamentary majorities. Hence in terms of allocating government time to the "wrong" party, the error is fairly small. Although two out of ten postwar elections produced the "wrong" winner, the resulting parliaments lasted for a total of only fifty months. This argument does not justify this type of result, but it does put it into perspective. If considered important, the problem could be overcome with a minor reform, rather than the wholesale electoral reforms proposed recently.

What does this alternative conception of the purpose of an election do for reformers' arguments of fairness and justice? Electoral reformers may, as Rogaly (1976) asserts, advocate "parliament for the people" but their reforms will *not* produce "government for the people"—instead there would be "government for the party politicians." A PR system will almost inevitably mean that no party controls a majority of seats in parliament, so that government is created *not* as a result of an election, but as a consequence of post-election party maneuvering. As in recent PR elections in Holland, Belgium, and Ireland, the new government will not be known after the "people have given their verdict" in the election but will have to await what deals the party managers can put together away from voter control. PR reforms could, of course, lead to a situation where governments change without politicians bothering even to call an election—as happens frequently in Italy[2] and has occurred recently in the German Federal Republic.[3] We should not forget that Britain's only postwar move towards coalition government—the Lib–Lab pact of 1977–78—was put together to *prevent* a general election occurring because of the unpopularity of both parties. The conclusion is clear: Given our assumptions about the prime purpose of an election, PR systems are not just unfair and unjust, but profoundly undemocratic.

"All organization is bias" says Schattschneider (1960), and it is about time that the advocates of electoral reform got off of their moral high-horse and admitted as much. The reforms *will* produce proportionality of parliamentary representation, but they have to argue that this is the important purpose of an election. The reformers, of course, ignore the government tenure argument because it exposes the political bias of their case, which is to provide a disproportionate amount of government tenure (in coalition) for small center parties. The present system does produce approximate proportionality of government tenure and can be defended on the grounds that elections are about producing governments. It is, of course, much more than a matter of PR versus PT. It is a matter of stopping small center parties from hijacking British governments.

NOTES

1. This comment refers specifically to the recent PR debate in Britain. The classic statement against PR by Hermens (1941) does consider ethical arguments.

2. In 1983, Italy's forty-third government since 1945 collapsed, leading to only Italy's tenth general election in the same period. Clearly, the typical process is for government to change without resource to elections.

3. In Germany, the party with the *most* government experience is the *smallest* of the three main parties, the Free Democrats. This party has been in coalition with one or the other of the two largest parties, the Social Democrats and Christian Democrats, for twenty-seven out of thirty-four years in the period 1950–1983.

6

Seats, Votes, Redistricting, and the Allocation of Power in Electoral Systems

R. J. Johnston

Electoral reform is an issue that refuses to go away in many countries. There may be periods when it is kept alive by only a small group of protagonists (as in Britain; see Bogdanor 1981), but these are punctuated by episodes of considerable activity and generalized support. The United Kingdom is experiencing one of these episodes at the present time. It began with the electoral resurgence of the Liberal Party in 1974, being stimulated by a major mismatch between that party's percentage of the votes cast (19.3, 18.3) at the two general elections and its percentage of the seats won (2.2, 2.0). Since then, it has been carried forward by the new Social Democrat Party which, along with its Liberal allies, has set electoral reform as a major political goal (Liberal/SDP Alliance 1982). The political debate has been matched by increased academic interest. And yet, it will be argued here, the arguments for electoral reform have not been seen through to their logical conclusions.

Arguments for electoral reform are not peculiar to countries that use the first-past-the-post (plurality) system; in France, several different systems have been tried over the last century in attempts to delete the voting power of certain social groups and the political base of certain parties (Campbell 1958); and in Germany there have been arguments for abandoning the present system and adopting first-past-the-post (Conradt 1970). Because it is the first-past-the-post system that is currently under considerable attack, it forms the focus of the present chapter. Most attention is paid to the British case, although many of the arguments apply equally well elsewhere. The basic objective is to identify the problems of the first-past-the-post system and to evaluate the potential of other systems in the alleviation, if not cure, of those problems.

THE ILLS OF FIRST-PAST-THE-POST

Nearly all analyses of electoral systems focus on their potential for electoral distortion—defined as the difference between a party's proportion of the votes and its proportion of the seats. Both theoretical (Loosemore and Hanby 1971) and empirical (Gudgin and Taylor 1979) investigations have shown that the first-past-the-post system is more likely to produce distortion and produces greater distortions than do other commonly-used systems. Thus, the case for electoral reform is that replacement of the first-past-the-post (FPP) system will equalize (or more nearly so) votes and seats, so that each party's political power will be approximately equal to its electoral support.

The fullest empirical statement of the ills of the FPP system has been provided by Rae (1971; O'Loughlin 1979 has updated Rae's analyses). He has shown that: 1) FPP is more likely to deny representation to parties than is any other system; 2) the mismatch between votes and seats is greater under FPP; 3) minority parties—those with less than twenty percent of the votes—are seriously disadvantaged by FPP; 4) the largest party almost invariably gets a greater percentage of the seats than the votes under FPP; 5) most parliaments elected by FPP have a manufactured majority, in that one party gets more than fifty percent of the seats without getting fifty percent of the votes; 6) the average number of parties needed to produce a parliamentary majority is much less under FPP than any other system; and 7) changes in party support between elections are magnified by FPP. In addition, the constituency-delimitation procedure is open to abuses, of which the most common are malapportionment and gerrymandering. The first was outlawed in the United States by a series of Supreme Court decisions beginning with *Baker v Carr* in 1962 (Dixon 1968), although it has only recently been legally challenged in the United Kingdom. Gerrymandering is more difficult to control—except where the electoral interests of a well-specified group, such as ethnic minorities in the United States (O'Loughlin and Taylor 1982; O'Loughlin 1982) are concerned. Even when the redistricting is undertaken by neutral commissions, political control of the redistricting agenda and commission interpretation of its task can substantially influence the electoral outcome (Johnston 1982a; 1983).

The case against FPP has recently been bolstered by analyses which suggest that its role in exaggerating the impact of electoral change has been reduced. Rae's (1971) analyses suggested that the average swing in voter support for particular parties was magnified by a factor exceeding 2.0 when the allocation of seats was inspected. The reasons for this have been conclusively demonstrated as a function of the variance in the frequency distribution of the percentage of votes won by a party (Taylor 1973; Gudgin and Taylor 1979; Johnston 1979).

A decline in the magnification effect was first brought to academic attention by Tufte (1973), who showed that the frequency distribution in American voting was developing a bimodal shape. This stimulated considerable interest in the "case of the vanishing marginals" (Mayhew 1974) and the cause of the new bimodal distribution (see Ferejohn 1977; Fiorina 1977). More recently, a similar phenomenon has been observed in Great Britain. There, for a long time, the cube law was treated as the best representation of the relationship between votes and seats; if S_A is the proportion of the seats won by A, V_A is its proportion of votes, and S_B and V_B refer to party B, then in a two-party system $(S_A/S_B)=(V_A/B_B)^3$ (see Johnston 1979; Gudgin and Taylor 1979). Laakso (1979), not confining his work to the two-party situation, has argued that raising (V_A/V_B) to the power of 2.5 provides a better fit than the power of 3 for recent elections. Curtice and Steed (1982), however, argue that the power has declined even further, to a value of about 2. The result is that, as in the United States, there are many fewer marginal seats than previously (assuming that the party system remains relatively unchanged).

The validity of these last two arguments is difficult to establish. Using Laakso's (1979) measure of the deviation from proportionality in a multiparty system, the value for the power has ranged from 1.8 to 4.5 over the four elections in 1970, 1974 (February and October), and 1979. Graphing these values (Figure 6.1) suggests that increased disproportionality (i.e., more marginal seats)

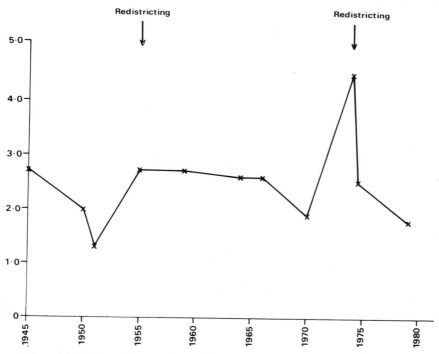

Figure 6.1. The Seats:Votes Ratio (Using Laakso's 1979 a_{opt} Measure) for the United Kingdom, 1945-1979.

is brought about by redistricting, after which a combination of migration, population change, and voter accommodation to the new constituency environment leads to a decline in the number of marginals and the power of the seats:votes ratio.

The conclusion derived from Figure 6.1 is tentative. Data for three other cases (Figure 6.2) give no clear indication of a similar pattern. For New Zealand, where redistricting takes place every five years—after the census—the data show that, in most cases, the value of Laakso's a_{opt} parameter increased over the se-

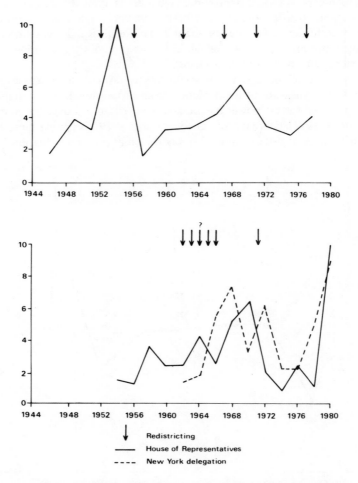

Figure 6.2. The Seats:Votes Ratio (Using Laakso's 1979 a_{opt} Measure) for *Top* New Zealand, 1947–1978, and *Bottom* the United States House of Representatives, 1954–1980, and the New York Delegation to the United States House of Representatives, 1962–1980.

quence rather than declined (1972–75 is the exception to this). For the United States House of Representatives, a somewhat similar trend occurred in the late 1960s, following the "reapportionment revolution" of the early years of that decade. In the 1970s, the parameter remained low—indicative of gerrymandering—except for 1980. Finally, for the state of New York alone in the voting for the United States House of Representatives, there is a clear indication that redistricting at the beginning of each decade creates a gerrymander, but that over the decade this is diluted, presumably as the result of population changes.

The implications of these findings suggest that in Britain, where redistricting is undertaken by a neutral commission, once every fifteen years, the effect of the commission's work is to create marginal constituencies. Over time, because of a variety of processes (probably reflecting population change and voter socialization) the number of marginal constituencies declines. In the United States, on the other hand, where redistricting is undertaken by partisan agencies, the effect of redistricting is to create safe constituencies. Over time, again because of a variety of processes, the number of marginal seats increases. Further exploration of these findings is beyond the scope of this chapter. They suggest— as Gudgin and Taylor (1976) did several years ago— that a nonpartisan cartography is impossible with the FPP system. Such conclusions, if later verified, add yet another criticism to the case against FPP. Is there, then, any defense for FPP?

FIRST-PAST-THE-POST AND THE ALTERNATIVES

Most of the presumed ills of the FPP system can be summarized by stating that it fails to take account of the voters' preferences. Many voters do not even have their first preferences taken into account. Those in constituencies where their candidate wins, waste that fraction of the total vote for the candidate (and thus the same fraction of each elector's vote) that is in *excess* of the total needed to win the seat. Those in constituencies where their candidate loses *waste* all of their vote—it is irrelevant to the final outcome of the election (in terms of the allocation of seats). In any one constituency, the number of *effective* votes may be relatively small. For each party, the proportion of its votes that are effective is crucial to electoral success (hence gerrymandering).

How, then, can one ensure that all votes are equally effective? One proposed method—adopted for elections to the Australian House of Representatives—is to require electors to rank order all candidates preferentially, and to count votes in such a way that the elected member for each constituency is preferred, by a majority, to all other candidates. No solution to this problem may be available, because of the Arrow theorem of indeterminacy, but the Alternative Vote (AV) system seeks to approach it (as does the French double-ballot system).

There is, however, a major disadvantage of the AV system. If one party has, say, forty percent of the first preference votes, but those who do not rank the party first, rank it last, then it may fail to win any seats. This would only occur if it won forty percent of the votes in each constituency, of course, but the greater the number of constituencies in which it fell below fifty percent in the first preferences, the greater the probability of it being underrepresented in the allocation of seats. Taylor and Gudgin (1977) have shown that this is the fate of the Australian Labor Party.

Preferential voting alone is therefore insufficient. Where it is undertaken in multimember constituencies, the results are more likely to produce an allocation of seats roughly in accord with the interparty distribution of votes. Thus, the AV system adopted for multimember constituencies—the single transferable vote (STV) system—is strongly promoted by those seeking electoral reform to achieve proportional representation (PR).

The STV system will not necessarily produce PR, however. Of crucial importance is the size of the constituencies—the larger the constituency, the greater the proportion of votes that are effective. Also critical is the number of members per constituency—those with even numbers favor the party with fewer votes (especially in a two-party contest), whereas those with odd numbers favor the largest party (Paddison 1976). Thus the system is open to both redistricting abuse and the unintentional effects of nonpartisan redistricting—as the Irish are well aware. The result may be that, in a close fight, the largest party does not win the most seats (as in the 1982 Maltese general election).

An alternative to STV is the *party list* system that is widely employed in Western Europe (Carstairs 1980). In this, constituencies are usually very large (thirty or more members in some cases), and PR is virtually assured. Electors have one vote only, however, although most systems allow them to express a preference, within their chosen party, for particular candidates. This, according to the proponents of STV, operates against the interests of individuals who do not wish to follow a single party line. To them, the list system achieves PR at the expense of voter freedom in expressing preferences for candidates rather than parties.

A number of other, hybrid, electoral systems are employed and have been considered by proponents of electoral reform seeking to replace FPP. Of these, only the German system has been widely canvassed. This combines FPP in single-member constituencies, which provides individualized representation, with provincial (Land) lists. The combination ensures PR. It is preferred by some. Majority opinion among British electoral reformers (expressed most recently in Lakeman 1982), however, favors STV: it allows the maximum expression of voter preferences; its abuses are relatively easily controlled; and it produces a solution close to PR. The latter is crucial, because the goal of elections in Britain (as in Australia, New Zealand, and all Western European countries except France) is to produce a Parliament from which a majority government can be formed.

THE ACHILLES HEEL

So far so good. The logic of the above argument points clearly towards some form of PR; only in this way will the ills and potential abuses of FPP be avoided. Or will they?

As just stressed, most of the arguments for PR take place in the context of parliamentary democratic practice, whereby a (if not the) major purpose of electing a parliament is to produce a government with majority support there, and thus with a mandate to govern. The argument of electoral reformers opposing FPP is that this mandate is frequently given to a party with majority support in the parliament but with only minority support among the voters. With PR, this would not happen. Any majority in the parliament would represent a majority of the voters. Thus PR would not only allocate parliamentary seats fairly, it would also allocate *power* fairly. "One man, one vote, one value" would be ensured.

Or would it? If, under PR, a single party achieved a majority of votes and seats, then a mandate to govern could be assumed. But most proponents of PR presume that this would rarely happen. No party would receive majority support, so no party would have a mandate to govern. A coalition of parties would be needed to create a majority, and it is in this that the strength of PR is grounded, according to many (see Lakeman 1974; Finer 1975; Rogaly 1976; for a contrary view, see Chandler 1982).

Coalitions are produced as a result of interparty bargaining. The assumption of the PR protagonists is that in this bargaining, each party's power is equivalent to its seats in the parliament. Unfortunately, this is rarely (if ever) so. Some parties have much more bargaining power (relative to the total in the system) than they do seats; some have much less.

This conclusion has been derived many times, from analyses based on games theory (Brams 1975; Laver 1981). Some of the analyses are relatively sophisticated mathematically, but the basic argument is extremely simple. A party can only bargain with potential partners in a coalition if its votes are valuable to them. Thus in a parliament of 101 members, with a simple majority of fifty-one, a party is of no value to a group of other parties with forty-four votes between them if it has only five. Nor, more importantly, is it of much value to them if they have fifty-three votes; they have a majority without the extra five. Thus, bargaining power is available only in situations where a party's votes are crucial to the coalition's majority; only then can it argue its particular policy line and get support for its constituents' opinions.

A simple index of bargaining power has been devised as the ratio between a party's percentage of the seats and the percentage of coalitions that it can defeat by a withdrawal of support. (This is outlined in a number of places—e.g. Taylor and Johnston 1979; Johnston 1979. For a summary see Johnston 1982b.) A ratio in excess of 1.0 indicates that the party is more powerful than its seat allocation, whereas one of less than 1.0 indicates a paucity of power relative to seats.

To illustrate this index, ratios have been calculated for election results in New Zealand if PR had been employed instead of FPP (see Table 6.1). Seats were allocated among the three main parties (four since 1972) according to their percentage of the national vote total. (Note that this analysis does not refer to the full House of Representatives. Elections to this are split into two parts, both using FPP. Four seats are reserved for the Maori electorate. The remainder are allocated to the "European" electorate, with the number of seats being increased in line with population growth—Jackson 1973. Only the "European" votes and seats are analyzed here.) Nearly all of the results indicate the over-allocation of power to the small parties, especially to Social Credit prior to the introduction of the fourth—Values—party in 1972. In a hung parliament, the bargaining power of small parties may be much greater than their representation—but not necessarily so, as indicated by the ratio of "Other" in 1978. As a consequence, larger parties have less bargaining power than their seats would apparently entitle them to, although again this is not always the case as indicated by the 1975 and 1978 results.

The New Zealand situation suggests that small parties are advantaged under PR, but it must not be assumed that this is always the case. Balinski and Young (1982) have recently produced a "fair" allocation of seats in the European Parliament, and analysis of the relative power of the ten countries in this plan indicates that it is the medium-sized countries that are particularly advantaged (Table 6.2). Furthermore, other analyses have shown that the power ratio may be very sensitive to small changes in the distribution of seats (Johnston 1982b); defections and/or by-elections could significantly influence the distribution of power.

This index can be refined in a variety of ways (as in Johnston 1979; see also

Table 6.1 PR, Seats, and Power in Recent New Zealand Elections

	Seats Under PR				Power Ratio			
Election	Labour	National	Social Credit	Other	Labour	National	Social Credit	Other
1978	36	36	14	4	0.83	0.83	2.14	0.00
1975	34	41	7	5	0.43	1.06	2.07	2.90
1972	42	36	6	3	1.04	0.40	2.42	4.83
1969	36	36	7	1	0.74	0.74	3.81	0.00
1966	32	30	11	0	0.76	0.81	2.21	—
1963	33	36	6	1	0.77	0.70	4.22	0.00
1960	33	36	7	0	0.77	0.70	3.62	—
1957	37	34	5	0	0.68	0.75	5.07	—
1954	34	30	8	0	0.71	0.80	3.00	—

Table 6.2 Seats and Power in the European Parliament, 1980

Country	Fair Share Allocation of Seats (Proportion)		Proportion of Power	Power:Seats Ratio
West Germany	97	(0.224)	0.212	0.949
Italy	89	(0.205)	0.174	0.848
United Kingdom	88	(0.203)	0.167	0.822
France	83	(0.191)	0.147	0.767
Netherlands	22	(0.051)	0.099	1.958
Belgium	15	(0.035)	0.056	1.607
Greece	14	(0.032)	0.050	1.553
Denmark	10	(0.023)	0.039	1.700
Ireland	10	(0.023)	0.039	1.700
Luxembourg	6	(0.014)	0.017	1.252

Source: Based on data in Balinski and Young 1982.

Laver and Underhill 1982). The method of analysis can also be extended by taking account of the issues in which each party is most interested and the strength of its commitment to each. (Batty 1974, 1976 has used Coleman's 1973 work in this context, but it has not yet been applied to the situations described here.) With refinement and extension, it is likely that the mismatch between seats and power will increase rather than decline.

PR, Power, and Politics

The implication of these analyses is that PR, however desirable it may be for other reasons, is very unlikely to allocate power to parties within a parliament in proportion to their (fair) allocation of seats there. Thus, the electorate can have little confidence that the coalitions that emerge reflect the "will of the people," any more than they do under FPP. Some argue otherwise, that parties can enter the bargaining rooms with clear directions from the electorate; a strong rebuke to this position is provided by Chandler (1982). In systems with many parties, the combinatorial possibilities are manifold, and no party can hope to obtain guidance from the electorate on all of these; furthermore, the combinatorial probabilities are very sensitive to the actual configuration of seats, and parties cannot prepare for all eventualities. In systems with relatively small numbers of parties, one may be extremely powerful and can be responsible for major shifts in policy without any reference to the electorate (as happened in West Germany in 1982).

Is there, then, any case for PR? Although it makes more effective use of votes, and reduces the chances of either intentional abuse or unintentional bias in the allocation of seats, it does not ensure that the formation of governments is readily influenced by, and a reflection of, the electorate's wishes. It does ensure that minority opinion is represented in the parliament, and it allows new parties to develop parliamentary credence that might otherwise be denied them. But is this worth the trading in of the benefits of majority government by a party with known policies?

Clearly this is a difficult, if not impossible, question on which to obtain an answer from the electorate. Proponents of electoral reform (PR) rarely pose it. They argue for fairness in the seats:votes relationship and do not present the electorate with the problems of government formation in a multiparty situation, which not only comprises many competing interests (including, perhaps, groups committed to only one policy, who may be powerful enough to wield a virtual veto), but is probably quite volatile in its allocation of power relative to small changes in the composition of the parliament. To the extent that they don't raise these issues, the proponents of PR are disingenuous.

It may be that PR is the preferable system for electing a parliament only when the government is not created out of a majority there. Thus, as in the United States, there would be a separation of the executive and the legislature. Each branch would be able to initiate legislation, but would have to obtain the support of the other in order to get it enacted. In this way, the legislature, in responding to initiatives from the executive, might more readily represent the (perceived) will of the electorate, and the executive may have to construct separate legislative majorities for different measures. In this way, the interparty bargaining and debate would be more explicit, and therefore accountable to the electorate. More importantly, parties would not be effectively disenfranchised on all issues if they were not members of a permanent parliamentary majority coalition which formed the executive.

It would seem, therefore, that PR may bring "fairness" in the allocation of seats relative to votes in the conduct of parliamentary elections, but it would almost certainly not allocate parliamentary bargaining power equally among the various political parties—if one of the main purposes of a parliamentary election is to produce a majority government. But if the production of government were to be separated from the election of parliament, then PR would appear to be well-suited for providing an accountable legislative assembly which voted upon executive proposals. The major difference between the two models is that in the first, a permanent parliamentary coalition is needed, whereas in the second, separate coalitions may be needed on different issues. With the latter, the parties need not then bargain away their interest in certain policies in order to obtain concessions on others, if they are to be in the government. Nor, if they are not in the government, need they lose all bargaining power. PR with a separate executive and legislature allows parties to retain their bargaining position on each issue until it is decided—although they may then have to bargain with others over "policy packages."

Two types of political systems appear best suited to this solution at the present time. The European Parliament is elected on a quasi-PR basis; seats are allocated to countries in a relatively fair procedure (though see Taylor and Johnston 1978; Balinski and Young 1982) and only in Great Britain are the members not elected on a PR system. As yet, however, the Parliament has no major legislative powers, and the executive (the European Commission) is not directly elected. The other type comprises countries in which the executive and the legislature are elected separately, but PR is not used. The United States is clearly the main example. The introduction of PR for the election of Congress—basically the House of Representatives—might ensure that public opinion is better represented there. The deep entrenchment of the two main parties and their financial security, plus the present method of operating Congress (notably the committee system), mean that any changeover would not be straightforward, however.

Elsewhere, in countries where legislature and executive are not separated, introduction of PR will produce the inequalities in political power noted here—and made apparent in recent years in West Germany, Italy, and the Netherlands, and also in France prior to 1958. To be effective in these countries, the introduction of PR will require much more fundamental constitutional reform. Without that, PR will not necessarily bring political benefits to the United Kingdom. But, is the upheaval worthwhile in order to equalize the seats:votes relationship?

CONCLUSIONS

The arguments about electoral reform are frequently phrased in terms of electoral fairness, of equalizing the ratio between seats and votes for all parties contesting an election (except those with minimal support). But such phrasing omits reference to the crucial, and intended by its proponents, consequence of electoral reform: the reallocation of political power. If the argument is extended to incorporate this consequence, then this essay has suggested:

1) that the logic of electoral reformers with regard to the unfairness of the FPP system is undeniable;
2) that either the STV or the party list system, and especially the former, is much preferable to FPP;
3) that achievement of fairness in the allocation of seats is no guarantee of fairness in the allocation of power; and
4) that as a consequence, there is no guarantee that PR will produce more responsive, accountable, and representative government.

Only, it seems, if the elected legislature is separated from the elected executive can improvement in the nature of representative government be expected. This requires, in most countries, a major constitutional change much more significant than the mere changing of the electoral system. It is upon that major issue that debate should focus.

PART III
PLURALITY VERSUS
PROPORTIONAL REPRESENTATION:
HOW MUCH DIFFERENCE?

7

Electoral Systems:
A Question of Degree
or of Principle?

Richard Rose

Debates about electoral systems are often cast in terms of absolutes, both scientific and moral; seemingly small technical differences can be described as major issues of principle with political consequences of the first magnitude. In fact, the differences between electoral systems are matters of degree, not kind. This statement is true in worldwide comparisons, for there are some common features between elections with and without choice (Hermet, Rose, and Rouquié 1978). Similarities are much greater when comparisons are made within competitive party systems.

Properties of electoral systems can be made to appear important by using hypothetical examples of how an electoral system *might* work in the abstract, or by selecting a single empirical example from manifold election results. But electoral systems are not employed in the abstract; they function in concrete historical contexts. The same electoral laws can work very differently as social settings vary, for example, the differences between the old solid South and the North in the United States, or between England and Northern Ireland within the United Kingdom. Electoral systems are but a means to larger political ends, ends that may be agreed between parties, as in the maintenance of proportional representation (PR) systems in most of Europe today, or means that may be highly contingent and contested, as in the very frequent switching between electoral systems in France in the past half century.

The extent to which electoral systems differ in degree, not kind, is examined here empirically. This chapter also asks to what extent it is reasonable to regard an election as determining absolute control of the government of a country. The conclusion is that electoral systems are necessary but relatively unimportant in their influence upon the government of a country (contrast this with Finer 1975).

OVERLAPPING PROPERTIES OF ELECTORAL SYSTEMS

By definition, any electoral system will have a degree of representativeness, that is, the number of representatives elected will not be completely independent of the votes cast. We could not conceive of an honest electoral system in which parties receiving zero votes took one hundred percent of the seats, and in which parties with one hundred percent of the votes won zero seats. The question of representativeness—that is, the relationship between a party's share of votes and seats—is a matter of degree, not kind.

The degree of distortion between seats and votes will be greatest in an election for a single office, when only one candidate can be elected and the also-rans get nothing. A presidential ballot can, at best, be representative of a majority of votes only when a second ballot is used to guarantee a majority, as in France. In the United States, it is possible for a presidential candidate to win all of the powers of office with less than half the vote, as Harry Truman, John F. Kennedy, and Richard Nixon all did in the post-1945 era. Abraham Lincoln was elected president in 1860 with only 39.8 percent of the popular vote. Single-member plurality elections for a parliament or congress overcome the gross disproportional element by holding a number of winner-take-all ballots simultaneously in different constituencies. A party failing to win anything with a substantial minority of the vote in some constituencies can offset this by winning other seats with a small lead. The apportionment of seats may distort, but does not completely negate, the preferences of electors. There is a correlation between a party's share of the vote and its share of seats.

Empirically the question is: To what extent are PR systems more representative than plurality systems (as in Canada, New Zealand, the United Kingdom, and the United States) and other non-PR systems (the French and Australian majority systems and the Japanese single nontransferable vote). The first point to establish is whether there is a difference in kind, that is, whether all PR systems are more representative than all non-PR systems, or, alternatively, whether there is an overlap, with some PR systems less representative than some non-PR systems. The second point to establish is the degree of difference between the two systems. The Index of Proportionality used here to compare electoral systems is calculated as the sum of the difference between each party's share of seats and its percentage share of votes, divided by two and subtracted from one hundred. The closer the index is to one hundred, the more exactly proportional is the relationship between seats and votes.

A comparison of PR and non-PR systems in Western nations shows that the two types of system overlap in their empirical results. The most representative plurality system, the United States House of Representatives, is at least as proportional as seven of the seventeen PR systems. The least proportional PR system, Spain, is more disproportional than five of the seven non-PR systems (Table 7.1).

Table 7.1 Comparing the Proportionality of PR and Non-PR Systems, 1982

PR Systems	Index of Proportionality
Austria	99
Germany	98
Denmark	97
Ireland	97
Netherlands	97
Sweden	96
Iceland	96
Switzerland	96
Finland	95
Italy	95
Israel	94
Belgium	94
Portugal	93
Norway	91
Luxembourg	90
Greece	88
Spain	84
Average	94

Non-PR Systems

United States (House, 1980)	94
Japan	91
Canada	88
Australia	87
Britain	85
New Zealand	80
France	79
Average	86

Source: The most recent general election reported in Mackie and Rose (1982), updated by the author for countries with an election in 1982.

(The Index of Proportionality is calculated as the sum of the differences between each party's share of seats and its share of votes, divided by two and subtracted from one hundred).

The overall difference of degree between systems is relatively small, eight percent. The average index of proportionality for PR systems is ninety-four percent, and for plurality systems, eighty-six percent. The difference between the most proportional PR system, Austria, and the most proportional plurality system, the United States, is only five percent. The difference between the most disproportional PR and non-PR systems, Spain and France, is also only five percent. The range of variation is as great among PR systems (from ninety-nine to eighty-four percent) as it is among non-PR systems (from ninety-four to seventy-nine percent).

In order to understand the degree of representativeness of an electoral system, we must go beyond simple generalizations derived from theories of PR and plurality systems. We must explain substantial differences among PR systems, and substantial differences among plurality systems. Two types of differences can be readily illustrated here.

One type arises from the nonuniformity of electoral law within and between nations. Scholars are agreed that an electoral district's magnitude, that is, the number of representatives elected in a single multimember constituency, affects the degree of proportionality in the system (Rae 1971). A 150-seat national district, as exists in the Netherlands, can give representation to far more parties than a three- to five-seat district, such as is found in Ireland.

Among European PR systems there are very substantial differences in district magnitude *within as well as between* nations. In Sweden, the smallest constituency elects two members and the largest forty-nine, and in Italy, the range is from one to thirty-five (Table 7.2). The rationale for such disparities is normally the desire to maintain a link between natural geographical or administrative boundaries and electoral constituencies. The individualist philosophy of the United States Supreme Court, that legislators represent electors, not communities, is not commonly accepted in Europe. Within-nation differences in district magnitude qualify any generalization about the operation of proportional representation. Where the number of representatives returned by a constituency can vary within a nation by twenty times or more, then the quota necessary for a party to win a seat can vary greatly, too.

The size and spatial variation of the popular vote of parties is a second major determinant of the degree of proportionality of an electoral system. Unlike the number of representatives elected in a district, this influence cannot be determined by electoral law. It reflects a complex of political and social conditions within a country, and varies from constituency to constituency.

Plurality electoral systems are especially sensitive to the distribution of votes between parties. In theory, two parties could be very competitive in every constituency, but if in each constituency the same party always wins fifty-one percent of the vote, then the favored party would win one hundred percent of the seats. It is also theoretically possible for a party to win an absolute majority in Parliament with only one-quarter of the popular vote, by winning fifty-one seats in every one hundred by a margin of a few votes, and gaining no votes in the other forty-nine constituencies. Table 7.1 shows that, notwithstanding the theoretical potential for very disproportional distribution of seats in relation to votes, in empirical fact, votes tend to be distributed territorially in ways that distribute seats proportionally, even in plurality systems.

The British electoral system illustrates how gross discrepancies in the de-

Table 7.2 Constituencies in Proportional Representation Systems

	Total Seats	N Constituencies	Seats per Constituency	
			Average	Range
Austria	183	9	20	6–39
Belgium	212	30	7	5–48
Denmark	175	18	10	2–40
Finland	200	15	13	1–26
Germany				
a) Direct	248	248	1	0
b) PR	248	1	248	0
Ireland	166	41	4	3–5
Israel	120	1	120	0
Italy	630	31	20	1–35
Luxembourg	59	4	15	6–24
Netherlands	150	1	150	0
Norway	155	19	8	4–15
Spain	300	52	6	1–33
Sweden	349	29	12	2–49
Switzerland	200	26	8	1–35

Sources: Mackie and Rose (1982); Inter-Parliamentary Union (1976, Table 9).

gree of disproportionality can occur between different parties contesting seats under the same electoral system. The Liberals regularly poll ten to twenty percent of the vote, and spread their vote relatively evenly throughout Britain. In consequence, the Liberals win very few seats. By contrast, Nationalist parties in Scotland, Wales, and Northern Ireland regularly poll only a very small fraction of the popular vote in the United Kingdom, but win a more nearly proportionate number of seats in the Westminster Parliament. In the extreme case of Northern Ireland, where major British parties do not contest seats, seventeen seats (2.6 percent of the Westminster total) can be won by candidates polling less than 1.3 percent of the total United Kingdom vote.

The extent to which plurality systems discriminate against all but the strongest party in the allocation of seats reflects the social and geographical concentration or dispersion of a party's electoral support. Catchall parties with a heterogeneous basis of support are most likely to have their support widely dispersed, and therefore either do very well (e.g. the British Labour or Conservative party) or very badly (the British Liberals). The important point here is that the outcome is not a function of electoral laws, but of political and social influences.

To understand the workings of electoral systems in practice, we must consider *both* generic properties of the system and specific national contexts. Variations in national or subnational contexts can produce different results from the same electoral system. Broadly speaking, the countries that depart from their ideal-type properties in Table 7.1—that is, disproportional results in PR systems such as Spain, and proportional results in disproportional plurality systems, such as the United States—represent the greater strength of national context as against abstract properties of electoral systems. Those countries that tend to conform to prototypes, such as Austria and France, may be described as systems in which the national context tends to reinforce given properties of an electoral law. The workings of an electoral system cannot be understood simply in terms of definitional and abstract properties; they must be evaluated by the analysis of an electoral-system-in-a-political-system.

ELECTORAL SYSTEMS AND PARTY GOVERNMENT

An electoral system is but a means to the end of determining control of the government. In Western nations, an election is neither a necessary nor a sufficient condition for control of the government changing hands. Where a coalition of parties governs, it is twice as likely that the coalition will be altered in the midst of a Parliament as after a general election. Moreover, where coalition government is the norm, at a general election the electorate is likely to increase support for some parties in the coalition and reduce support for others (Rose and Mackie 1983, pp. 129–37). In France and the United States, where the president is directly elected, the installation of a president is not sufficient to constitute a government. A president must appoint a cabinet (and in France, a prime minister as well), and come to terms with a separately elected legislature.

Insofar as electoral systems are viewed as means to the end of constituting government, the most common generalization is that the plurality system secures government by a single party manufacturing a parliamentary majority from a minority of votes. By contrast, a PR system is presumed to create coalition government, because it divides seats in Parliament among so many parties that none wins an absolute majority.

Here again, differences between electoral systems are differences of degree, not kind (Table 7.3). There is no tendency for non-PR electoral systems to produce a two-party Parliament. In the six countries reviewed here, there are an average of five parties in each Parliament, and as many as nine parties in the British Parliament. None of the systems examined has only two parties. (Whether the United States Congress has any nationwide parties electing its members is a debatable point). At the latest general election in each of these countries, the largest party did win more than half of the seats, but this is not invariably the case in five of the six countries examined. In France, no party normally wins as much as half of the seats in the Assembly, notwithstanding the relatively high degree of disproportionality in the French system.

PR systems tend to have an average of eight parties, but the number ranges from a low of three to a high of thirteen parties. Notwithstanding the tendency toward more parties in Parliaments elected by PR, in two of the fourteen countries, Austria and Spain, one party had an overall majority in Parliament in 1982. In eight of the fourteen countries examined, one party has won an absolute majority at least once in the postwar era, and it has been a frequent occurrence in Austria, Ireland, Norway, and Spain.

All Parliaments examined here, whether elected by PR or non-PR systems, have three or more parties. The difference in the total number of parties is a difference in degree, not kind, for four of the PR systems have no more parties than the average non-PR system, and eight have no more parties than the non-PR system with the most parties, the United Kingdom. The difference in the number of seats won by the largest party at the latest general election is noteworthy, but not evidence of a difference in kind. Most non-PR systems have not consistently produced a majority party government at every postwar election, and a majority of PR systems have, at some time since the war, produced a single-party majority government. Of the twenty countries examined in Table 7.3, less than half consistently conform to the stereotype of single-party government under a non-PR system or multiparty coalition government under PR.

The disjunction between the electoral system and the type of government is further emphasized when the actual composition of governments is compared with their strength in Parliament. Logically, there are at least four types of government: single-party majority, single-party minority, multiparty majority coalition, and a grand coalition in which one party has more than half the seats in Parliament but shares office with other parties. The disposition of seats in Parliament does not determine whether a country has a single-party government (whether with a majority or a minority) or some type of coalition. The decision about how many parties constitute the government, and whether or not the government has a majority of seats in Parliament, is determined according to the national context, and specific situational factors. In the extreme case of Austria, all four types of government have been formed in the postwar world. In Ireland, Fianna Fail has dominated postwar Irish politics, but often it has governed as a single-party minority government (cf. Flora 1983, chapters 3–4).

Parties that win a majority of seats in a national Parliament are often de facto coalitions. The United States Congress—whether considered a four-party system of two types of Republicans and of Democrats or a no-party system of 535 members, each with his own electoral constituency—is an extreme example of nominal labels masking complex and shifting coalitions. In Britain, the construction of the Cabinet is openly spoken of as a task of coalition-building within the majority party, balancing members along many dimensions, including left–right differences within the majority party. The larger the party, the more likely it is to be a coalition of factions, loosely defined tendencies, and those oriented toward a few vague overarching symbols of party unity (Rose 1964).

Table 7.3 The Relationship Between Electoral Systems and Single-Party Majority Government, 1982

	Parties Winning Seats	Largest Party's Share Seats	Largest Party Wins Half of Seats
	(Latest Election)		
	N	percent	(Percent of Postwar Elections)
Non-PR Systems			
Australia	3	43	20
Britain	9	53	91
Canada	3	52	54
France (Fifth Republic)	6	56	28
Japan	6	56	53
New Zealand	3	51	100
Average	5	51	58
PR Systems			
Austria	3	52	45
Belgium	13	20	7
Denmark	9	34	0
Finland	8	26	0
Germany	3	45	11
Ireland	4	45	33
Israel	10	40	0
Italy	12	41	11
Luxembourg	6	41	0
Netherlands	12	31	0
Norway	7	42	40
Spain	10	58	33
Sweden	5	48	8
Switzerland	13	25	0
Average	8	39	13

Source: Calculated from Mackie and Rose (1982), updated for 1982 by the author.

THE IMPLICATIONS

By definition, democratic governments have fundamental features in common; the character of the electoral system is *not* one of these features. Democratic governments require the recognition of the rule of law, otherwise constitutional provisions are invalid, and the rights of freedom of speech and free association, otherwise free elections cannot meaningfully be held. There is no minimum requirement for social and economic prosperity, as is shown by the existence of free elections in some developing countries such as India (cf. Weiner and Ozbudun 1984). Nor is there any reason to regard free elections as a necessary or sufficient condition for the introduction of welfare state programs (Flora and Heidenheimer 1981).

To argue that a subordinate part of a constitutional system can transform it, is to show a faith in constitutional engineering that cannot be justified empirically. The introduction of PR into Northern Ireland provides an instructive example of the way in which fundamental cleavages are *not* overridden by a change in electoral system (Rose 1976). The new electoral system was introduced in the belief (or, at least, the hope) that it would produce a middle-of-the-road coalition government. In fact, the tendency to represent seats in proportion to votes has meant that it guarantees Protestants a majority of seats in a Northern Ireland Assembly. The coalitions formed there have been between different groups of Unionists. The chief party of the Catholic minority, the SDLP, now abstains from the Northern Ireland Assembly, not on the grounds that the electoral system is unfair, but rather arguing that Northern Ireland should not exist.

The case for or against a given electoral system will depend more upon many national contextual factors than upon arguments derived from abstract principles, for the way in which a system actually works depends upon the interaction of election law and social and political conditions. Variations in national party systems display differences in kind far greater than the differences in degree between electoral systems (cf. Lipset and Rokkan 1967; Rose and Urwin 1969). This fact is appreciated by politicians, who are likely to change their views about which electoral system works best by its consequences for their own party.

The consequences—both good and bad—of changing an electoral system cannot be known for certain, for so much hinges upon the behavior of individual political leaders in forming, or deciding not to form, particular parties at particular historical conjunctures. Nor can the results of electoral reform be controlled. An electoral law can only propose how votes should be counted; it cannot determine how they are cast.

Countries with free elections can normally claim to be democratic, whatever electoral system they use; political attention is concentrated upon questions of what government does, rather than how it is chosen. Particular decisions are required about electoral matters from time to time, e.g. reassigning seats to districts as a result of population movements. But these measures are not constituent concerns of government. The status of government depends less upon how elections are conducted than upon whether free elections exist.

8

Two Incompatible
Principles of Representation

Dieter Nohlen

The problems of classifying electoral systems are sometimes the result of deficient information about particular systems. More fundamentally, however, they arise from the lack of a widely accepted conceptual framework and by differences in terminology. There exists, it is true, the basic differentiation between majority/plurality systems and proportional representation (PR), but there is no clear and uniform understanding in the comparative literature on electoral systems of what is meant by the terms "majority rule," "plurality system," "PR," etc. In addition, there is the category of so-called mixed systems, used as a residual category, the meaning of which varies considerably from one author to another. Problems of classification arise especially when electoral systems consist of contradictory elements, when a given electoral system is composed of elements belonging (in the traditional way of classifying electoral systems) to the plurality system as well as to PR. The West German electoral system is one example of this. Similar cases exist in those electoral systems in which the seats are allocated according to a formula of PR in many small-sized constituencies. In such a system, the actual threshold of representation will be high and will cause a considerable degree of disproportionality. The overall election results will no longer correspond to the principle of PR. Should such a system where the seats are allocated according to a formula of PR, but where the electoral outcome will be disproportional, still be classified as a system of PR? What defines PR, and what defines majority/plurality systems? The answer to these questions of classification have far-reaching consequences for the normative assessment of electoral systems, for the definition of functions one ascribes to electoral systems will influence one's choice. As far as PR is concerned, its main function may consist of achieving a parliamentary representation of the socio-political groups in accordance with their numerical strength in the electorate; in that case the assessment should be based on the question of whether a given system of PR really succeeds in reaching that functional goal.

Furthermore, there are many differences in the comparative literature concerning the attribution of the various elements to the two basic types. Does a five percent threshold of representation constitute a "strongly non-proportional" element within a system of PR, as Giovanni Sartori (1984) maintains, or does it serve, as I would argue, as a functional equivalent for the missing division of the entire election territory into separate electoral districts, and is such a threshold, therefore, not totally compatible with the principle of PR?

A good example of the fact that most attempts to classify the various electoral systems rest on normative premises is G. Sartori's (1984) recent distinction between strong and feeble electoral systems. The chosen terminology (strong versus feeble) already contains a judgment, on which, however, I don't want to center my criticism. Sartori classifies the electoral systems according to their manipulative effect on the voter, which can be either "constraining" or "unconstraining":

"An electoral system that unquestionably exerts a manipulative influence, will be classified as being a *strong* electoral system. Conversely, if an electoral system exerts no such influence or exerts it only minimally, I propose to class it as a *feeble* electoral system."

According to this conceptualization, majority/plurality systems belong in the class of the strong electoral systems, while systems of PR are classified as feeble electoral systems, and "a pure PR system is a no-effect system." Concerning the effects of electoral systems, Sartori argues that all electoral systems tend to have a reductive effect on the number of parties, and he then adds "that the multiplying effect of PR is an optical illusion prompted by the historical sequencing of electoral systems."

Consequently, Sartori's interpretation of the effects electoral systems may exert is based on the conception of an unipolar continuum on which all electoral systems can be located—an analytical model developed in the context of the West German debate on electoral systems of the late 1960s and early 1970s by Wildenmann, Kaltefleiter and Schleth (1965), and by Meyer (1973). According to this conceptualization, a system of "pure" PR which produces a degree of almost exact proportionality between votes and seats is the starting point (zero) on the continuum, from which all "nonpure" systems move away. Plurality systems are located at the largest distance from this starting point. Meyer (1973, p. 189, author's translation) describes this conceptualization as follows:

"The influence of the electoral systems on the chances of the political parties extends from the most exact degree of proportionality between the votes gained and the share of seats, to a more or less continuously increasing degree of disproportionality which restricts the chances of the minor parties and leads to a situation where only two parties will have a chance of winning seats."

The essential factor of this differentiation of electoral systems lies in the distinction between a "pure" proportional system, on the one hand, and all other electoral systems on the other hand. Sartori subdivides the latter category into two classes of electoral systems, those which he terms "strong electoral systems" and those which he calls "strong–feeble electoral systems," a mixed class containing nonproportional or low-proportional electoral systems. The central point of Sartori's conceptualization resides in the fact that the basic categories of his classification rest on just one function, the "constraining effect" on the voter or (and this Sartori strictly separates) the "reductive effect" on the number of parties. Since the no-effect assumption applies to just *one* principle of representation, the whole range of electoral systems is judged from the point of view of the deviation from the "no-effect situation." This view naturally leads to judgments based on a one-dimensional concept: the greater the distance from the starting point, the better the premises of the conceptualization will be met, and the "stronger" a given electoral system will be. But do those scholars like Meyer or Sartori present convincing arguments for their basic assumption that all electoral systems have to be conceptualized as being located on just one *uni*polar continuum?

Theoretically and empirically, the evidence points in a different direction. Undoubtedly, there are two principles of representation: the majority/plurality one and the PR one. These should be considered as two antithetical principles of political representation—politically, systematically, and with regard to the history of ideas. A bipolar model is, therefore, the more logical one. The majority/plurality system, as well as PR, stand for specific political goals which they are intended to reach, and they both are located at the opposite ends of a bipolar continuum, separated from each other by zero in the middle. First, from the perspective of the history of political ideas, one should keep in mind that the principles of representation are considerably older than the electoral systems. This is especially true in the case of the principle of PR, which was developed mainly on the basis of two ideas, on Mirabeau's (1834, p. 7) conception of representation as a "mirror of the Nation,"[1] and on the idea of the "best" election, a graduated preferential electoral process, in order to find the "véritable voeux de la nation."[2] These ideas of representation were developed by the French rationalists of the eighteenth century, and, therefore, were well established long before workable systems of PR were invented.[3] Secondly, if one tries to find the prerequisites for the implementation of PR, one has to look at the specific sociopolitical conditions which preceded its application historically. As I have already stated, the demand for PR arose in the context of the deeply rooted social changes of the late nineteenth century, and was connected with the rise of socialist and labor parties; its implementation took place together with the democratization of voting rights and the introduction of universal suffrage. Historically speaking, PR was not at all intended to be a "no-effect-system"; on the contrary, PR was used deliberately by special political interests as a tool with which those interests tried to achieve their socio-political goals.

In order to prove the bipolarity of electoral systems and to theoretically establish the assumption that both forms of representation have to be conceived of as *principles* of representation, a more detailed argumentation is necessary. This leads to the constructive part of this chapter, which centers around the basic distinction between the two alternative principles of representation (functional/ political representation versus social/proportional representation) and the two types of formulae for translating votes into seats (the majority/plurality formulae versus the PR formula). This distinction is often overlooked in the comparative literature on electoral systems, thus causing serious misunderstandings, and leading to the many problems of classification.

Majority/plurality systems and PR systems can be defined according to two criteria: the principle of representation and the formula of decision, i.e. the formula used to translate votes into seats. Let us first consider the two types of formulae of decision: Under the majority/plurality formulae, the gaining of a seat in Parliament depends on a candidate or a party winning the required majority or plurality of votes. The election law reads as follows: The candidate or party who wins a majority or plurality of the votes cast in a given territory shall be elected.

Under the PR formula, the gaining of a seat usually depends on the share of votes which the various candidates or political parties can attain. Candidates or parties who have been able to win a required number of votes (quota) will be elected. A political party is given that number of seats which accords with the number of votes it gained in the election.

This leads me to the following definition: The formula of decision (used in the process of translating votes into seats) determines the winner and loser in an election. It concerns the disaggregate situation of how votes are translated into seats. Under the majority formula, the candidate or party who obtained more votes than all the other competing candidates or parties combined will win the seat. Under the plurality formula, the candidate or party who gained more votes than the second strongest competitor will win the seat. Under the PR formula, the number of seats won by any party will be equal to the share of votes polled by it.

Let us now consider the principles of representation inherent in the majority/plurality systems and in PR. When defining the principles of representation, I pose the question as to the political goals of political representation concerning the aggregate nationwide outcome of elections. I pose the question about the ends intended by the two basic types of electoral systems, the majority/plurality systems and the systems of PR. What is the political objective of majority/ plurality systems? Under majority/plurality systems, the goal is to attain a parliamentary majority for one party or for a party alliance. The essential factor consists in enabling a political party which has not attained a majority of votes to form a majority party government. This is the desired political goal of the principle of majority representation: a single-party government based on a minority of votes. The basic function of a plurality system (and the criterion for evaluating its effects) is its ability to produce governments.

What is the goal of PR? PR systems intend to reflect, as exactly as possible, the social forces and political groups in the population. The share of votes and of seats for the parties should correspond approximately to each other. This is the basic function of the principle of PR and the criterion of effectiveness of a proportional system.

Electoral systems should be classified and evaluated according to the principles of representation. The formulae of decision are secondary in rank and do not determine the question of definition and classification of the electoral systems. The principles of representation and the formulae of decision relate to each other like ends and means; while a wide scope of possibilities exists for the means, there are only two alternative ends. On the one hand, the plurality formula of decision may be combined with various other elements in a system of PR, i.e. a system which follows the principle of PR, and the overall effects of which will produce a high degree of proportionality between votes and seats; examples of this are Finland, Denmark, and the Federal Republic of Germany. On the other hand, one can envisage a system in which the seats are allocated by a formula of PR, like the quota in STV, which nevertheless produces election results that reflect the principle of majority representation, because the distribution of the election territory in small-sized constituencies will prevent a high degree of proportionality. In this conceptualization, the type of a mixed system does not exist. There are just majority/plurality systems and proportional systems which correspond *more* or *less* to the respective principles.

A pragmatic argument for this conceptualization is the fact that the principle of representation is very often decided on the constitutional level. Hence, the question which principle of representation should be chosen is a matter of constitutional law, whereas in most cases all other provisions of an electoral system are dealt with by simple legislation (see Table 8.1). Constitutions also sometimes stipulate that certain administrative units shall serve as constituencies, or that the right of the political parties to take part in the allocation of seats depends upon the attainment of a certain percentage of the total votes cast. The most important political decision, however, relates to the principle of representation which necessarily includes (as we have shown) the decision for a specific social and/or functional concept of parliamentary representation.

The conceptualization suggested here (which I have dealt with extensively elsewhere; see Nohlen 1978, 1983) places the evaluation of electoral systems on a new basis. The assessment of the electoral systems does not follow the one-dimensional evaluation based on just one criterion anymore; on the basis of the two principles of representation, the electoral systems are judged by criteria derived from alternative principles and are quite distinct. Thus systems of PR are no longer evaluated according to the criterion of the plurality system, and the plurality system is no longer judged by the criterion of PR. This reorientation

Table 8.1 Principle of Representation and Electoral System in
Eighteen West European Countries

Countries Where the Principle of Representation is Included in the Constitution		Countries Where the Electoral System is Decided Upon by Simple Legislation
	Constitutional Article	
Austria	26, paragraph 1	Federal Republic of Germany
Belgium	48, paragraph 2	Finland
Denmark	31, paragraph 2	France
Iceland	31, paragraph 1	Great Britain
Ireland	12, paragraph 3	Greece
Luxembourg	51, paragraphs 5 and 6	Italy
Netherlands	92, paragraph 2	Sweden
Norway	59, paragraph 3	
Portugal	151–155	
Spain	68, paragraph 3	
Switzerland	73	

of the criteria prevents those interpretations that evaluate a given electoral system by the opposite principle of representation and which cannot yield results of any significance, since one should expect from the very outset that, for example, any system of PR will not be able to fulfill those functional expectations that a plurality system will meet quite easily. As far as the "constraining" or "reductive" effects of electoral systems are concerned, plurality systems are usually superior to the system of PR. In this regard, they are (to use Sartori's terminology) the "stronger" ones. But they are not "stronger" when the aim that should be achieved is that of PR. In such a case, systems of PR are usually the "stronger" ones.

My conceptualization of electoral systems leads to the following two general conclusions:

1) Electoral systems should be classified and judged in accordance with the degree to which they meet the principle of representation that they are supposed to follow. They should not be judged on whether they fulfill any of the functions of the other principle of representation. This does not, of course, exclude the possibility of a comparative analysis, but it prohibits judgments that are based on the criteria of the "wrong" principle of representation. It is in this context that one should discuss the question of whether thresholds of representation affect the principle of PR in general, or only from a certain level on, or methodically speaking, whether an electoral system must follow its principle of representation without any exception at all. The West German Constitutional Court, for example, has examined the question of whether the five percent threshold of

representation contained in the West German election law is compatible with the principle of PR. In its positive judgment, the Court argued, however, that a barrier of five percent should form the upper limit of such a threshold, and it barred any further change that would strengthen the "constraining effect" of the electoral system as incompatible with the principle of PR. Consequently, if the West German legislature would like to strengthen those effects, for example by raising the five percent barrier, it would first have to opt for the other principle of representation (i.e. the principle of majority representation); only after having done so would the West German Bundestag be allowed to introduce a considerably higher threshold of representation. In this context, one should also mention that the disproportional effects in the so-called meliorated system of PR in Greece are almost incompatible with the principle of PR. These conclusions about the constitutional and legislative limitations of electoral systems are of utmost importance for anyone who is interested in the reform of a given system and wants to escape the impression of manipulation.

2) Any debate about the principle of representation one wants to opt for, should, first of all, be carried out in connection with democratic theory; it should, secondly, take into account the specific historical and socio-political situation under which an electoral system has to operate. Leaving those two aspects aside, any discussion about the advantages or disadvantages of electoral systems becomes rather useless, because—as we know—answers to normative questions like the assessment of electoral systems depend, to a certain degree, on the analyst's (normative) democratic positions; secondly, those questions are contingent and related to time and space. These two premises are often unconsciously overlooked or even consciously neglected. However, these theoretical and historical prerequisites must be taken into consideration, especially if one discusses not only minor technical questions of electoral systems, but concentrates on questions regarding the principles of representation.

NOTES

1. The famous phrase reads as follows: "Les états sont pour la nation ce qu'est une carte réduite pour son étendue physique; soit en partie, soit en grand, la copie doit toujours avoir les mêmes proportions que l'original."

2. I am thinking of the ideas of de Borda and Condorcet; see Misch (1974), pp. 16ff.

3. The best source of information on the expansion of PR in the early decades after the creation of practicable systems is still the report of the Société pour l'Etude de la Représentation Proportionnelle of 1888.

9

The Effect of District Magnitude and Properties of Two-Seat Districts

Rein Taagepera

Plurality and Proportional Representation (PR) rules are part of the same quasi-continuum, if one takes into account the district magnitude (the number M of seats in the district). Apply various PR seat allocation rules (such as d'Hondt, Sainte-Laguë, or Largest Remainder) to the case where $M=1$, and nearly all of them will yield the same outcome as does the plurality rule. Exceptions include the Irish Single Transferable Vote, which for $M=1$ would become similar to the Australian absolute majority procedure. As district magnitude is reduced, a PR system gradually starts penalizing the small parties, an effect reaching its strongest degree when M becomes "one."

District magnitudes used in practice tend to be either $M=1$ (in Anglo-Saxon countries, in particular), or in the range from six to twenty (in most West European countries). A few countries apply a PR formula nationwide, making the country one single huge electoral district: $M=150$ for the Netherlands, and $M=120$ for Israel. In some other countries (such as Denmark), nationwide adjustment seats lead to an effect analogous to that of a very large district magnitude. Very few countries use an average M larger than one but smaller than five. In fact, contemporary Ireland and Japan seem to be the only countries divided into three to five seats, with an average of about four. No country seems to use an average district magnitude of around two or three. Yet, such magnitudes might offer a combination which moderates some of the less desirable features of both plurality and large-magnitude PR.

The gerrymander problem largely arises only with single-seat districts. As will be discussed later, gerrymander becomes rather difficult when all districts are mandated to have two seats allocated on the basis of a PR rule. If a stable two-party alternation is considered a desirable goal, two-seat districts might assure it even better than does the plurality rule in single-seat districts. The latter can lead to permanent one-party hegemony, as was the case in the pre-1970 United States South, and still is in India. It will be shown that $M=2$ may automatically lead to an outcome analogous to "bipartisan gerrymander" practiced in some single-seat two-party systems: both major parties would be assured one of the two seats in the district as long as each of them obtains at least one-third of the district vote. (This assumes the d'Hondt distribution rule. With the Largest Remainder or Sainte-Laguë rules, the second-largest party is assured a seat with as little as a quarter of the votes.) Electoral campaign activity would be reduced in districts with expected votes distribution close to fifty/fifty, with excitement over closely contested races shifting to districts where the major parties' vote distribution is close to 1:2, so that seats could go 1–1 or 0–2. Except for doing away with the horse-race-like excitement of "first-past-the-post," the two-seat districts could, apparently, achieve everything the single-seat districts can for assuring stable two-party alternation—and they could reduce the possibility of partisan gerrymander and of one-party hegemony.

In the unusual circumstances where the public is severely dissatisfied with both major parties, two-seat districts would make the emergence of a new major party (such as the British Labour Party in the early 1900s) easier, compared to single-seat districts. However, the fourth and fifth parties that plague many PR systems would be blocked by $M=2$ almost as effectively as they are with $M=1$. Regional parties (such as Scottish Nationalist, or Parti Québécois) would be easier to start with $M=2$ (compared to $M=1$), but it would be harder for them to gain local control. With two-seat districts the Parti Québécois would not have an absolute majority in the provincial legislature. Ethnic minorities in the United States would find it easier to gain representation with $M=2$, even without attempts at paternalistic gerrymander in their favor (which occasionally backfire).

In the following pages, some effects of district magnitude will be reviewed. Our empirical knowledge of the outcomes for single-seat districts on the one hand, and for multiseat districts on the other, should enable us to interpolate for some probable characteristic effects of two-seat districts.

PROPORTIONALITY PROFILES

When looking for a way to graphically express the deviation from PR, one's first thought is to plot the parties' percentage of seats against their percentage of votes, as is done in Figure 9.1a for Japanese elections 1963–1980. While the overrepresentation of the large Liberal Democratic Party is well visible, the severe underrepresentation of some of the small parties is masked by the overcrowding in the bottom left corner. Proper perspective is established by shifting to Figure 9.1b, where the quantity plotted on the y-axis is the "advantage ratio'' (percent seats/percent votes). Identical to Dahl's (1956, p. 114) "index of advantage" and Gallagher's (1975, p. 506) "proportionality index," this ratio was apparently first plotted against percent votes by Laakso and Taagepera (1978) for Nordic countries, and by Taagepera and Laakso (1980) for most other West European countries. The latter article also discusses the general uses and limitations of such "proportionality profile" plots. Regardless of how a particular electoral system should behave according to theoretical analysis or the intentions of some founding fathers, the proportionality profile shows how the system actually penalizes or favors various parties, either systematically (depending on their vote size) or in a biased manner (offering different parties at the same percent vote different bonuses or penalties), or possibly completely erratically.

Japan's profile was chosen as an example of the technique because Japan (along with Ireland) has the lowest district magnitude ($M=4$) practiced in any country with multiseat districts. A systematic bonus for larger parties is well in evidence, and so is the penalization of small parties. It is also easy to see, in Figure 9.1b, that at the same percent of votes, Komeito tends to do much better than the Communists. Despite such variety, the "break-even percentage" seems to be around 15 percent—this is the vote share at which the typical party would shift from underrepresentation to overrepresentation. Depending on district magnitude (and other factors), the break-even percentage in other countries can be appreciably lower or higher, as illustrated in Figure 9.2.

Figure 9.2 shows the average proportionality profiles for Japan (from figure 9.1), and also for elections with extremely large district magnitude (Netherlands, $M=150$) and elections with single-seat districts (United States House). The curve shapes are similar, but the break-even percentage is seen to increase as the magnitude decreases. In the Netherlands, parties with more than five percent votes already start receiving a large-party bonus, while in the United States House of Representatives, even a party receiving forty percent of the votes suffers a smaller-party penalty.

Not all electoral systems yield proportionality profiles with a definable break-even percentage. Elections where second preferences are taken into account either explicity (Australia and Ireland) or through a second round (France), yield formless "wide scatter" profiles. Even for systems presenting a well-defined pattern of vote size dependence, the break-even percentage can vary appreciably for the same district magnitude, depending on various other features of the electoral law and national history. Furthermore, for plurality in single-seat districts, very small localized parties tend to have a reduced penalty, compared to medium-sized nationwide parties—see Taagepera and Laakso (1980) for plots illustrating all these qualifications. Nonetheless, the patterns shown in Figure 9.2 do correctly express the main message: *For single-round single-preference elections, the vote share at which parties stop being penalized for smallness tends to increase with decreasing district magnitude*. The average relation between break-

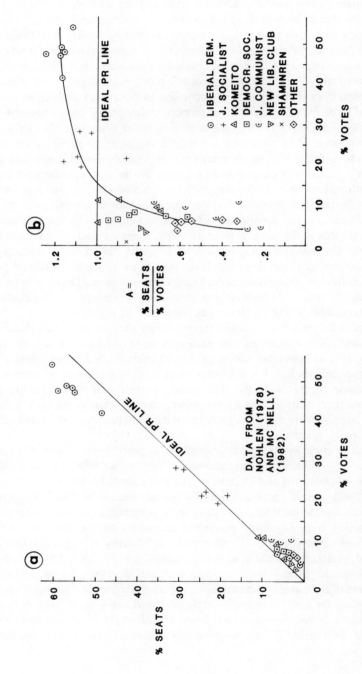

Figure 9.1 Two Ways to Graph the Deviation from Proportionality in Japanese Parliamentary Elections 1963–1980: a) Percent Seats Versus Percent Votes, and b) Advantage Ratio Versus Percent Votes.

even percentage (B) and magnitude is approximated by the simple equation (Taagepera 1983):

$$B=45/\sqrt{M}. \tag{1}$$

For two-seat districts, this empirical equation would yield an average break-even percentage of thirty-two percent, and the approximate expected curve shape is shown as a dashed curve in Figure 9.2. Given the variations for individual

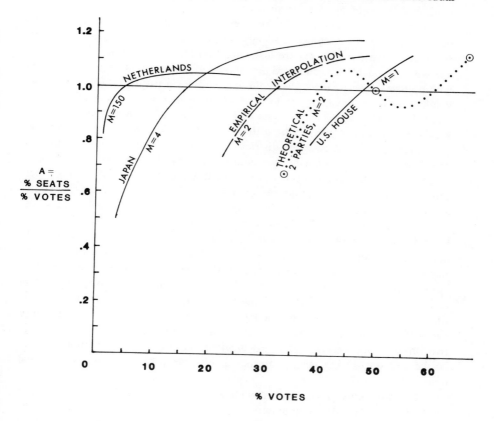

SOURCES: NETHERLANDS--
TAAGEPERA & LAAKSO (1980);
JAPAN--FIGURE 1;
U.S.--TAAGEPERA (1983).

Figure 9.2 Proportionality Profiles for Electoral Systems with Various District Magnitudes.

countries on which the equation is based, two-seat districts could be expected to have break-even percentages ranging from twenty-five to forty percent, depending on the local political culture and details of electoral rules. Possibly due to an ingrained two-party philosophy, B tends to be rather high in the United States, compared to other countries with single-seat districts, such as Canada ($B=30$). Hence, one could expect that two-seat districts under United States conditions would yield a break-even percentage considerably above thirty-two percent, which implies that there would be little encouragement for third party formation or the split of an existing party.

Theoretically, proportionality profiles for two-seat districts could have some peculiarities, if one assumes that only two parties are present, and that party strengths in various districts are distributed normally around the national average with reasonably low standard deviations (cf. Owen and Grofman 1982) and with no party-specific bias. Under these conditions a fifty/fifty vote nationwide would lead to an advantage ratio of $A=1$ for both parties. Assuming that the d'Hondt seat allocation formula is used, a nationwide thirty-three/sixty-seven vote would put the minor party right at the borderline of obtaining or not obtaining one of the seats in the two-seat districts. For a normal (or any other symmetrical) distribution, the minor party would be successful in one-half of the cases. Since it would thus obtain twenty-five percent of the seats, with thirty-three percent of the votes, its advantage ratio would be 0.75. This would leave seventy-five percent of the seats for the major party, with sixty-seven percent of the votes, corresponding to $A=1.125$. These outcomes are plotted in Figure 9.2. It might be tempting to join those points with a smoothly increasing curve, but this would not do, if one considers small deviations from the fifty/fifty votes constellation. Suppose the vote goes forty-nine/fifty-one. If the vote distribution in districts does not deviate drastically from the national average, both parties would still obtain one seat each, in every district. Now the smaller party's advantage would be fifty/forty-nine$=1.02$, while for the large party it would be down to $A=$fifty/fifty-one$=.98$. Such a counterintuitive trend may continue up to about a forty-five/fifty-five votes constellation. For a wider disparity in votes, the minor party is likely to start losing seats at an increasingly steep rate, as suggested by the dotted curve in Figure 9.2.

Would the kink in the curve mean that, if the opinion polls indicated a close tie, both parties would try to underbid the other in their campaign efforts in order to increase their advantage ratio? Not at all. The party with more votes is still likely to carry more seats and dominate the assembly, but the swing at fifty/fifty is nearly zero. Single-seat districts tend to magnify the seat ratio, building solid parliamentary majorities out of even minor disparities in votes. In contrast, the two-seat districts would theoretically seem to have an opposite effect, which would be undesirable from the viewpoint of securing stable parliamentary majorities. However, the theoretical kink at fifty/fifty votes is likely to be evened out in actual cases through the effect of even minor third parties, or of geographical distribution irregularities and biases. It should be noted that the curve for the United States House of Representatives, in Figure 9.2, also deviates markedly from theoretical predictions such as the "cube law." The best guess on the effect of two-seat districts is still the dashed "empirical prediction" curve in Figure 9.2.

It should be noted that with three-seat districts the two-party competition would again be shifted back to the fifty/fifty region. Both parties would be rather certain of receiving one seat, and competition would center on who gets the remaining one. However, with three-seat districts, a third party might become overly easy to maintain, so that a succession of coalition governments might result.

EFFECTIVE NUMBER OF PARTIES

Since small district magnitudes impose large penalties on small parties, the number of parties should decrease with decreasing M. Such an effect has, indeed, been observed in various studies using various indices, starting at least with Rae (1967). The unweighted number of parties participating in elections is not always meaningful since some parties may be negligibly small. When the vote distribution for five parties is fifty/forty-five/two/two/one, the system actually is closer to a two-party, than to a five-party, system. The confusion can be avoided through the use of the "effective" number (N) of parties, defined by Laakso and Taagepera (1979) on the basis of the well-known Herfindahl-Hirschman concentration index (HH):

$$N = 1/HH = 1/\Sigma p_i^2 \tag{2}$$

where P_i is the fractional share of the i-th party. For a votes distribution twenty/twenty/twenty/twenty/twenty, HH is $5(.20)^2 = .20$, so that $N=5$, as one should expect. For the constellation fifty/forty-five/two/two/one, however, HH is $.50^2 + .45^2 + .02^2 + .02^2 + .01^2 = .4534$, so that $N=2.20$, well in line with the intuitive notion that the system involves two major parties plus a smattering of small parties which even taken together cannot have the effect of a fullblown third party. The Rae-Taylor fractionalization index (F) can be calculated from N:

$$F = 1 - HH = 1 - 1/N. \tag{3}$$

For the examples above F assumes the values .80 and .55, respectively. While the information content of N and F is identical, the meaning of N might be easier to visualize.

Even when the electoral laws stay the same, the effective number of parties can change appreciably over time. From 1956 to 1972, N rose from 4.2 to

7.6 in the Netherlands elections, in line with an average West European rise from 3.6 to 4.5 (Laakso and Taagepera 1979). When plotting N versus district magnitude M, scatter is appreciable, but the expected trend nonetheless emerges: *The effective number of parties tends to increase with increasing district magnitude.* The average relationship could be approximated with the following equation, if one goes by party shares of votes (Taagepera 1983):

$$N(\text{votes}) = 1.25(2 + \log M) \tag{4}$$

where decimal logarithms are used. The correlation is slightly improved by using the party shares of parliament seats (instead of votes):

$$N(\text{seats}) = 1.15(2 + \log M) \tag{5}$$

These equations express the empirical observation that countries with single-seat districts typically tend to have an effective number of 2.5 parties competing in elections, with somewhat fewer ($N=2.3$) obtaining seats. For ten-seat districts the typical effective numbers of parties are 3.7 on the votes level and 3.4 on the seats level. However, the values for individual countries depend heavily on the local tradition. Austria switched, in 1970, from rather low-magnitude districts to large districts and, as one would expect on the basis of Equation 1, the advantage ratio for Austria's minor third party (FPÖ) jumped from around 0.7 to 1.0. However, in the absence of new issues, no new parties emerged merely to take advantage of the new rules. With a multiseat PR system which even before 1970 was fairly hospitable to new party emergence, Austria's party constellation continues to behave as if it were subject to the pressures imposed by single-seat districts. As a reverse example, India continues to have relatively many parties despite the incentive for fusion supplied by its single-seat districts.

How many parties could one expect with two-seat districts? The equations above suggest averages of 2.9 and 2.6 effective parties, respectively, but the actual number for a given country could be as low as two or as high as more than three. With the conditions and traditions prevalent in the United States, the lower part of this range would be more likely. The emergence of third parties would become easier in principle, but (as in Austria) none would be likely to be formed.

GERRYMANDER IN TWO-SEAT DISTRICTS

The classical gerrymander, as practiced with single-seat districts, can be shown to become almost impossible with two-seat districts. Assume that there are only two parties, and districts of equal size. With single-seat districts, a party with slightly more than twenty-five percent of the vote but with absolute gerrymander control could theoretically gain a majority of seats by dividing the country into districts where one's own party has either zero percent of the votes, or slightly over fifty percent.

In the case of two-seat districts and the d'Hondt rule, the theoretical minimum vote needed to gain seat majority would be slightly more than 33.4 percent. (One could try to gerrymander for 33.4 percent of the vote, and hence one of the two seats in all districts but one, and for 66.7 percent in the remaining one. Or one could aim at 66.7 percent in slightly more than half the districts, with zero percent in the rest. In any combination of these two strategies, the votes needed would amount to a minimum of 33.4 percent.) It can be shown that, in general, control through perfect gerrymander with M-seat districts and the d'Hondt rule requires at least a fraction $0.5M/(M+1)$ of the votes. For five-seat districts, the minimum vote needed would be 41.7 percent. The limit for large M is of course fifty percent. Thus, compared to the one-seat districts, the two-seat districts raise the theoretical gerrymander threshold by one-third of the total possible range (33.4 percent, compared to the total range from twenty-five to fifty percent).

The thresholds would be different for different allocation rules and for a different number of parties, but the message would be the same: the two-seat districts have a markedly higher theoretical gerrymander threshold, compared to single-seat districts.

In actual practice, successful partisan gerrymander in single-seat districts requires many more votes than twenty-five percent. It is typically a device through which a party with about fifty percent of votes buys itself extra insurance. Even then it can backfire badly, as Scarrow (1982), and also Grofman (1982), have described in the case of New York. The same applies to paternalistic gerrymander in favor of an ethnic minority such as California's thirty-fourth Congressional district, expressly designed to have a Latino plurality, at the cost of uncannily imitating the shape of the original Gerry's Mander. While a Latino eventually won the decisive Democratic primary in 1982, the outcome was by no means assured (see Hume 1982), and slight changes in demography or ethnic consciousness could turn a safe seat into systematically wasted votes, from the Latino viewpoint.

With PR in two-seat districts, a minority group conscious of its identity (be it based on class, language, race, religion, or any other feature) would not need paternalistic gerrymander in order to gain representation, if they have at least one-third of the vote in the general area. Gerrymander itself would become prohibitively difficult. It is one thing to tailor for districts with an adequate safety margin over fifty percent of votes, and another to do it with safety margins over sixty-seven percent votes (for two seats). As for tailoring districts to win one of the two seats with as few votes as possible, the safe range may become impractically narrow, with thirty-three percent meaning failure and fifty percent meaning overkill.

Besides the classical single-seat gerrymander where district *boundaries* are altered, the same term has been applied occasionally to alterations in the *number* of seats assigned to a given multiseat district. The issue mainly arises when these districts involve relatively few seats, as is the case in Ireland and Japan. With district magnitudes varying from three to five, the specific number could have an appreciable effect on the representation of a party with about 20 percent of votes in a given region. Regardless of the seat allocation rule followed, such a party would tend to gain representation within a five-seat district, and fail to obtain it in a three-seat district.

In Ireland, the 1969 electoral amendment act increased the number of three-seat districts in the west, where the governing Fianna Fail party was strong, and four-seat districts in the east, where Fianna Fail was weaker. When Fianna Fail nonetheless lost the 1973 elections, the new Fine Gael and Labour coalition government undertook a reverse tailoring of district magnitudes (1974), but nonetheless lost heavily in the 1977 elections. The next amendment (1980) was left to an independent commission, and officials of various parties seemed to agree that the game of district magnitude gerrymander could not affect the political outcomes in any appreciable way (Zimmerman 1982).

In Japan, the potential district magnitude gerrymander has been overshadowed by malapportionment. Even after the 1975 corrections, the vote of some rural residents weighed 2.9 times more than the vote of some urban ones (McNelly 1982).

It may be concluded that if a system allows low-magnitude districts of various sizes, magnitude gerrymander games may arise, even if, in retrospect, they are not worth playing. If the alternatives available should include a choice between single-seat, two-seat, and three-seat districts, the game would not only be as attractive as it was in Ireland in 1969–1976, but it may offer genuine payoffs: the party in control of reapportionment could establish three-seat districts in regions where it is very weak, and single-seat districts (with gerrymandered boundaries) in regions where it is strong. Such a combination of gerrymander of boundaries *and* of magnitudes could lead to a truly superior gerrymander, where a party could assure itself of permanent assembly majorities with vote shares as low as forty percent or possibly even thirty percent. Evidently a mix of single-seat and two-seat districts should not be allowed. However, in a system where only two-seat districts are allowed (with possibly a single-seat or three-seat district in the capital city, to avoid ties), the magnitude gerrymander is made impossible, and the classical boundary gerrymander is made very difficult (as noted earlier). Gerrymander of any type is not likely to be a problem in a system of two-seat districts.

The last issue to be briefly discussed is "bloc voting," or "at-large elections," as they are called in the United States. The heavy minority penalization in single-seat districts can be made even more severe by giving the plurality winner all of the seats throughout a wider area. In many United States cities, a black minority could win council seats under a single-seat ward system which penalizes dispersed minorities but not the geographically concentrated ones. Such minority representation is sometimes thwarted by a switch to at-large elections whereby the whole city is made a single district, with the winner-take-all rule. The multiseat district, usually conducive to proportional representation, is thus converted into a tool of absolute control by the majority. The larger the district magnitude, the worse off the minority parties or groups are likely to be. It is as if district magnitude had become even smaller than "one," as far as its effect on minority representation is concerned.

The winner-take-all rule, if applied to two-seat districts, could be expected to lead to a slightly higher minority penalty, compared to single-seat districts. Such a half-hearted at-large approach would seem to serve no conceivable purpose. The only reason for mentioning it is to alleviate the concerns of American minority leaders, conditioned as they are to the misuse of multiseat districts for bloc vote. Compared to single-seat districts, two-seat districts used with any PR allocation rule would represent a moderate step toward more minority representation.

10
Electoral Systems and Constitutional Restraints
William H. Riker

The discussion about the choice of an electoral system has been much confused by the fact that most actual choices have been made with the intention of promoting partisan advantage rather than with the goal of incorporating sound constitutional principles into governmental structure. Most of the conscious decisions to retain (as in England in 1884) or return to (as in New York City in 1947) plurality systems, with their strong tendency toward a structure of two parties, reflected the calculations of advantage by the leadership of the two major parties. On the other hand, most of the conscious decisions to adopt (as in France in 1945 and in Germany in 1919) proportional representation (PR) systems with their tendency to perpetuate multipartyism reflected the prior existence of three or more parties, spawned (typically) by systems of majority voting (Riker 1982b). As a consequence of this historical fact, much of the academic dispute on the relative merits of PR and plurality voting have been no more than ideological exercises in the justification of one interest or another in a fight for political control. Very few of the participants in the academic debate have been concerned with generalizing about the consequences of electoral systems. Rather, they, just like the politicians, have sought to persuade rather than to analyze.

My intention in this chapter is to attempt to raise the quality of the debate by raising it above these merely partisan and ideological considerations. I would like to discuss instead the constitutional issues considered from the point of view of the successful operation of the whole society.

CONVENTIONAL UNTRUTHS

Owing to the lamentably unscientific state of political science, it is necessary first, however, to clear away some widely disseminated and obviously ideological untruths before one can begin to examine the merits of alternative systems.

The first such untruth is the assertion that minorities are not represented in a two-party system. This is the main ideological justification urged against plurality voting and in favor of PR, which John Stuart Mill expected would give to all minorities of the size (total population/number of seats) at least one seat. But it is a wholly false argument, and the tip-off to its falsity is the common observation that two-party politics is characterized by subservience to special interests, all of which are, of course, minorities. How can such subservience occur if the minorities are not represented? The answer is, of course, that minorities are indeed represented, probably somewhat better in a political system like that of the United States than in officially proportional systems like those of Scandinavia.

The representation of minorities in the United States system is a consequence of the fact that annual legislation is incremental in nature. The statute books are not completely rewritten after each election. Rather, legislatures make marginal revisions and, given the massive body of existing public policy, the marginal revisions are invariably tiny in comparison to what is already in statutes and decrees. Legislators undertaking these marginal revisions are doubtless inspired, in part, by their personal and partisan conceptions of public policy, but they are also driven by the exigencies of reelection, either for themselves or for their parties. In making calculations about the effect of marginal policy revisions on a prospective reelection, legislators of course know that the bulk of their support in the previous election will be maintained. Hence, their chief concern is with a relatively small proportion of votes at the margin. The calculation goes something like this: One begins with the votes the legislator received in the last election (v_{t-1}). To this one adds, algebraically, a demographic variable, say (d), namely the net result from the loss by death and emigration of the legislator's supporters balanced by the gain from new eligibility by maturation or immigration of supporters of the legislator's party. This demographic variable is typically, I suspect, close to zero, but nevertheless negative, because new eligibles tend to be less securely loyal to a candidate or party than deceased or emigrating ones. A second negative term, (a), counts those previous supporters whom the legislator has consciously or unconsciously alienated since the last election. But the calculation ends with a positive term, (c), namely those previously indifferent or previously opposed whom the legislator has converted. Thus the legislator's expected votes in the next election, v_t, are:

$$v_t = v_{t-1} + d - a + c.$$

The last two terms (a and c) on the right side are probably quite small in comparison with the first term (v_{t-1}), and yet a and c are the terms that, at least, the legislator can expect to influence, and these only partially. Consequently, the legislator's attention is concentrated on these terms, seeking to retain the allegiance of those small groups who are listening to the siren song of the opposition and seeking to convert, with his or her own siren song, small groups of opposition voters who seem to be tractable. Because of the legislator's concentration on these two marginal groups, the content of a substantial amount of legislation is directed at satisfying the interests of minorities of voters who currently stand between the parties. Since most minorities of voters are at one time or another in this marginal position, their interests are well served, probably too well served, in any two-party system. Furthermore, if the members of any group feel poorly served, they have only to become marginal in order to attract attention.

A second conventional untruth is that governments operated under PR are unstable. It is certainly true that there are some pathological instances of instability, as in the French Fourth Republic or the Weimar Republic, but these are perhaps matched by the instability of presidential governments that whirl from dictator to dictator. In a recent and elegant study, G. Bingham Powell (1982) has shown that, for the period 1967–76, if a government consists of a party with a majority in parliament, its duration and hence its stability are about the same whether elected by plurality methods (as in Britain, Canada, or India) or by PR methods (as in Austria, Ireland, Turkey, or Japan). Even without a majority party, coalitions under PR systems are almost as stable as those with majority parties, provided the system does not have extremist parties (e.g., in West Germany, the Netherlands, Norway, and Sweden). The attribution of short duration and instability seems to be accurate only for those PR systems that are plagued with extremist parties (e.g., in Belgium, Denmark, Finland, and Italy). Instability seems, indeed, to be a function, primarily, of extremism and of the motivation of extremists to mix things up repeatedly, each time in the hope that they can come out on top. Since there is no systematic relation between extremism and PR, except that this electoral method *sometimes* and *in some forms* gives extremists a slightly better chance of holding office, it is difficult to say that there is any straightforward causal relation between PR and governmental instability. Even presidential systems, which are, on average, the most stable kinds of governments, display considerable instability when the president and the legislative body are controlled by different parties. This is especially true if the president disobeys the law as, for example, Nixon in the United States covered up theft and Allende in Chile systematically confiscated property.

THE UNFAIRNESS OF ALL ELECTORAL SYSTEMS

The two falsehoods just exposed are crucial to the reformist arguments for PR and plurality rule. The argument for PR rests on the normative premise that electoral systems ought to provide representation of opinions and on the (false) observation that plurality systems fail to represent minorities. Assuming (mistakenly) that PR improves the representation of minorities, it is then recommended as an appropriate reform. This reformist argument is, of course, ideological nonsense. The effectiveness of PR is, at least, doubtful. And the normative premise about the function of electoral systems is only partly true. On the contrary, the main and ineradicable function of an electoral system is to provide a set of officials. One hopes that they will be representative in some way or another.

It is worth pointing out that *all* electoral systems are unfair in ways that we do not fully understand, an observation that is elaborated in Riker (1982a). The argument that electoral systems fail to be representative runs as follows:

1) From exactly the same set of individual values and preferences, two electoral systems may produce quite different results. If one could rank the systems in a moral hierarchy, then one result might be better than another. But, in fact, the systems are more or less morally indistinguishable in that all are, in one way or another, morally deficient. The plurality system is deficient in that it fails to assure the selection of Condorcet winners, while the Hare system, for example, is deficient in that it fails to ensure monotonicity. While, to my mind, the failure to ensure monotonicity (to ensure, that is, that a changed vote for a losing candidate will help him on towards victory) is the *worst* possible sin an electoral system can commit, I recognize that other people have other perspectives. In any event, any pair of electoral systems is likely to produce different results and both cannot be truly representative of identical tastes and values.

2) Owing to the essential disequilibrium of political preferences, it is unlikely that the outcomes of elections will be ordered, that is, they will not be arranged so that the first alternative is decisively ahead of the second, and so on until the next to last is decisively ahead of the last. While this makes some difference in single-member districts where, typically, one out of two or three candidates is to be elected, it makes a great difference in some PR systems where several parties are, by definition, intended to be ordered—and may well not be.

3) Even worse, and again owing to disequilibrium, all elections are subject to manipulation in the sense that artificial arrangements of the agenda (e.g. the media's or politicians' strategems to affect the salience of issues) have as much effect on the outcomes as the values of the electorate. In my opinion, most elections are manipulated, so the result is certain to be unrepresentative. As a result of these facts, the representativeness of all electoral systems is likely to be less than what one might hope for. Indeed, PR is no more likely than plurality voting to be representative. Since, furthermore, representation is only a secondary function of elections, it is easy to reject the ideological claims of the supporters of PR.

It is just about as easy to reject the similarly ideological claims of the supporters of plurality elections. The argument for plurality is almost entirely negative—seldom has it been claimed positively that plurality voting is a method of obtaining the most representative results in elections. In the plurality system, only first-place preferences of voters are counted and, if the voters' second, third, etc. place preferences are counted, the plurality choice is typically upset. It is this fact about plurality systems that makes their supporters wary of claiming great positive merit for them. But it is possible to claim that they at least produce a stable government—and, by implication, that alternative systems do not. Powell's evidence, already cited, fairly disproves this claim.

So we are left with the demonstration that the typical partisan and ideological claims of advocates of either system are just exactly that, namely partisan and ideological and untrue. Proper examination of the two systems requires that we start from a broader intellectual base.

THE FUNCTION OF CONSTITUTIONS

The broader base is a statement of what one wants out of a constitution. Of course, the first thing a constitution must do is provide for the selection of officials. Indeed, the whole point of a constitution, written or unwritten, rationalized or customary, is to provide for regular succession, rather than perpetual coup d'état or civil war. Any constitution that successfully provides for regularized and undisputed successions is in some sense a successful one, even if the regularity is no more than the inheritance of absolute monarchy. The experience of many ages suggests, however, that it is prudent to consider the preferences of politically relevant groups in determining the succession, simply to assure that they will not be offended by the chosen rulers and rebel against them. In the modern world, the "politically relevant" have come to be most adults, which is why we think that democratic representation is necessary. It is thereby hoped to guarantee that the politically relevant (i.e. all adults) will be reasonably satisfied that their interests have been protected in the process of selection.

The way best to protect the diverse interests in the body of all adults is, however, not entirely clear, especially since, as indicated previously, representation is not particularly straightforward. One cannot simply say that an elected body is representative in the sense that it is the result of a true and fair amalgamation of voters' preferences and values, when we know that *no* method typically produces true and fair amalgamations. Furthermore, since the reason for this disconcerting state of affairs lies not in the method of amalgamation, but rather in the nature of political values and preferences, there is no hope that some magical new invention of a better representative system will allow us to obtain a true and fair amalgamation.

The world has not made representation easy for us, and it is worth pointing out why. Much of the motivation for the invention of new electoral systems is a belief that a new method of counting will resolve the inherent contradictions in opinions and values in society. That this is false is easily seen in the situation of the so-called paradox of voting:

Person 1 prefers a to b, b to c, and hence a to c.
Person 2 prefers b to c, c to a, and hence b to a.
Person 3 prefers c to a, a to b, and hence c to b.

In the usual commentary on this situation it is pointed out that a majority (1,3) prefers a to b and another majority (1,2) prefers b to c, so that, for consistency, the social choice should be a to c. In fact, however—and this is the paradox—only a minority (Person 1) prefers a to c. Because the paradox is usually presented in this form it is commonly assumed that the difficulty is in the summation. But no. The difficulty is in the way the *individuals* have arranged their preferences. Suppose the people in society decide by some unspecified method to implement alternative a, then Person 2 discovers society is enforcing the absolutely worst alternative against him, and Person 3 discovers the next to worst is being enforced. A similar result occurs if either b or c is implemented. Whatever is implemented, all but one person is against it. This fact has nothing to do with the method of counting and of choosing (because the method was left wholly unspecified), but is a direct consequence of the preferences or values held in society. Given any reasonably complicated social situation, where, for example, two or more criteria are involved in people's decisions among alternatives, it is the case that something like the paradox of voting occurs (Plott 1967; Riker 1982a). Hence, in most realistic political situations, the distribution of public opinion is such that any chosen alternative is opposed by a group strong enough (given time and proper organization) to replace it. Not surprisingly, therefore, any chosen and enforced alternative appears to many people to be tyrannical. Typically, they put up with what they conceive of as oppression mainly because they expect to be among the favored on other issues.

This fact is what makes representation so difficult. Any choice by what, superficially, appear to be fair methods is, in some other sense, unjust. The essential constitutional problem of representation is not, therefore, simply reflecting public opinion, but rather reflecting public opinion in so *cautious* a way that significant elements of society (e.g., majorities) are not opposed to the reflection.

CONSTITUTIONAL RESTRAINTS

The constitutional problem of representation is one of finding appropriate restraints on the process of representation so that officials display proper caution. There is one well-recognized and well-tested way of inducing caution, and that is to construct government so that no choices at all are made until the choice passes an extremely difficult test, e.g., an extraordinary majority. There are many institutions that thus slow down government, and one of the most famous is the so-called separation of powers. By means of this arrangement, officials expressing the views of different constituencies can block each other's action until an alternative is found that satisfies public opinion aggregated in several different ways.

The most well-known kind of separation of powers is the tricameral legislature found in the United States (originally copied from Great Britain, which has, however, now lost that system). In the United States system the three legislative houses (President, Senate, and House of Representatives) are chosen by the people arranged in three different structures of constituencies, and are voted on at different times so that the officials in each of the three houses never have quite the same mandate and often—even typically—speak for different interests. By contrast with a system in which the whole legislature and executive is elected from one kind of constituency at one time (as in, for example, India), it is possible—and, indeed, frequently the case—that a minority interest be placed fully in charge of the whole government. The contrast between the two systems is then that, in the United States system, three kinds of officials must agree to produce a statute or a policy, while in India only one kind need agree. One extreme example of the difference was Sanjay Gandhi's sterilization program, which ultimately led his mother to adopt all the expedients of the tyrant—except for one: she allowed an election, which of course, she lost.

The separation of powers in the Constitution of the United States is not, however, the only kind of restraint on the representative process. Another is federalism which, entirely apart from its other constitutional significance, is important for restraints on legislatures. It locates authority over nominations for national office in processes and politicians not controlled, or selected by, national officials. Hence, leaders of national political parties cannot force members of the national legislature to follow the policies of the national leaders simply because the national leaders have no control over the nomination, or, more importantly, the renomination of national legislators. This feature of federalism might be described simply as political decentralization, and it seems to be increasingly characteristic of Canada and possibly India, as well as the United States.

A third form of restraint on representation is multipartism. This restraint is especially appropriate for parliamentary governments. In parliamentary governments, the danger always exists that an executive with a large parliamentary majority is liable to interpret its majority as a mandate, and thus to engage in what has traditionally been called majority tyranny, but which, as I have just shown, is a kind of minority tyranny. One way to control that tendency is to weaken the executive coalition by forcing it to be composed of several parties, any one of which can bring the government down by withdrawing from the coalition.

CONCLUSION

Of the three main devices to restrain the tyranny of temporary majorities (separation of powers, political decentralization, and multipartism), only multipartism is closely related to some particular method of election. It is true that a PR system can usually be made to produce a large number of political parties, though most constitution writers of the last generation sought to structure PR to minimize, not maximize, that number. The separation of powers and political decentralization are not logically related to any method, although historically both have been constitutionally associated with plurality elections.

The inference from this fact is, I believe, that either kind of electoral system is adequate for representation. Indeed, the kind of election is, itself, not very important compared with the overwhelming importance of constitutional restraints. Constitution writers might as well adopt the electoral method that is most comfortable for the people who will use the constitution they produce, plurality or PR as the case may be. What is more important for constitution writers is that they recognize that neither method of election can produce a true mandate or a true popular will. If they recognize that central and essential fact, then their problem is to restrain elected officials so that their actions can be easily blocked or vetoed by, and in the name of, the real majorities that oppose so-called mandates or the so-called popular wills.

PART IV
THE SINGLE
TRANSFERABLE VOTE

11

Proportional Representation with the Single Transferable Vote: A Basic Requirement for Legislative Elections

George H. Hallett, Jr.

"No State shall...deny to any person within its jurisdiction the equal protection of the laws." 14th Amendment to the United States Constitution.

"The Equal Protection Clause requires substantially equal legislative representation for all citizens in a State regardless of where they reside.

"(a) Legislators represent people, not areas.

"(b) Weighting votes differently according to where citizens happen to reside is discriminatory." Syllabus of Reynolds v. Sims (377 U.S. 533), United States Supreme Court.

"And the right of suffrage can be denied by a debasement or dilution of the weight of a citizen's vote just as effectively as by wholly prohibiting the free exercise of the franchise." From the Opinion of the Court in Reynolds v. Sims.

"The conception of political equality from the Declaration of Independence, to Lincoln's Gettysburg Address, to the Fifteenth, Seventeenth and Nineteenth Amendments can mean only one thing—one person, one vote." Opinion of the Supreme Court in Gray v. Sanders (372 U.S. 368), quoted in the Opinion of Reynolds v. Sims.

"A government is republican in proportion as every member composing it has his equal voice in the direction of its concerns...by representatives chosen by himself." Thomas Jefferson, quoted in the Opinion of Reynolds v. Sims.

"Wesberry [v. Sanders (376 U.S. 1)] clearly established that the fundamental principle of representative government in this country is one of equal representation for equal numbers of people, without regard to race, sex, economic status or place of residence within a State." Opinion of the Court in Reynolds v. Sims.

"Representative schemes...become archaic and outdated. But the basic principle of representative government remains, and must remain, unchanged—the weight of a citizen's vote cannot be made to depend on where he lives." Opinion of the Court in Reynolds v. Sims.

"We concluded [in the Wesberry case] by stating: 'No right is more precious in a free country than that of having a voice in the election of those who make the laws under which, as good citizens, we must live. Other rights, even the most basic, are illusory if the right to vote is undermined. Our Constitution leaves no room for classification of people in a way that unnecessarily abridges this right.' " Opinion of the Court in Reynolds v. Sims.

IMPROPRIETY IN SINGLE-MEMBER DISTRICTS

These quotations from the highest court in the United States were written primarily to establish substantial equality in the population of legislative districts under the single-member district system of election. They overrode, and continue to override, countless laws of states and municipalities, citing the superior law of the United States Constitution. The Constitution, in turn, was, in this respect, based on the fundamentals of democratic self-government.

But note that every one of these quotations, on examination, applies just as clearly to the unsuitability of using a method of election which inevitably leaves large numbers of voters without representatives of their own choosing. This includes the single-member district system itself, for any method of choosing legislators from single-member districts has to disregard the minority in every district. Millions of voters across the country are regularly left with "representatives" whom they voted against because they were outvoted in the district where they resided. Though they are all sorts of people, they form together a major class of unrepresented citizens just as surely as if they had been denied "the free exercises of the franchise." And, as I hope to demonstrate, they are neglected "unnecessarily."

When this is understood by those in authority—which may take a little time—some form of proportional representation (PR) may be required constitutionally for all legislative elections in this country. "PR" and "one person, one vote" are identical concepts.

How strikingly the single-member district system of election may fall short of this concept has just been illustrated by my own city of New York. Our thirty-five council members, all elected now from single-member districts, are all, without exception, nominees of the Democratic Party. The highest vote received by any of them in their latest (1982) election was 43,781 for Carol Greitzer in the

3rd Councilmanic District of Manhattan (36,609 in the Democratic column, 7,172 in the Liberal). But in all the districts 230,507 voters—over five times that many—voted the Republican ticket and elected no council members except one regular Democrat whom the Republicans endorsed. Some of the Liberals and Conservatives also supported Democratic winners, but nearly a quarter of all who voted for candidates in the final council election voted only for losers (295,579 out of 1,222,863 or 24.17 percent). All of these people are "represented" by council members whom they voted against.

This gross distortion was due to the fact that the council members do, in reality, represent areas, not just people. To get represented, people have to be assigned to voting areas where people of like inclination are in a plurality. The "weight of a citizen's vote" does "depend on where he lives." In this case, the districts represented were so carved out that only Democrats were anywhere in a plurality. Even in the special circumstances of New York City it would have been possible to give the constitutionally required equal treatment to Democrats and non-Democrats alike, but not in single-member districts.

It is hardly ever possible with single-member districts to come anywhere near giving satisfactory representation to all the voters. One of the most obvious requirements, then, for an acceptable method of electing legislators is that more than one member be elected together from each district or at large. Not just two members (with an occasional exception where isolation of small numbers in a large area may make it unavoidable), but enough members in each district or at-large to make "one person, one vote" a reality in each district if the election method is right.

The usual method of electing several members together from one district or at-large—giving each member as many votes as there are members to be elected —is even farther from constitutional requirements than single-member districts. Its usual result is to give all the places in each district to one ticket.

PART-WAY METHODS FALL SHORT

It is interesting to note that the simple methods devised to give some representation to minorities also fail to meet the constitutional test. Take limited voting, which usually results in some minority representation. A simple example will illustrate the difficulties. Suppose one hundred voters, with three votes each, are electing five candidates and there are two parties, A with fifty-five votes, B with forty-five. If each party nominates and votes for three candidates only, A will elect three and B two, which is appropriate on the "one person, one vote" principle. But if A tries to elect four, and divides its voters into four groups with different sets of three candidates for that purpose, while B stays put with three candidates, the best A can do is to give each of its four candidates $(55 \times 3)/4$ votes, which is forty-one or forty-two. This is less than B's forty-five votes per candidate and the B minority will elect three to the majority's two. But if A turns out to have sixty votes to B's forty, the maneuver will work. A can then give each of four candidates $(60 \times 3)/4$, which equals forty-five votes, more than B's forty. A elects four times as many as B, though the right proportions required by "one person, one vote" are still three and two, twenty votes per member elected. If the two parties do not know the exact strength of both, as in most larger elections, either distortion is possible.

Cumulative voting sometimes presents similar situations, though it makes the party maneuvering that it promotes less difficult. From 1870 until its recent abolition, it was used for all members of the Illinois House of Representatives, with districts electing three members each and each voter having three votes which he could cumulate on one candidate or "distribute the same, or equal parts thereof, among the candidates, as he shall see fit" (from the Illinois Constitution). The usual result was two candidates elected in each district by the party with the most votes there, and one by the other major party. In fact, the parties frequently nominated only the number they thought they could elect, and cumulated their votes for either two or one. If the result was uncertain, they would presumably each nominate two, which was likely to be safe. If the larger party tried to elect all three, it might be in trouble. Suppose Party A turned out to have fifty-five percent of the votes and gave each of three candidates a fifty-five percent vote, while party B with forty-five percent cumulated on two candidates, giving 1½ votes of each of its voters to each of its candidates. The forty-five percent vote of Party B would then give each of its candidates $.45 \times 1½ = .67½$ times as many votes as there were voters, more than the .55 times for each of A's three candidates. The majority A would elect one, the minority B would elect two. With cumulative voting, advance calculation of party strength and party discipline to act accordingly is sometimes necessary to avoid disaster.

PARTY LIST SYSTEMS NOT GOOD ENOUGH

The party list systems of PR used in most of the countries of western Europe and in Israel meet the constitutional criteria so far as political parties are concerned. They divide the seats available in a multimember district among the parties in approximate proportion to the votes cast for the party lists, with a great variety of methods of selecting the winning candidates within each party. They do not offer proportionality on any other basis than that of political party. If an ethnic group, for example, wants to elect some of its own people, it has to form a party for the purpose, or act dividedly within some of the parties.

Perhaps the most serious defect of the party list systems is that most of them require complete adherence to one party. There is no facility for splitting party votes. The voter has to pretend, in voting, that all of the candidates of the party he chooses are better than all other candidates. In voting, he gives support to all of the party's nominees and the ones that he helps elect may sometimes be candidates that he does not like. He may or may not be given a choice of particular candidates within a party, but only at the expense of accepting the whole party ticket for the party apportionment.*

Defective as most of our American voting methods are in some respects, they regularly allow the voters to vote for any of their favorite candidates, and never require any distortion of a voter's preference in order to vote at all. I hope we are never tempted by other gains to give up this valuable asset.

THE SINGLE TRANSFERABLE VOTE

The one system of election which passes muster, logically and constitutionally, is PR with the single transferable vote. This is the kind of PR used in all public elections in the Republic of Ireland since 1920, for all recent elections in Northern Ireland under mandate of the British Parliament in order to protect the Catholic minority, and for a considerable part of the public elections in Australia, including the upper house of Parliament and, since 1907, the dominant lower house of the province of Tasmania. It is the only form of PR widely advocated in Great Britain and the United States.

This system of election is specifically designed to provide "equal representation for equal numbers of people," real majority rule with due representation for all sizable minorities. In all its minor variations, it provides the following steps to that end:

1) "One person, one vote" is taken literally as well as in principle. It provides a single vote for each voter in a district electing several members or at-large.

The number of members per district is crucial, for it is not possible to give separate representation to more, widely differing groups of people than there are members being elected together. With an occasional smaller number in an isolated district, perhaps, it would seem desirable to allow due separate representation in every district to the larger competing groups. An effort should be made to recognize enough such groups so that most voters will not have to compromise very much to find satisfactory representation in one of them. A convenient number per district or at-large which would almost always meet this test is nine, the number elected together in each of New York City's community school districts under this form of PR for six times now. Seven or five members will usually work quite well.

In most cities, and even in some of the smaller states, election at-large would be feasible and desirable. Where districts seem necessary, it would usually be feasible to make them permanent, and to allot each district one more or one fewer member whenever the

---

*A seldom used variant lets the voter cast votes for candidates on different party lists (panachage), but with each such vote helping the candidate's whole list for the party apportionment.

census so indicates. Most recent proposals for New York City have used the five boroughs as permanent districts, with a given number of Council members divided among the boroughs after each census, in proportion to their population. When PR was in use for the Council some years ago, the number elected in each borough depended on the size of the actual vote in the borough, but total population is now generally accepted for apportionments. The usual freedom from any need for redistrictings under PR can be a great boon.

2) The "quota" sufficient for election under this system is not the simple quota found by dividing the total vote by the number of candidates to be elected, but almost always the smaller "Droop quota," which is the smallest number that cannot be beaten. With one vote for each voter in a nine-member district, for example, any candidate who receives more than one-tenth of the vote is sure of election, for it would not be possible for ten candidates to get more than a tenth of the vote each. The general formula for the Droop quota is to divide the total number of valid ballots by one more than the number of candidates to be elected and add one to the result, disregarding fractions.

3) No candidate is allowed to keep more than the quota. To prevent votes from being wasted on candidates who do not need them or cannot be elected by them, the system gives each voter a preferential ballot. Either on a paper ballot or (prospectively) on a voting machine the voter is invited to express an order of choice; first, second, third, and other choices for as many or as few choices as he wishes. This is his instruction to the counting officials to count his single vote for his first choice if it can help elect his first choice; if it cannot, it is to be transferred to his second choice; if it cannot help elect his second choice either, it is to be transferred to his third choice, and so on.

4) If a candidate has more than a quota of first choices, he is declared elected. Just the quota of ballots that he needs, including any that have no second choice, are left to elect him, and the rest are taken for transfer to each voter's second choice or the earliest of his choices who is not also elected. The question of which ballots to transfer as surplus and which to leave in the quota is met variously in different sets of rules, but in no case does the method used deprive any voters of an effective vote, as does the corresponding single-member district division into constituencies by arbitrary boundary lines on a map. The dividing line between the quota and the surplus merely decides which of the voters concerned help elect their first choice and which help a second or later choice after their first choice has been elected by others. Both groups are well treated.

5) After all surpluses have been transferred and no candidate has more than the quota he needs for election, the lowest candidates are declared defeated one at a time. As each one goes out, all his ballots that have further choices are transferred so that their votes will not be wasted. Each transferred ballot takes its vote to the voter's next choice among the candidates still in the running—neither elected nor defeated. As candidates reach the quota in this process, they are declared elected and receive no more ballots, or new surpluses are created for them and then immediately transferred, which comes to the same thing.

At this point it is sometimes objected that the lowest candidate is not necessarily the fairest candidate to defeat. Another candidate who is "everybody's second choice" but few people's first choice might occasionally be a more readily acceptable representative of a quota of voters than a candidate who defeated him on early choices and went on to win. By complicating the rules considerably this possibility could be guarded against before each candidate is defeated, but probably most people would prefer the simplicity of the present rule, which is widely accepted. The procedure regularly followed corresponds to what the voters would probably do if they were all there in person and deciding what to do next—the smallest group would give up first and disperse to other candidates with an apparently better chance. In theory, the procedure is a succession of run-offs, all in one election. This objection is not a constitutional defect, for the voters who might, some of them, be better pleased to have the defeated low man as their representative get representation by helping to elect other candidates that they like. This and other technical objections raised by some analysts to this well-proven system of election are more curiosities than serious faults. They would usually not be noticed by the people involved or do any practical damage.

6) The process of successive defeats and transfers is continued until the desired number have completed their quotas and been declared elected or until only the desired number are left undefeated. In the latter case the remaining candidates are all elected whether they are quite up to the quota or not, but it is a matter of interest—and often required—to transfer the ballots of the runner-up to their next choices for continuing candidates. This usually shows that all the successful candidates have the support of a quota or very nearly a quota of voters and exactly or very nearly exactly the same number that elected each of the other candidates. In the 1980 school board elections in New York City, for example (the May 1983 elections have not yet been analyzed at this writing), the voters who helped elect one of the nine winners in each of the thirty-two districts were either nine full quotas (ninety percent of the valid ballots) or ninety percent within one percentage point. No less than seventy-six percent, a large majority in every district, saw their very first choice elected.

In view of the variety of representation always secured in proportional elections, it is always probable that a considerable part of the "exhausted" ballots that do not technically elect anyone (the ten percent necessarily left in this category in the school elections) would be found, on examination, to have been marked for candidates elected by others. This was verified in one of the Worcester elections of nine Council members, where I was in charge of the count and was permitted to have the exhausted ballots examined when the count was over.

In short, this system of election regularly gives nearly all the voters satisfactory representation on approximately equal terms.

EASIER VOTING DECISIONS

It also, in important ways, makes voting and campaigning easier. In many situations, the voter is saved from any worry about wasting his vote. His preferential vote is insurance against that. He can safely vote his real order of choice as far as he has any, and no later choice will ever hurt an earlier choice. This is true because no later choice is ever counted unless and until all earlier choices are elected or defeated.

If you have a favorite candidate but don't think he has much chance of election, you can simply give him your first choice anyway, with later choices to fall back on. Your first choice is always counted.

If you like two or more candidates and don't know much about their chances, you can give your early choices to all of them and be pretty sure of helping to elect one of them if any of them has a chance.

If you can't find out about all of the candidates, you can give your early choices to as many of them as you do know something about and have reason to think well of. You can only elect one. If there are good candidates you haven't been able to discover, they may be good representatives for others.

If you are interested in a slate, you can help it by giving early choices to all its candidates in any order. Of course, you can leave out any particular candidate that you wouldn't like to see elected.

You can always make up your own slate. There is no strategic reason why you have to distort your own wishes. If you vote for five or six, you usually have an excellent chance of helping to elect one. Most of the ballots are effective without having to go farther than that to later choices. But you can safely mark more choices than are being elected. In a Queens proportional election of council members, I once helped elect a first choice, and the next time a tenth choice because several of my choices had been elected by others before my first choice was defeated.

Voting will always be worthwhile. You are almost sure to be a winner.

EASIER CAMPAIGNING

It is a remarkable but demonstrable fact that, under proportional representation with a single transferable vote in any of its variations, a group of voters united in support of any group of candidates, even across party lines, can always be sure to elect as many of its candidates as it casts quotas of votes, simply (1) by nominating or supporting at least that many candidates and (2) by giving all of its candidates the first consecutive choices of all its voters in any order or orders. This is evident if you think about it. Any surplus votes for any of the group's candidates will be transferred to other candidates of the group, so that no candidate of the group will use up more than his quota. And whenever any candidate of the group is defeated, all of his votes will be transferred to other candidates of the group, but not give any candidate votes above his quota. So when the number of the undefeated candidates of the group is reduced to the number of its quotas, all the quotas will be filled and the candidates with those quotas elected.

The representation of the group goes even beyond that. If it gets some support for its candidates from outside its own group, and has a fraction of a quota left over beyond a full quota, the combination may give it an additional elected member. And, in any case, any of its ballots that are left over after the election of its candidates will transfer their votes to other candidates if later choices are marked on them for such candidates, so even that remnant of voters will get some representation by candidates its members think well of.

Campaigning for a slate under this method is relatively easy, for there is no need to risk offending voters by suggesting a precise order of choice. Votes for all of the candidates on the slate in each voter's own order of preference among them will give the slate maximum help, so long as other candidates with a chance of election are not put ahead of any slate candidates who prove to have a chance of election. The Cincinnati City Charter Committee, the independent group which, for many years under PR elected a majority of the Council of nine, or at least four out of nine, used to instruct each of its nine candidates to get all of the first choices he could for himself and then urge the voters to give their next eight choices to all the other charter candidates in any order.

MAJORITY RULE ASSURED

The Cincinnati experience illustrates this method's assurance of majority rule as well as of minority representation. Whether the charter committee or the Republican organization elected a majority of the council, its majority was based on five quotas or near-quotas of votes. Since one quota was one-tenth of the valid vote plus one (disregarding fractions), five quotas corresponded to a bare majority of the votes cast. Even after the few elections when four were elected on each side with one independent, any majority vote in the council was cast by council members elected by five quotas or near-quotas, corresponding almost surely to a majority of the votes (bearing in mind especially that each candidate elected by transfers gave up a few votes beyond the quota that he did not need, but which could not go to other candidates because they had no further choices for candidates still in the running).

In a larger body elected from a number of districts, as in Ireland's Dáil Eireann, the districts would have populations roughly in proportion to the numbers of members they elected (in the United States they would have to) and in each district with an odd number of members the majority of members would correspond almost surely to a majority of the voters, while in districts with an even number any half of the members would correspond to somewhere near half the voters. The net result would be a fair likelihood that any majority in the elected body would correspond to a majority of voters.

NO NEED FOR PRIMARIES

Political parties may, but need not, participate in elections under PR with the transferable vote. The school board elections in New York City are nonpartisan and at a different time from other elections.

If political parties do participate, the elimination of a primary will be one of the system's great advantages. The transferable vote will select the candidates to represent each party without the need of a special primary election. Candidates are regularly nominated by petition. Our latest proposals in the New York legislature for proportional city council elections would permit any candidate who was an enrolled member of a party to use the party name on his petition and on the ballot. The candidates favored by the party organization would be indicated on the ballot by the party emblem in addition. This would set up a party primary on the final election ballot, to be decided by those who vote for the party's candidates.

Even without such information on the ballot, the voters would decide which candidates of a party, and how many, are elected. When PR was used for five elections of the New York City Council some years ago, the party organization was permitted to decide which candidates could use the party name on the ballot, but a number of independent Democrats and Republicans won anyway. These included Genevieve Earle, a member of the charter commission which put PR on the ballot for adoption, and later served as Minority Leader in the council, being elected three times as an independent and then twice with Republican support; James A. Burke, a Democratic Assemblyman who was denied his party's support, but came in first in the Queens Council election anyway, and later became Borough President; and Stanley M. Isaacs, who was denied endorsement by his Republican Party after distinguished service as Manhattan Borough President, and then was elected to the council ahead of the endorsed Republican who was also elected, and served on the council with his party's endorsement for many years afterward, the only Republican who remained after PR was discontinued.

REPRESENTATION OF ETHNIC MINORITIES

Much of the election discussion of late, both among students of election methods and in the courts, has been centered on ethnic representation. Blacks and Hispanics have been emphasizing the importance, to them, of electing people of their own background, not merely people sympathetic to their problems and interests. At-large or multimember elections without PR have sometimes been broken up by court order, in order to give ethnic minorities a chance to win. The Voting Rights Act requires examination of many redistrictings and election law changes by the United States Justice Department, in order to make sure that ethnic opportunities for success are not being prejudiced, and New York City's last city council election was delayed for a year for failure of a redistricting to pass muster.

It is significant to note that when the best form of PR was adopted for the New York City school board elections, it was submitted to the Justice Department under the Voting Rights Act and approved. It had previously been approved for constitutionality by the highest courts of New York, Massachusetts, and Ohio, and the Ohio approval was appealed unsuccessfully to the United States Supreme Court.

Though no free method of election can guarantee that ethnic minority candidates will be elected if its opportunites are not availed of by actual voters, it has been clear right along that the rules of this election method offer the best of opportunities. There have been some notable examples. Adam Clayton Powell was elected to the New York City Council by PR without major party support as the first black member of the council. In Cincinnati, Theodore M. Berry was elected, chiefly by the black community, to the city council under PR and became the council's vice-chairman. When PR was narrowly abolished, so was the black community's representation for several elections. Later, Mr. Berry was elected again, despite the absence of provision for minority representation, and this time was elected chairman of the council with the title of Mayor.

The 1973 New York City school board elections were analyzed by the United Parents Associations for their ethnic composition. It was found that seventy-one members, twenty-four percent of the 288-member total elected throughout the city, were black, coming from twenty-three of the thirty-two school districts; that thirty-eight members, thirteen percent of those elected, were Puerto Rican, coming from eighteen districts; and that one Chinese member was elected from a large Manhattan district containing a good part of Chinatown. This was much better from an ethnic point of view, as analyzed by a Board of Education study, than the results of any of New York's congressional, state legislative, or any recent council elections.

NO LONGER "DIVIDE AND CONQUER"

One thing that frequently blocks ethnic representation under ordinary plurality elections is the competition of two ethnic minority candidates for a single place, or of two different ethnic minorities for the same place. In a heavily Hispanic district, two Hispanic candidates and one non-Hispanic white candidate will contend for one place, and the non-Hispanic candidate will slip in with much less than the combined Hispanic vote. Or a black and an Hispanic candidate will divide the ethnic vote and make it impossible for either to win. A notable confrontation of this kind took place in the 1976 primary election that gave Edward Koch his start toward the New York mayoralty. There were seven candidates in the Democratic primary, and a forty percent vote for one of them was required for nomination without a runoff. Two of the candidates, both former or present Borough Presidents and widely popular outside their ethnic bases, divided the large ethnic vote, Percy Sutton of Manhattan, black, and Herman Badillo of the Bronx, Hispanic. Together they polled fifty thousand votes more than Koch, and it seemed probable that either, by himself, would have been right up among the leaders. As it was, they came in fifth and sixth in the Democratic primary and neither was included in the runoff.

One of the special merits of the single transferable vote, applied for one or several places, is that more candidates than are to be elected can divide the minority vote, any kind of minority, without depriving that minority of its rightful share of success. In a multimember district under PR, there is frequently room for both black and Hispanic candidates to win, but if more minority candidates are running than there are votes to elect them all, that does not of itself reduce the minority representation—any minority candidate defeated can pass on votes to another such candidate as next choice if voters support them both.

I ran into an instructive situation of this kind in 1980, when I was asked to finish up the school board count in District 9 in the Bronx for a count director who could not complete the assignment. Quite a number of the candidates were Hispanic, recognizable by their names, and between them they had about a third of the first choices. But none of them stood out above the others, and when I took over, five of the nine places had been filled with full quotas, none of them Hispanic. The Hispanic candidates were worried. Then the lowest Hispanic candidates began to be defeated and as each one dropped out his votes transferred predominantly to the other Hispanics. The next three quotas completed were for candidates of that group and they finished with three of the nine successful candidates, just the share that the voters' first choices indicated as appropriate.

The defeat of candidates who seem logical winners because of competition for their constituencies is one of the commonest misadventures of plurality voting. Two liberals may be defeated by a minority conservative, or vice versa. The dominant party may lose its seat by having one of its members run independently. Not infrequently, such situations are created artificially by persuading extra candidates to run. And quite frequently, candidates with good qualifications refrain from running so as not to be ''spoilers'' and hand over the place to someone they don't want by dividing his opposition. In PR with preferential voting, such situations are taken care of as an extra bonus. A group of like-minded voters does not lose out by having more candidates than it can elect.

WHAT KINDS OF REPRESENTATION SHOULD BE PROMOTED?

Some of the ethnic districting required by the courts has been protested by different groups that were divided by it. What about the rights of other minorities? The Sovern Charter Commission that just reported in New York City and rejected the Citizens Union's urgent proposal of PR for the all-Democratic city council, explained, regretfully it said, that it had put the representation of ethnic minorities ahead of party minorities when it decided it could not favor both. (Ironically, PR for the whole council would surely have done better by both minorities.)

What kinds of minorities should get separate representation? The answer of PR with the single transferable vote is to let the people decide. Any group that puts up or supports candidates and polls as much as a quota of votes can be sure of electing its share. Often the same candidate will represent more than one minority, e.g. a Spanish Republican in New York City. With the present emphasis of ethnic minorities on electing their own people, it is very unlikely that their interests will be neglected under this most responsive method of election. But every other minority has the same chance. The election method is neutral and should be left so.

The more general use of PR with the single transferable vote can mean a great deal for our country, or any country. It can transform our legislative elections from contests to win all the spoils of victory for one group and keep other people out to invitations to all citizens to come in and take part in a great cooperative democracy. This salutary development may even eventually be court-required on its merits. Without waiting for that, it is overridingly worth working for. "No right is more precious in a free country."

12

An Electoral Basis for Responsible Government: The Australian Experience

J. F. H. Wright

The meaning of the term "responsible government" is a matter of some confusion. Unless an electoral system ensures that elected governing bodies are accurately representative, a government can be fully responsible to the elected body but dedicated to the implementation of policies that are not supported by a majority of the people. Considerations of logic, justice, and efficiency require that there should be no conflict between the two concepts of responsibility.

A practical electoral system, besides ensuring accurate representation, must also ensure that it is possible to form an effective government, and should lead to stability consistent with responsiveness to public opinion. For long-term stability, governing bodies must be capable of winning and retaining the confidence of the people, and this can only be expected when the electoral system guarantees effective representation.

The basic failure of any single-member-district system to provide for representation of a large proportion of voters is sufficient to disqualify such systems for use in countries claiming to be democratic. An acceptable electoral system must be based on multimember electoral districts. In several countries, list systems of proportional representation (PR) give reasonably accurate representation of parties, but allow very little participation by voters in the actual selection of the candidates who fill the vacancies.

Quota-preferential or single transferable vote systems of PR are based on acceptance of the fact that a geographically defined district will inevitably contain people with political views varying over a wide range. They are designed to allow groups of voters who agree about the kind of representation they want to accumulate their votes so as to obtain that representation. With such systems, high proportions of voters are likely to see the election of the candidates they have chosen to support, so that there is a reasonable prospect of elected bodies being capable of winning and holding the confidence of the voters. Quota-preferential systems thus provide, as no other kind of system can, a realistic basis for the functioning of responsible government.

PREFERENTIAL SYSTEMS IN AUSTRALIA

The Australian experience provides a large amount of evidence on the use of both majority-preferential (alternative vote) and quota-preferential (STV) systems in elections of various sizes, the largest being elections of the two houses of Parliament. The House of Representatives is elected from single-member districts by the Ware preferential method. In 1983, there were 125 districts and approximately 8.5 million votes, with an average per district of almost seventy thousand. The Senate consists of sixty-four Senators, ten from each of the six states, two from the Australian Capital Territory and two from the Northern Territory. The Senators from the states are elected for terms of six years, half being elected in each state at each regular half-Senate election by a quota-preferential method, with each state an undivided electoral area. Territory Senators are elected by the same method for three-year terms. Legislation passed late in 1983 provides for an increase in the number of Senators from each state to twelve, with a corresponding increase to 148 in the membership of the House of Representatives.

From the beginning of self-government in Australia, there has been a readiness to innovate, and many features of the electoral arrangements are unusual. The first use of preferential voting in single-member districts was in Queensland in 1893, and plurality systems had been replaced by preferential systems in all states by 1936. Preferential voting was introduced for both houses of the Federal Parliament in 1918.

Following the use of a quota-preferential system in 1897 to elect ten of the thirty-seven members of the Tasmanian House of Assembly, an improved quota-preferential system was introduced for the entire House in 1907. Known locally as the Hare-Clark system, it provided for the election of six members from each of five electoral districts. It has continued in use, with some changes, to the present time. The most important change was the increase in membership from thirty to thirty-five in 1958, with seven to be elected from each district rather than six. Twenty-four general elections of the House have been conducted with this system. This is the world's longest continuous application of a quota-preferential system in public elections.

In 1953, a quota-preferential method was specified for all local-government elections in New South Wales for filling three or more vacancies. After a return to a majority-preferential method between 1968 and 1974, the quota-preferential method was reintroduced in 1977 and is currently in use.

In 1948, the majority-preferential method used for elections of the Federal

Senate was replaced by a quota-preferential method similar, in principle, to that used in the Hare-Clark system, but differing in some important details. With over eight million voters, this is the world's largest application of a quota-preferential method.

The Legislative Council of New South Wales was elected indirectly before 1978, when a quota-preferential system similar to that used for Federal Senate elections was adopted. This has been used in two elections, in 1978 and 1981. In South Australia, a similar system was adopted for elections of the legislative council in 1981, replacing a list system of PR which had been used for two elections, in 1975 and 1979.

At present, majority-preferential methods in single-member districts are used in elections of the lower houses of New South Wales, Victoria, Queensland, South Australia, and Western Australia, the Legislative Council of Tasmania, the Federal House of Representatives, and the Legislative Assembly of the Northern Territory. The Legislative Councils of Victoria and Western Australia are elected from two-member Provinces with overlapping terms, so that, in effect, a single-member-district system applies. The Tasmanian House of Assembly, the Federal Senate, and the Legislative Councils of New South Wales and South Australia are elected by quota-preferential methods. Of Australia's fourteen parliamentary bodies, ten are elected by majority-preferential and four by quota-preferential methods. In all cases, voting is compulsory[1] and in some, the indication of the voter's order of preference for all candidates is required for a valid vote.

From an examination of the results of the many elections held with systems of both kinds, it is possible to examine claims made by both supporters and opponents of such systems. They have been applied against a background of Westminster-style Parliamentary tradition, and with a highly disciplined party system. The present party structure developed over roughly the same period as that in which the transition from plurality to preferential systems occurred.

SINGLE-MEMBER-DISTRICT MAJORITY-PREFERENTIAL-SYSTEMS

The introduction of preferential voting in single-member districts in the last few years of the nineteenth century followed recognition of the fact that plurality elections had often given results noticeably inconsistent with the wishes of the voters. The expectation was that the change would provide both a wider range of choice for voters and more accurate representation of voters and parties.

In fact, as shown by examination of the results of a large number of elections up to 1980 (Wright 1980, pp. 57–84), these expectations have not been realized. More recent elections have followed similar patterns. It has been unusual for parties to endorse more than one candidate each in an electoral district, the choice of candidates for endorsement being made within the parties.[2] Voters have been practically limited to a choice between parties.

The proportions of seats won by parties with single-member-district preferential systems have rarely corresponded with their voting support. The party structure is essentially one of confrontation between the Australian Labor Party and a coalition of the Liberal Party and the rural-based National Party, previously known as the National Country Party and earlier as the Country Party. Results of the Federal House of Representatives elections of 1980 and 1983 give some indication of the distortions that the system can produce. In 1980, first preferences for the conservative coalition totaled 46.29 percent, and for the Labor Party, 45.15 percent. It has been estimated (Parliamentary Library, Australia 1980, p. 11) that 50.2 percent of all electors who recorded valid votes preferred the coalition to Labor. With this distribution of support, the coalition won seventy-four seats and Labor fifty-one. In 1983, Labor received 49.48 percent of the first preferences and the coalition 43.75 percent. It has been estimated (Parliamentary Library, Australia, 1983, p. 32) that the change in support for Labor was 3.6 percent. In this case, Labor won seventy-five seats and the coalition fifty. A change of 3.6 percent in support for Labor increased its proportion of seats from 40.8 percent to 60.0 percent.

In the House of Representatives election of 1954, Labor candidates received 50.03 percent of first preferences, but won fewer seats than the coalition. In 1961, and again in 1969, it was estimated (Mackerras 1980, p. 251) that Labor was preferred to the coalition by more than half the voters, but in both cases the coalition won more than half the seats. In the election of the South Australian House of Assembly in 1968, Labor candidates received 51.98 percent of first preferences but won only nineteen of the thirty-nine seats.

Australian results also allow the examination of the performance of single-member-district systems in providing representation of voters. It has been usual for a substantial proportion of voters, usually between forty percent and fifty percent, to indicate as their first preferences candidates who are not elected. As each party tends to endorse only one candidate in a district, voters who do not see the election of their first-preference candidates are left nominally represented by people with opposing political views. The 1983 House of Representatives election left 3,885,545 voters, 44.77 percent of those who cast valid votes, in this position. In 1980, the number was 3,863,180, or 46.51 percent. For the sixteen House of Representatives elections since 1949, the median proportion of voters who did not see the election of their first-preference candidates was 44.98 percent.

The concept of "one vote, one value" is often mentioned by politicians and others, and it is suggested that the placing of district boundaries so that enrollments (numbers of registered voters) are uniform or almost so would put the concept into effect.[3] Before 1977, enrollments in districts for the House of Representatives were allowed to vary by up to twenty percent from the average within each state. Before the 1977 election, there was a redistribution with the tolerance reduced to ten percent. In the election immediately following the redistribution, the Liberal-National Country Party coalition, preferred to Labor by 54.6 percent of the voters (Mackerras 1980, p. 251), won eighty-six seats (69.4 percent) while Labor won thirty-eight (30.6 percent). The Liberal Party, with fewer votes than Labor, won sixty-seven seats. The National Country Party, with a quarter of the votes of the Labor Party, won half as many seats. The 1981 election of the New South Wales Legislative Assembly was held immediately after a redistribution with 10 percent tolerance. Labor received 55.7 percent of the first preferences and won sixty-nine of the ninety-eight contested seats, that is, 70.4 percent. Obviously, reduction of variations in enrollment has had very little effect on accuracy of representation.

The Australian experience thus shows that, even with preferential voting, single-member-district systems still fail to give effective representation to large numbers of voters, do not give seats to parties in accordance with their voting support, and allow party machines to dominate the choice of people who are offered as candidates. As machinery for linking voters and governments in systems of responsible government, single-member-district systems in Australia have failed convincingly.

MULTIMEMBER-DISTRICT
MAJORITY-PREFERENTIAL SYSTEMS

While Australian experience with multimember majority-preferential systems is more limited, the failures have been more spectacular. The largest example was in elections of the Federal Senate from 1919 to 1946. In all ten elections with this system, the results were unsatisfactory. On two occasions, parties with less than half the votes won majorities of seats, and on eight occasions, parties or coalitions with more than forty percent of the votes won three seats or less. In 1948, the system was replaced by a quota-preferential system of PR.

QUOTA-PREFERENTIAL SYSTEMS

There were technical defects in the quota-preferential Hare-Clark system introduced in Tasmania in 1897 and improvements were made when the system was introduced for the whole state in 1907. The 1907 version included provision for the use of a Droop quota instead of the simple quota in the earlier version, and provision was made for the transfer of surplus votes of elected candidates by the Gregory or exact procedure (Piesse 1913, p.44). With this procedure, there is no selection of papers for transfer, and therefore no element of chance. All papers showing next preference for a continuing candidate are credited to the candidate at the appropriate transfer value.

The system introduced in 1907 and first used in 1909 provided for the election of six members from each of five electoral districts, the same as those used to elect five members to the Federal House of Representatives. It was used in seventeen elections from 1909 to 1956. In 1917, a new procedure for filling casual vacancies by reexamination of the ballot papers forming the quotas of vacating candidates was introduced. This, in effect, allows the voters who lose their representatives to choose the successors. It also has the effect of encouraging parties to endorse more candidates than they expect to see elected.

Although it might seem that a quota as small as 14.29 percent would have led to the election of many independents, this did not happen. In the seventeen elections, with 510 seats filled, only twenty-six were won by non-major-party candidates. Throughout the period of use of the system in this form, agreement between voting support for the parties and the winning of seats was consistently good.

Experience showed that the election of an even number of members from each district caused some problems. A party could win more than half the votes in a district but fail to win more than half the seats. In two elections, in 1955 and 1956, each of the two parties won fifteen seats. A Select Committee on electoral Reform, set up to consider possible changes (Tasmania House of Assembly Select Committee on Electoral Reform 1957), expressed the view that "a majority of electors within an electorate should be guaranteed the right of returning a majority of elected members." Its recommendation for "the election of seven instead of six members from each of the five existing Commonwealth State electorates" was adopted, and a seven-member-district system has applied to all elections since.

In four of the six elections after the change to seven-member districts, one party or the other has won a majority of seats. In the other two cases, neither party received more than half the votes. In 1959, Labor, with 44.51 percent of first preferences, won seventeen seats and the Liberal Party, with 41.51 percent, won sixteen. Labor was supported by two independents and formed the government. In 1969, the major parties each won seventeen seats, the other seat being won by a candidate of a new Centre Party. Having been a prominent Liberal, he was elected after the transfer to him of later preferences of votes of people who had given their early preferences to Liberal candidates. He supported the Liberals and was made Deputy Premier in a Liberal government but broke with the government in 1972, precipitating another election, in which he was not a candidate.

Although the normal practice in other states is for the parties to each recommend an order of preference for their candidates, this is not usually done in Tasmania. Each party usually endorses seven or more candidates in each district and the voter has a choice between about twenty candidates. With this range of choice, about seventy percent of voters have seen their first-preference candidates elected and another twenty percent have seen the election of candidates early in their preference order. Candidates conduct their own campaigns, all seeking first-preference votes. The exercise of the freedom of choice given to voters by the system has sometimes allowed new candidates of parties to replace senior members who have failed to retain the support of the voters.

Although voting is compulsory and the marking of preferences for at least seven candidates is required for a valid vote, the number of invalid votes has not been high, varying in recent years between three percent and five percent. In the 1982 election, use was made for the first time on a statewide basis of a system of rotation of the names of candidates on ballot papers so that all names had approximately the same exposure in the favored positions. Voters and electoral staff appeared to cope with this without serious difficulty and the percentage of invalid votes remained below five percent.

After more than seventy years of PR, Tasmania still has essentially a two-party system. In most of the other states and in Federal politics, there have been three or more parties for many years. There have been attempts to establish the National Party in Tasmania but these have not succeeded. The difficulty of establishing new parties is undoubtedly associated with the freedom of choice within parties available under the Hare-Clark system. If there is a serious attempt to set up a new party, the existing parties endorse candidates chosen to attract the votes of those who might support the new party. If such candidates are elected, they have to be accommodated within the parties and the effect over the years has been that the characteristics of the parties have been influenced considerably by the voters.

The quota-preferential system used in elections of the Federal Senate is based on the use of each state as a single electoral district. Senators are elected for six-year terms, with an election every three years for half the seats, except in the case of dissolution, when all seats in each state are filled in a single election. A random-sampling procedure has been used for the selection of papers to be transferred in the distribution of the surplus votes of elected candidates, but this will be replaced in future elections by the exact or Gregory procedure.

As with most other preferential systems in Australia, an indication of preference for every candidate has been required for a valid vote. This provision, carried over from the previous majority-preferential system, has led to disturbingly large numbers of invalid votes. In future elections, a valid vote may be recorded by indicating preferences for ninety percent of the candidates or by endorsing a party "ticket" by a single mark on the ballot paper.

In normal half-Senate elections, each party has usually endorsed only three candidates in each state and urged its supporters to follow party "how-to-vote" recommendations. Most party supporters have followed these recommendations but many voters have supported non-major-party candidates, some of whom have been elected in every recent Senate election. There has been some resistance to party tickets within the parties and, in 1980, substantial numbers of party voters in two states did not follow party-recommended preference orders.

Results in elections of the New South Wales and South Australian Legislative Councils, and of other bodies such as the House of Assembly of the Australian Capital Territory and local-government bodies in New South Wales, have been consistent with those discussed. In New South Wales local-government elections, there have been some cases of recounts, involving the taking of new samples in surplus transfers, leading to changed results. Although there have been no such cases in parliamentary elections, they could occur, and the use of the exact procedure as in the Hare-Clark system would be preferable.

The results of Australian use of majority- and quota-preferential systems show that majority systems are unsatisfactory in many respects. Quota-preferential systems have performed much more satisfactorily, but some features of the systems used have prevented the full benefits of the method from being realized. The method incorporated in the Hare-Clark system is technically the best and the exact-transfer procedure has been shown to be feasible and effective. In most applications of quota-preferential methods, the requirement for marking preferences for all candidates has caused unnecessary problems for voters, and should be removed. Only in Tasmania is there a satisfactory provision for filling casual vacancies, the procedure used there being sound in principle and satisfactory in practice. In Tasmania, too, extensive experience with the Hare-Clark system has convinced the parties of the desirability of leaving their supporters free to choose within as well as between parties.

It is important to realize that the difference between majority and quota-preferential systems is not merely one of mechanics, but relates to the basic principles of representative government. Where majority systems are designed to provide representation only for majorities, and thus exclude large numbers of voters from effective representation, quota-preferential systems provide, as nearly as is practicable, for representation of all voters. Only systems which do this can be acceptable in systems of responsible government.

NOTES

1. Failure to record a vote is an offense under the laws relating to all parliamentary elections in Australia. Since voting is by secret ballot, there is no real compulsion to vote, as an unmarked ballot paper can be placed in a ballot box.

2. Public primary elections are not held in Australia.

3. The allocation of seats in the House of Representatives to states and the placing of district boundaries are based on numbers of enrolled voters, not population. Enrollment of those eligible to vote is compulsory.

13

The Single
Transferable Vote and Proportional
Representation

Richard S. Katz

Electoral systems often are grossly classified into two groups, those based on majority (including plurality) election of candidates and those based on proportional assignment of mandates to party lists. The single transferable vote (STV) electoral system is particularly difficult to classify using this scheme. STV has customarily been considered to be a form of proportional representation (PR), has been supported on grounds of its fairness (i.e., proportionality), and has tended to yield distributions of seats in legislative assemblies that closely approximate the corresponding distributions of popular votes. On the other hand, the defining characteristic of PR systems is allocation of mandates based on a party's total vote in each constituency. STV does not have this characteristic; votes are cast only for candidates as individuals, and at no point in an STV election do party totals ever need to be computed. Indeed, as is the case for all of the majority systems, but for none of the ordinary PR systems, it is possible to conduct STV elections without parties or other combinations of candidates at all.

In this chapter, I want to do two things. The first is to examine STV's claim to being called PR, by comparing the actual performance of STV systems with list PR and with single and multimember majority systems, all used at the national level. The second is to explore the consequences of STV on the "partyness" (Katz 1980) of politics. In both cases, I will try to go beyond simple relationships to shed light on the actual operation and effects of STV. The overall objective is to provide a more informed basis for evaluating proposals to adopt the STV system in countries currently using PR or majority systems (Finer 1975; Pasquino 1979).

STV AND INTERPARTY COMPETITION

Proportionality

Although the proportionality of the outcome might better be interpreted as a consequence of the electoral formula than as its defining characteristic, it clearly is the principal basis of STV's claim to being called PR. Consider the relationship between shares of seats (S) and votes (V) obtained by parties winning at least two percent of the vote in national elections using STV.[1] In the case of perfect proportionality, all of the points would lie on the line $S=V$. An ordinary least-squares regression[2] shows the best straight-line predictor of S from V to be, instead:

$$S=1.10\ V-2.10.$$

While this equation indicates greater proportionality than is found in single-member majority systems[3] for which the equivalent relationship is:

$$S=1.22\ V-6.14,$$

it still indicates a degree of proportionality lower than that reported by Rae (1971, p. 89) for proportional systems:

$$S=1.07\ V-0.84.[4]$$

One of Rae's findings, however, was that, among the PR systems, district magnitude as indicated by the average number of members returned per district is a major determinant of proportionality. A more valid comparison, therefore, would be STV against large-district majority and small-district PR systems. The only national large-district majority system is the Japanese system of single nontransferable voting (Curtis 1971). For this system,[5] the best linear relationship between seats and votes was:

$$S=1.19\ V-2.96,$$

slightly more proportional than single-member majority systems, but much less so than STV. For PR systems with small districts and no national or regional distribution of remainders,[6] the best straight-line fit was:

$$S=1.13\ V-2.11.$$

Surprisingly, for comparably small districts, pure PR systems appear to be less proportional than STV.

The explanation of this anomaly lies in the treatment of small parties by the two types of electoral systems. The formal thresholds of exclusion are considerably lower in the PR systems, both because even the smallest list PR system had a higher district magnitude than the largest STV system, and because the threshold for Sainte-Laguë and Largest Remainder formulae are lower than the threshold for STV in comparable districts (Lijphart and Gibberd 1977). In fact, however, many parties win representation with national vote totals well below the average district threshold of exclusion, and the expectation that PR would be more charitable to small parties is contradicted by the data. In the elections considered here, the average party with between two and seven percent of the vote received .48 percent of the seats for each one percent of the vote in the PR systems, but .65 percent of the seats in the STV systems. Moreover, there were more parties in this category in the PR systems (twenty-eight percent) than in the STV systems (fifteen percent). In particular, there were proportionately more than twice as many parties in this range in PR systems that were excluded from the legislature altogether. The cumulative effect of this is to pull the lower end of the regression line down and to the right, thus increasing its slope and making its intercept more negative.

Although these national figures support the idea that STV is properly regarded as a form of PR, further consideration reveals a more mixed picture. PR traditionally is associated with a proliferation of political parties because of its low threshold of exclusion (Rae, Hanby, and Loosemore 1971). Indeed this is one of the arguments often raised against it.[7] Given the apparently more favorable results achieved by minor parties in STV systems, one would expect this to be particularly so for them. In fact, minor parties are more common in the PR systems. Underlying the entire process is a difference in the behavior of minor parties. PR systems tend to nationalize electoral processes. As a result, minor parties are likely to present candidates in all constituencies, including those in which they have no hope of gaining representation, increasing their percentages of the vote without increasing their shares of the seats. STV, however, tends to localize and personalize politics. Minor parties usually present candidates only where they have a reasonable chance of election; their vote and seat shares, thus, are more likely to be comparable. Ironically then, the greater proportionality of STV systems is indirectly the result of the parties in them behaving as would be expected in majority systems (Katz 1980).

Positive Responsiveness

At least in the sense that large differences in vote shares are reflected in large differences in seat shares, all democratic electoral systems are reasonably proportional. For practical politics, however, this is often far less important than the degree to which electoral systems faithfully translate small shifts in vote shares to the parliament. Although one party or coalition may occasionally win a massive parliamentary majority, or may control the parliament over a long period of time, to do both simultaneously is extremely rare. Instead, most parliaments tend to be divided nearly evenly between government and opposition, with a small shift in seats sufficient to reverse the balance. Even if one party is advantaged in the translation of votes to seats, an electoral system ought to be positively responsive (May 1952) in the sense that, when a party's share of the votes goes up, its share of the seats should not go down.

Although obviously of greatest importance when control of the parliament is at stake, the question of positive responsiveness is not relevant only then. Indeed, for many purposes, the absolute aggregate outcome of an election, taken in isolation, may be less important than the changes that occurred from the previous results. Gains by the government will be interpreted by the press and by politicians as an endorsement of its program and personnel, while gains by the opposition, even if they are not sufficient to produce a new government, will be interpreted as a signal that a change of course is required. Notwithstanding the ready availability of vote totals, however, this interpretation is regularly based on gains and losses of legislative seats. When the trends run in the same direction, even though their magnitudes may be quite different, the general thrust of the interpretation may be accurate. If a party or coalition gains seats while its share of the votes is declining, the interpretation will be unfounded. For example, the victory of the Fine Gael–Labour coalition in the 1973 Irish election was attributed by the press to the "fact" that, "Their concentration on prices and other social and economic issues proved of greater attraction to the electorate than the Fianna Fail emphasis on national security and Northern Ireland" (*Times* 1973a; see also Taylor 1973, and *Times* 1973b). But, as compared to the previous general election, the combined first preference vote of the coalition *declined* from 51.1 percent to 48.8 percent.

Indeed, of the three major electoral systems considered here, STV was the least positively responsive. In over fourteen percent of the cases in which a party had candidates in two successive elections, its vote and seat shares moved in opposite directions. In several cases, the failure of the STV system to reflect shifts in popular opinion altered the final outcome of the election. (The Japanese system was even less positively responsive, with a negative relationship between changes in seats and changes in votes in twenty percent of the cases.)

This apparent perversity has three sources. The first, which is common to all pure district systems, is the ineffective use of remainders. Election outcomes are rarely unidirectional; a party may gain votes in some districts while losing votes in others. With large electorates, vote share is nearly a continuous variable. Seat share, however, is distinctly discontinuous, especially with small districts. Small shifts in vote in some districts, if the vote shares are near one of the points in the seats/votes relationship at which jumps in the seat shares appear, can alter the overall seat shares, while much larger vote shifts in the opposite direction in other districts have no effect. This principle underlies attempts to gerrymander, to which STV is as susceptible as single-member systems. Indeed, because the points in the relationship between seats and votes at which discontinuities occur is a function of the number of members to be elected from the district, STV may be even more amenable to manipulation within the constraints of compact districts and equal population per representative (Craig 1982; Mair 1982).

The vote totals to which reference has been made here, as is the usual practice, are the totals of first preference votes cast for each party's candidates. The actual election is determined, however, by the distribution of votes to individual candidates after transfers have occurred. The second potential source of perversity stems from the transfer of votes. If voters' preference orderings of the candidates are not single-peaked, a likely eventuality where preferences are determined by personality, locality, and religion, as well as by party (Sacks 1970), then it is possible for a candidate, and, by extension, his or her party, to be better off with fewer first-preference votes (Doron and Kronick 1977). Similar perversity is possible with the two-ballot majority and alternative vote systems. Under the Japanese system, no candidate is ever better off as an individual with fewer rather than more votes, but a party can be seriously hurt if one of its candidates is *too* popular and draws support that is superfluous for him, but needed by his copartisans.

The third, and most important, source of perversity also stems from the transfer process. Parties may not keep all of the votes with which they were credited after the first count (Cohan, McKinlay, and Mughan 1975). Some will be transferred from a candidate of one party to a candidate of another. Other votes will become nontransferable. Although, perhaps, votes of this sort *ought not* to be counted as party votes in the first place (Katz 1981), they do contribute to the apparent nonresponsiveness of the aggregate results.

The question of nontransferability becomes of particular importance, however, with regard to interparty alliances, and in fact provides an explanation of the 1973 Irish result. In 1969, Fine Gael and Labour competed as independent parties. As is usual, so long as a candidate of the party of origin remained eligible to receive votes, the vast majority of votes transferred strictly within party; when no candidate of the party of origin remained, roughly half of the votes from each party became nontransferable. In 1973, Fine Gael and Labour presented a joint program and agreed to form a coalition government if they jointly obtained a majority in the Dáil. Each also requested that its supporters give their lower preference votes to the candidates of the other, rather than allowing them to become nontransferable or go to candidates of Fianna Fail. The pattern of transfers while a candidate of the party of origin remained was very similar in the two years. Once all the candidates of the party of origin had been eliminated, however, the difference in the behavior of Labour voters was dramatic. In 1969, roughly thirteen percent of the total Labour vote became nontransferable at some point in the count; in 1973 the figure was just over three percent, with virtually the entire difference going to candidates of Fine Gael (Katz 1980, p. 81).

As this suggests, the apparent positive responsiveness, or lack thereof, of STV, and indeed the apparent overall proportionality of the system, depends less on the formal characteristics of the electoral formula than on the behavior of voters. If voters rank all candidates of a single party, and allow their ballots to become nontransferable when no candidates of that party remain, then STV is simply a Largest Remainder PR system. If they rank candidates of a second party following those of their first choice, larger departures from proportionality *with regard to the distribution of first-preference votes* are possible. In particular, under these circumstances, the possibility that a candidate could be better off with fewer votes will apply to parties as well. If voters intermix candidates of different parties, proportionality is likely to diminish greatly, but so too is its logical precondition—that the object for which people vote is the party.

Number of Parties and Coalitions

Finally, the claim that STV will produce a more "PR-like" party and cabinet system must be examined. The evidence is idiosyncratic. It is also contradictory, with the Irish and Maltese experiences quite different from that of Northern Ireland. None of the evidence, however, suggests that moderate coalitions will form in limited multiparty systems.

In Malta, the 1962 election was the last in which more than two parties won seats in the legislative assembly. The electorate appears to be polarized, with virtually no votes transferred across party lines. Cross-party voting ought to be particularly common when a well-known and popular candidate is in contention; voters may defect from their regular party to support him and then return to its other candidates with their lower preferences. Yet, for example, only twenty-five votes of Premier Dom Mintoff's surpluses of 3,757 and 5,477 votes in the First and Second electoral divisions transferred across party lines in 1976; in 1981, the figures were thirty-seven votes of 12,262. At the level of elite behavior and party rhetoric, the system is divided similarly.

The Irish system has also evolved from multipartism to bipolarity, although one pole is the coalition of Fine Gael and Labour rather than a single party. Especially since 1981, the Irish have also experienced a resurgence of minor party success. Deputies from these parties and independents, although not numerous, on occasion have held the balance of power. However, since these deputies have been extremists rather than moderates, this can hardly be counted as a force for moderation, and indeed, it contributed to the Irish need for three general elections in eighteen months.

Given the polarized nature of Northern Irish society and politics, one might well have expected a bipolar system to emerge there, as it has in the other STV systems. In fact, the effect of STV has been just the reverse, allowing each pole to fragment into numerous and mutually antagonistic splinters. To a greater extent than any other system, STV removes the disincentives to fragmentation. Even if a party wins no seats, its votes need not be wasted since they can be transferred to other parties. As a result, each group of supporters of a particular leader or shade of opinion can afford to present its own candidates. The Northern Irish situation, in which there was little likelihood of any government forming, and in which the British planned to impose a power-sharing arrangement, only furthered this situation.

Looking at the interpartisan operation of STV, one sees a mixed picture, but one which hardly justifies a simple lumping together of STV and list PR. With regard to proportionality, STV lies intermediately between PR and single-member systems, although the experience of the STV systems considered has actually been more proportional than that of the pure small-district PR systems to which it was compared. The multimember plurality system of Japan was more proportional than the single-member systems, suggesting that at least part of the proportionality of STV stems from its multimember character. On the other hand, a major explanation of STV's apparent proportionality was the relatively greater number of local minor parties in STV systems rather than national minor parties in the list systems. In this respect, as well as with regard to the behavior of the national parties, STV appears more like majority than PR systems. Further, the positive responsiveness of STV was the lowest of the systems other than the Japanese; PR had the highest positive responsiveness. Again, if a simple dichotomy were to be drawn, it would be between list PR and majority, with STV and the Japanese system as subclasses of the latter.

STV AND THE NATURE OF PARTIES

If the standard by which an electoral system is to be judged were solely its faithful reproduction in the parliament of each party's share of the popular vote, list PR with large districts or a regional or national distribution of remainders would clearly be superior to STV, as both would be relative to any single-member system. There is ample evidence that any tendency of large-district PR to lead to a fragmented party system can be countered by a three percent or five percent exclusionary rule, while the threshold of exclusion for STV is no higher than for small-district PR. Moreover, the early experience of Ireland, with as many as six parties plus sixteen independents in a 153-member chamber, or Malta, with up to five parties and one independent in a forty-member chamber, and the current experience of Northern Ireland, show that STV is hardly immune to fragmentation.

Fairness in this numerical sense is not the only argument adduced to support STV, however. Lakeman, in this volume, among others, argues that a further advantage of STV is that it widens the range of choice open to voters, and thus the discrimination with which the popular will may be determined. In single-member systems, there are likely to be in each district two, or at most three, candidates with any chance of election. The voter thus has only two or three complete packages of policies among which to choose. In list systems, voters have a wider choice, but they can still only select the whole program of one party or the whole program of another. STV opens up the possibility of discrimination within each party's group of candidates, allowing voters to choose among tendencies, approaches, or emphases within the party.

Implicit in this is the assumption that there will be a basic policy coherence within each party and basic differences between parties. While the additional choice afforded to voters ought to allow them to exercise greater control over the party, the basic quality of party government should remain. Is the assumption that STV is uniquely suited to allowing voters to express their policy-relevant wishes, while retaining the essential character of parties as the vehicles through which public preferences are put into effect, warranted?

In fact, the possibility of intraparty choice is not limited to STV. The direct primary in the American majority system, the nomination of more candidates than a party elects in the Japanese system, and personal preference voting in list PR systems all allow voters, within the constraints of party nominations, to choose the particular candidates who will be awarded their party's parliamentary mandates (Katz 1984). To the extent that transfer votes do not cross party lines, STV might be seen as simply a form of intraparty voting, although there remains a substantial difference between intraparty choice under STV and the choice allowed in most other systems. Additionally, as the discussion in the last sections suggests, when transfer votes do cross party lines, there may be further differences between STV and list PR systems.

When transfer votes remain within a party, STV differs from other preference voting systems with regard to what Rae (1971, p.17) calls "ballot structure." Other systems require a choice that is essentially categoric; voters must support one candidate, or a few candidates, to the exclusion of all others. Even in PR systems with cumulation, which allow an ordinal choice in the limited sense that some candidates may be given two preference votes rather than one, each voter has only a limited number of votes and once a vote is given to one candidate it is irretrievably lost to the others. STV, however, allows a choice that is truly ordinal. A candidate can appeal for the second preference votes of those who strongly support someone else, and since those preferences will not become effective until the candidate given the first preference votes is either elected or eliminated, voters can give him or her their second preference votes without diminishing their support for the candidate they most prefer.

Moreover, when votes transfer across party lines, the choice allowed under STV is not, strictly speaking, intraparty at all. When a party's voters in a list system are allowed to express a preference among its candidates, the logic of the system is always to force this to be a choice of a candidate *within* a party.

Even in systems with panachage, in which the voter may support candidates of more than one party, each vote is firstly a partial vote for the candidate's party. Mandates are assigned to each list on the basis of the number of whole or partial votes received by any of its candidates; only secondly do the individual votes determine which particular candidates are elected. Thus, a partial vote for one candidate actually may contribute to the election of some other member of the same list.

Under STV, votes are given only to candidates. A large personal vote for one candidate does his or her copartisans no good unless it is transferred explicitly to them. Analogously, voters can support a particular candidate without embracing that candidate's party. Even the votes of a party's loyal supporters may be transferred to other candidates after all of its nominees are elected or eliminated. As a result, wise candidates will not restrict their quest for personal support to their own party, and they may try to attract personal support without necessarily encouraging support for other candidates of their party. The interpersonal competition that is characteristic of all systems with preference voting may thus tend to supersede interparty competition, rather than taking place strictly within party boundaries.

One effect of the personalism implicit in this system has been to undermine the salience of party for voters. Given its sixty years of uninterrupted democratic experience, one would expect levels of partisanship to be higher in Ireland than in the countries of continental Europe, where democracy was suspended by fascism or fascist occupation (Converse 1969). Ireland has neither the deep religious nor deep class divisions that some have argued may make a sense of partisanship superfluous in some continental societies (Shively 1977). Yet, in the Eurobarometer series, Ireland consistently ranks near the bottom in partisanship.

This is not to say that party is irrelevant; the high degree to which votes transfer within a party belies any such notion. The ties that bind voters to a party, and correspondingly, the forces that occasionally lead voters to cross party lines, however, are primarily personal, rather than ideological or to a national organization. In this respect, the need to compete for personal votes has had two effects on Irish politics.

Firstly, when a party has more than one candidate in a constituency, the candidates tend to divide the territory into personal bailiwicks. This minimizes the chances of direct clashes, which, when they occur, can be both bitter and disruptive (Chubb 1959, p. 196). It also minimizes the degree to which multiple candidates afford voters a real choice. This is more than simply a campaign device, moreover; outside of the cities, it is the organizing principle of Irish parties. Irish constituency parties come into existence only to fight elections; other than small national headquarters, the only organizations that have any continuing existence are the local branches, and the informal groups of branches that are the basis of a particular politician's bailiwick. In any given area, the identification of party and a particular politician is extremely strong.

That the result is not competition within a party which otherwise behaves as a team is made particularly clear when a seat becomes vacant. In the ordinary model of party competition, one would expect each party to campaign actively to gain the seat in a by-election. In fact, this does not always occur because it is not in the interests of the incumbent deputies of other parties for their parties to gain that seat. To win the seat would mean that there would be more incumbents at the next general election than the party is likely to be able to reelect. Moreover, the old deputies are hardly likely to want voters in their bailiwicks to be in any doubt as to whom they should vote for first.

Secondly, competition within parties tends to be on the basis of services rendered, rather than policy differences. The job of the Irish member of parliament tends to be "going about persecuting civil servants" (Chubb 1963). Constituency case work is part of the job of a member of parliament in any country. The impact of the electoral system is partially illustrated, however, by a contrast with Israel, which uses list PR with a single national constituency. There is a tendency for candidates to have bailiwicks in the weak sense that a list will have a candidate representing, for example, Haifa, one representing the Negev, and so forth. If a member of the Knesset receives a request for service from someone in another member's area, he is likely to forward the request to that member (Uslaner 1983). In Ireland, it is precisely by performing such services for voters in another member's area that a deputy can enlarge his bailiwick and secure his seat. Thus, not only is the extent to which voters actually are confronted with an intraparty choice limited by the bailiwick system; the choice they have tends to be one of personality and clientelism rather than policy.

EVALUATION

As effective democratic electoral system must strike a balance between two conflicting goals. On one hand, it ought to give each voter a range of choice adequate to allow expression of his or her true preferences, and then give representation to the preferences expressed roughly in proportion to their popular support. Carried to its logical conclusion, this could require a separate candidate for every voter and a representative body as big as the population. On the other hand, it must so limit choices that when the results are aggregated, a stable government emerges that can be said to be the choice of the people as a whole, or at least of a majority of them. Carried to its logical conclusion, this could require a system of two cohesive parties in which the party with the most popular votes wins all the parliamentary seats. All democratic electoral systems extant represent compromises between these two extreme positions.

Large-district PR gives great weight to fairness of representation at the expense of majority formation, although the fragmentation of most large-district PR systems may be the cause rather than the effect of the electoral system. Single-member systems perform well in the generation of stable majority governments, but only at the cost of severely restricted choice and grossly unproportional representation (Milnor 1969; Rae 1971). STV is one of three systems, the others being the Japanese single nontransferable vote system and small-district PR, that aim for a more central position. Is it the most desirable of these?

The Japanese system has a number of features that make it unattractive. It is the least proportional of the three systems, barely more proportional, in fact, than single-member election. It is also extremely nonresponsive to shifts in electoral opinion and disruptive of party unity.

As between small-district PR and STV, STV appears slightly more proportional in aggregate terms, but small-district PR is slightly more positively responsive. Moreover, with a regional or national distribution of remainders, small-district PR can be made far more proportional. The decision then comes down to the range and nature of the choice offered the voters. Since small-district PR can allow for intraparty preference voting, neither system need force voters to choose among complete party packages. The choice offered by PR, however, is a choice *within* party while the choice under STV is a choice without regard to party. The effect has been to offer voters under STV a wider choice, but one which, in terms of the arguments used by its advocates, is less meaningful. Small-district PR coupled with national distribution of remainders and intraparty preference voting thus appears the most effective in coupling a reasonable range of individual policy choice fairly represented with the kind of parties needed for effective implementation of the public will.

NOTES

1. The STV elections considered were the general elections of the Irish Free State and Republic of Ireland (1922–1982) and Malta (1921–1932 and 1947–1981), plus the Northern Ireland elections of 1973 and 1982.

2. While a curvilinear relationship would be more appealing theoretically, since it could be forced to go through the points (0,0) and (100,100), the straight-line fit in the region for which there are data is so good $(r > .99)$ as to make this added complication superfluous.

3. The equation for majority systems is based on the general elections of the United States (1946–1982), United Kingdom (1945–1979), Canada (1945–1980), New Zealand (1946–1981), and France (1958–1981). Rae's equation is $S = 1.20 V - 6.3$.

4. This comparison is marginally contaminated by the fact that 24 of the 146 points on which the equation for STV was based were among the 488 points that entered into Rae's calculation for proportional systems. The effect of this contamination is to reduce the difference in proportionality observed between STV and proportional systems.

5. Data are from the elections of the Japanese House of Representatives, 1947–1979.

6. Data are from Norway (1945–1981) and Sweden (1948–1968).

7. Majority electoral systems actually have a lower threshold of representation, if one can assume that a minor party can concentrate its supporters in a single district.

14

Some Logical
Defects of the Single
Transferable Vote

Steven J. Brams
*Peter C. Fishburn**

Every voting system has both practical and theoretical defects (Straffin 1980; Nurmi 1981, 1983; Bordley 1983; Merrill 1984). Since the single transferable vote (STV), or the Hare system, as it is sometimes called, is fairly widely used, and since its logical defects are not very well-known, we shall focus on it and its close cousin, the alternative-vote or successive-elimination method.

By "logical defects" we mean a voting system's incompatibility with certain formal conditions that mirror desirable democratic principles. Many such conditions have been proposed in the technical literature, but we shall limit ourselves to just three in this chapter: (1) invulnerability to truncation of voter preferences; (2) guaranteed election of Condorcet candidates without truncation; and (3) monotonicity.

The first condition is not well known, but of interest because it would seem, on first blush, that STV would satisfy it. The second condition extends the notion of a majority winner in two-candidate races to elections involving three or more candidates. The third condition is quite well known, though its failure for STV and related systems was proved only recently (Smith 1973; Doron and Kronick 1977). Monotonicity may be the most basic of the conditions in requiring that more first-place votes can never hurt a candidate, which to us seems a sine qua non of a democratic voting procedure.

Other theoretical problems can crop up under STV, but our purpose is not to present a full catalogue of its difficulties. In particular, because STV's abil-

*We would like to thank Bernard Grofman, Arend Lijphart, and Duff Spafford for valuable comments on an earlier draft of this chapter. Steven J. Brams gratefully acknowledges support for this research from the National Science Foundation under grant DAR-8011823.

ity to ensure proportional representation (PR) is dealt with by Richard Katz elsewhere in this volume, we shall not consider this aspect of STV here. However, in Chapter 17 we shall indicate how we think PR may be preserved with *non*-preferential voting under a district system, with at least one representative elected from each district, given allowance for a legislature of somewhat variable size.

STV was first proposed by Thomas Hare in England and Carl George Andrae in Denmark in the 1850s. It is presently used to elect public officials in several countries—including Australia, Ireland, Northern Ireland, and Malta—in local elections in Cambridge, Massachusetts, in school board elections in New York City, and in numerous private organizations. John Stuart Mill (1862) placed it "among the greatest improvements yet made in the theory and practice of government." But consider the following defects of STV:

1. STV is vulnerable to truncation of voter preferences. Under STV, as well as other preferential voting systems, voters rank the candidates from best to worst. By the nature of STV, which will be explained shortly, it would seem that "there is no tactical advantage to be gained by marking few candidates," as one society (American Mathematical Society, or AMS) that uses STV recently claimed (Brams, 1982). Yet, we shall show that there *may* be a "tactical advantage" to "marking few candidates"—that is, truncating one's preferences—and *not* following the advice proffered on the AMS's 1982 ballot: "It is advisable to mark candidates in the order of your preference until you are ignorant or indifferent concerning candidates whom you have not ranked."

Our first counterexample to this statement will illustrate how STV works. This example will also show that some voters can gain an advantage by truncating their preferences when two out of four candidates are to be elected. Our second example will illustrate STV's vulnerability to truncation when only one candidate is to be elected and there is no transfer of "surplus votes." This example will show that the simpler alternative-vote/successive-elimination procedure (sometimes called "majority preferential voting"), is subject to the same difficulties as STV. Both examples will then be used to illustrate the other two defects of STV and its variants (hereafter referred to as simply "STV" for convenience).

COUNTEREXAMPLE 1. Assume that there are three classes of voters, with the indicated numbers of voters in each class ranking the set of four candidates $\{x,a,b,c\}$ as follows:

> I. 6: *xabc*
> II. 6: *xbca*
> III. 5: *xcab*

Thus, for example, the 6 voters in class I rank x as their first choice, a as their second, b as their third, and c as their fourth.

Assume two of the set of four candidates are to be elected, and a candidate must receive a quota of 6 votes to be elected on any round. A "quota" (sometimes called "Droop quota") is defined as $(n/(m + 1)) + 1$, where n is the number of voters and m is the number of candidates to be elected. It is standard procedure to drop any fraction that results from the calculation of the quota, so the quota actually used is $q = [(n/(m + 1)) + 1]$, the integer part of the number in the brackets. The integer q is the smallest integer (6 in this counterexample) such that it is impossible for more than the specified number of candidates to be elected (2 in the counterexample) to win with first-place votes on the first round (the election of three candidates would require 18 votes, but there are only 17 voters). In fact, what happens is as follows:

First round: x receives 17 out of 17 first-place votes and is elected.

Second round: There is a "surplus" of 11 votes (above $q = 6$) that are transferred in the proportions 6:6:5 to the second choices (a, b, and c, respectively) of the three classes of voters. Since these transfers do not result in at least $q = 6$ for any of the remaining candidates (3.9, 3.9, and 3.2 for a, b, and c, respectively), then the candidate with the fewest (transferred) votes (i.e., c) is eliminated. His supporters (class III) transfer their 3.2 votes to their next-highest choice (i.e., a), giving him more than a quota of 7.1. Thus, a is the second candidate elected. Hence, the two winners are $\{x,a\}$.

Now assume that 2 of the 6 class II voters rank only x first: they do not indicate that they prefer b next, etc. The results are:

First round: Same as above.

Second round: There is a "surplus" of 11 votes (above $q = 6$) that are transferred in the proportions 6:4:2:5 to the second choices, if any (a,b, no second choice, and c respectively), of the voters. (The 2 class II voters with no second choice do not get their transferred votes distributed.) Since these transfers do not result in at least $q = 6$ for any of the remaining candidates (3.9, 2.6, and 3.2 for a,b, and c, respectively), then the candidate with the fewest (transferred) votes (i.e., b) is eliminated. His supporters (4 voters in class II) transfer their 2.6 votes to their next-highest choice (i.e., c), giving him 5.8, less than the quota of 6. Because a has fewer (transferred) votes (3.9), he is eliminated, and c is the second candidate elected. Hence, the two winners are $\{x,c\}$.

Conclusion: The 2 class II voters who ranked only x first induced a better, not a worse, social choice for themselves by truncating their ranking of candidates on the ballot. Thus, there may be a "tactical advantage" in "marking few candidates."

The reason for this in the counterexample is that 2 class II voters, by not ranking b second, c third, and a fourth, prevent b's being paired against a (their last choice) on the second round, by whom b would be beaten. Instead, c (their next-last choice) is paired against a and beats him, which is better for the class II voters.

Lest the reader think that a counterexample must turn on the allocation of surplus votes, we shall next give a counterexample in which only one candidate is to be elected, so the election becomes an elimination contest that ends when one candidate wins at least a simple majority.

COUNTEREXAMPLE 2. Assume there are four classes of voters, with the indicated numbers of voters in each class ranking the set of four candidates $\{a,b,c,d\}$ as follows:

> I. 7: *abcd*
> II. 6: *bacd*
> III. 5: *cbad*
> IV. 3: *dcba*

Since no candidate has a simple majority of $q = 11$ first-place votes (out of 21), the lowest candidate, d, with 3 votes, is eliminated on the first round, and his second-place votes go to c, giving c 8 votes. Because none of the remaining candidates still has a majority, b, with the (new) lowest total of 6 votes, is eliminated next, and his second-place votes go to a, who is elected with a total of 13 votes.

Now assume the 3 class IV voters rank only d first. Then d is still eliminated first, but since the class IV voters did not indicate a second-place choice, no votes are transferred. Now, however, c is the (new) lowest candidate with 5 votes; his elimination results in the transfer of his supporters' votes to b, who is elected with 11 votes. Because the class IV voters prefer b to a, it is in their interest not to rank candidates below d to induce a better outcome for themselves.

It is true that a first choice can never be hurt by ranking a second choice, a second choice by ranking a third choice, etc., because the higher choices are eliminated before the lower choices can affect them. However, lower choices can affect the order of elimination, and hence transfer of votes, so that—as the counterexamples demonstrate—a higher choice (e.g., second) can influence whether a lower choice (e.g., third or fourth) is elected.

We wish to make clear that we are not suggesting that voters would routinely make the strategic calculations implicit in these counterexamples. These calculations are not only rather complex but also could, on occasion, be neutralized by counterstrategic calculations of other voters in gamelike maneuvers. Rather, we are suggesting that the advice to rank *all* candidates for whom one has preference is not always rational under STV.

2. STV does not guarantee the election of a Condorcet candidate without truncation of preferences. A Condorcet candidate is a candidate who can defeat every other candidate in a pairwise contest with each. Note that in counterexample 2, that b is the Condorcet candidate: in a pairwise contest with c, 13 to 8; and in a pairwise contest with d, 18 to 3. If only one candidate is to be selected, as in counterexample 2, b would seem the evident consensus choice. Yet, b would not have won had there been no truncation by the class IV voters.

Indeed, truncation of preferences by the voters is, in general, required to ensure the election of Condorcet candidates (if they exist, i.e., if there is no paradox of voting) under ranking voting systems (Fishburn and Brams, 1983a).

To be sure, truncation is not the only device by which voters may ensure the election of a Condorcet candidate. They may also misrepresent their preferences to accomplish this end. For example, a single class II voter in counterexample 1 could ensure that c (whom he prefers to a) will be elected by pretending to have the preferences of class III voters.

The pioneering work of Gibbard (1973) and Satterthwaite (1975) established that virtually every voting system is vulnerable to manipulation by "insincere" voting (i.e., voting contrary to one's true preferences). What is less apparent is that "sincere" truncation, which does not involve announcing a false preference order, but rather an arrested true order, can also be used for manipulative purposes (Nurmi, 1982). The fact that truncation may be needed to guarantee the election of Condorcet candidates suggests that desirable ends may require manipulative means!

3. STV is not monotonic. A preferential voting system is monotonic if more first-place votes can never hurt a candidate. The non-monotonicity of STV is dramatically illustrated by counterexample 2. If the three class IV voters raised a from fourth to first place in their rankings, without changing their ordering of the other three candidates, b would be elected rather than a. Thus, candidate a would be hurt when he moves up in the rankings of some voters and thereby receives more first-place votes.

The fact that more first-place votes can hurt, rather than help, a candidate under STV violates what, in our opinion, is a fundamental democratic ethic. This defect does not afflict nonpreferential voting systems like plurality voting or approval voting (Brams and Fishburn, 1983b), though with runoffs these systems, too, become nonmonotonic (Fishburn, 1982). A catalog of other failings of preferential systems is recounted in a story told in Fishburn and Brams (1983b); Fishburn (1981) and Sidney (1981) analyze approval voting in multiple-winner elections.

Both plurality voting and approval voting suffer from being vulnerable to truncation of voter preferences, and both provide no guarantee that a Condorcet candidate will be chosen. On the other hand, STV provides some measure of PR (Hoag and Hallett, 1926; Lakeman, 1974), which nonpreferential voting systems make no claim to at all. We shall suggest, however, in Chapter 17 that PR might be preserved under a nonpreferential scheme in which district elections are only the first stage in a two-stage process.

PART V
ADDITIONAL-MEMBER
SYSTEMS

Personalized Proportional Representation: The "Model" of the West German Electoral System

Max Kaase

In democratic polities, the right of the people to freely choose among political alternatives has long been regarded as the core element of the democratic process. This is particularly true in those countries which have experienced a varied, discontinuous history of democratic institutions, like West Germany. The breakdown of the Weimar Republic and the ensuing totalitarian Nazi regime have consequently shaped the perspectives which inside and outside actors have brought to bear on designing West German political institutions after the end of World War Two. One example is the strict emphasis in the West German Constitution (*Grundgesetz*) on parliamentary versus plebiscitary modes of decision-making. One other example which one frequently hears, is the way in which the electoral system, as the procedure by which votes are translated into parliamentary mandates, was designed. To some outside observers, this system seems to work so well that it has even come to serve as a model for their own country— rightly or wrongly so (Nohlen 1978, pp. 312–13).

THE HISTORICAL BASES OF THE WEST GERMAN ELECTORAL SYSTEM

The long-standing controversy between proponents and adversaries of proportional representation (PR) has been particularly fueled by the failure of the first German democratic state between 1919 and 1933. By now it is generally accepted that the specific electoral system of the Weimar Republic was but one of a whole set of factors allowing the Nazis to attain power. Thus, it is frequently overlooked that the system on the one hand operated under strict conditions of PR, but on the other hand contained two (indirect) clauses that limited access of parties to parliamentary representation (Sternberger and Vogel 1969, pp. 257–58). Nevertheless, all analysts seem to be agreed upon the fact that the Weimar experience has shaped the way that politicians have approached the choice of an electoral system for the second German democracy (Sternberger and Vogel 1969, pp. 285–86; Meyer 1973, pp. 32–33; Pulzer 1983, p. 84).

The partition of Germany after the Second World War into four occupied zones each administered by one of the four Allied powers, did not in itself automatically create a separated Germany. However, the lack of truly integrative institutions, plus the increasing conflict between the Soviet Union and the three Western powers led to a situation where the two parts of Germany went different ways. Political parties were licensed by the Allied powers as early as 1945 (for details, see Sternberger and Vogel 1969, pp. 277–80; Kaack 1971, pp. 155–99). By contrast, the founding of the Federal Republic had to wait until May 23, 1949. This was made possible as a result of decisions made by the three Western allies and the Benelux countries at the London conference in 1948. They designed a parliamentary council (*Parlamentarischer Rat*) and assigned to it the main task of building a new constitution for West Germany. The corresponding laws issued by the West German states (*Länder*) creating that parliamentary council did not entail the assignment to also construct an electoral law for the *Bund*. Nevertheless, the parliamentary council, only one day after its constitution, selected a committee to deal with problems of a new electoral law (Meyer 1973, p. 29). The debates on these matters in the council contain, in a nutshell, all the well-known arguments from the general controversy on a majority rule versus PR. The composition of the council—CDU/CSU: 27 members, SPD:27. Liberals (FDP/DVP): 5, German Party (DP):2, Center Party (*Zentrum*): 2, Communists (KPD): 2—the traditional stance of the SPD against majority rule, and the vested interests of at least some of the small parties, made a decision in favor of a clear-cut majority rule system virtually impossible, in spite of what had happened to the Weimar Republic. It may suffice to say here that, after long deliberations and substantial conflicts in the council and with the three Western allies, the parliamentary council voted in favor of a system combining elements of majority rule and PR; in core, even then, the system, in its effect on mandates, was a system of strict PR.

This electoral law had to be passed by the minister-presidents of the West German states, who engineered two changes, one of which went directly against the explicit preferences of the parliamentary council, and undoubtedly had had an important impact on the political process in West Germany: the five percent clause barring all parties from parliamentary representation in the 1949 Bundestag which did not obtain at least five percent of the valid vote *in one of the states or one direct constituency seat* (Meyer 1973, pp. 42–46).

The West German electoral law of June 15, 1949, was only meant to guide the election to the first Bundestag on August 14, 1949. As a consequence, the controversy on the proper electoral law flared up again in 1952–53 and could only be resolved at all by the pressure to get a law. Thus, once more, the new law in 1953 was regarded as provisional, and it was not until 1956 that an electoral law was passed that, with minor changes, is still in operation today.

Just once more after 1956, at the time of the great coalition linking CDU/CSU and SPD, between 1966 and 1969, did the problem of changes in the electoral law rise to the surface. Although both parties had initially agreed upon implementing some kind of a majority rule system (available options are described in Wildenmann, Kaltefleiter, and Schleth 1965), for a variety of reasons both parties, but particularly the SPD, refrained, in the end, from going through with their initial plan (for details see Bredthauer 1973, pp. 45–96; Meyer 1973, pp. 57–74).

THE WEST GERMAN ELECTORAL LAW

In technical terms, the West German electoral system can be regarded as an "additional-member" system because, beyond seats allotted by the plurality rule on the constituency level, additional mandates are assigned via candidate lists on the state level. It must, however, be kept in mind that from the beginning, in the parliamentary council, the electoral law was explicitly chosen such that all votes cast should basically have the same impact on the distribution of seats in parliament and that all parties had equal chances for parliamentary representation (Meyer 1973, p. 45).

Thus, at no time was the electoral law meant to make up for distortions necessarily resulting from the single-member constituency plurality system. Rather, the majority rule aspect was introduced into the electoral system in order to improve and strengthen the relationship between the members of parliament and the citizens. Table 15.1 contains the relevant information on the West German *national* electoral laws since 1949 (the various state electoral laws are rather similar in principle).

Limitations of space do not permit any detailed presentation of the changes in electoral laws between the first and the now-existing laws. The core elements of the present electoral law are as follows:

1) West Berlin is excluded from participating in general elections because of the Four Power Status of West Berlin. It is represented in the Bundestag by 22 members elected proportional to electoral strength by the members of the Berlin state parliament.

2) West Germany is divided into 248 constituencies. In each, one candidate is elected directly to the Bundestag on the basis of the relative majority of votes (first ballot; see step 4).

3) 248 additional members of parliament are elected on the basis of state lists put up by the political parties.

4) Every voter has two ballots, the first ballot (*Erststimme*) for the constituency vote, and the second ballot (*Zweitstimme*) for the party vote.

Table 15.1 Core Regulations of West German Electoral Laws for General Elections since 1949

Year of General Election	Number of Constituencies	Number of Total Seats (Without Surplus Seats)	Number of Ballots	Protective Clause		One-Party Combination of Lists Across States	Calculation Procedure	Surplus Seats Kept Without Adjustment (Number Actually Occuring)	Voting Age
				Magnitude	Reach				
1949	242	400*	1	5 percent or one constituency seat	At least one state	Not applicable; seats were distributed on the state level only.	Strict PR; d'Hondt	Yes (2)	21
1953	242	484	2	5 percent or one constituency seat	Area of Federal Republic	Not applicable; seats were distributed on the state level only.	Strict PR based on second ballot; d'Hondt	Yes (3)	21
1957	247	494	2	5 percent or three constituency seats	Area of Federal Republic	Yes	Strict PR based on second ballot; d'Hondt	Yes (3)	21
1961	247	494	2	5 percent or three constituency seats	Area of Federal Republic	Yes	Strict PR based on second ballot; d'Hondt	Yes (5)	21

1965	248	496	2	5 percent or three constituency seats	Area of Federal Republic	Yes	Strict PR based on second ballot; d'Hondt	Yes (—)	21
1969	248	496	2	5 percent or three constituency seats	Area of Federal Republic	Yes	Strict PR based on second ballot; d'Hondt	Yes (—)	18
1972	248	496	2	5 percent or three constituency seats	Area of Federal Republic	Yes	Strict PR based on second ballot; d'Hondt	Yes (—)	18
1976	248	496	2	5 percent or three constituency seats	Area of Federal Republic	Yes	Strict PR based on second ballot; d'Hondt	Yes (—)	18
1980	248	496	2	5 percent or three constituency seats	Area of Federal Republic	Yes	Strict PR based on second ballot; d'Hondt	Yes (1)	18
1983	248	496	2	5 percent or three constituency seats	Area of Federal Republic	Yes	Strict PR based on second ballot; d'Hondt	Yes (2)	18

*To the total number of seats, some seats for Berlin have to be added (1949: 19; since 1953: 22). Because of the Four Power Status of Berlin, inhabitants of West Berlin cannot directly participate in general elections.

5) The distribution of mandates is *exclusively* calculated on the basis of the second ballots. Those parties not obtaining more than five percent of the second votes *on the national level* or getting three members elected directly in the constituencies will be excluded from parliamentary representation. The votes collected by such parties will be dropped from the calculation of mandates.

6) In the first step, the remaining (second) votes for the parties which have passed the five percent clause are used to calculate, *on the national level*, the total distribution of the 496 mandates to the parties. The calculation takes place according to the d'Hondt algorithm.

7) In the second step, the (second) votes gained by the parties in the ten states of the Federal Republic, *per party and within states*, are submitted once again to the d'Hondt calculating algorithm. The total seats allotted to a given party in step 5 are now distributed among the state party lists. (The CSU, the Bavarian sister party of the CDU, is regarded as a party in its own right.)

8) From the total number of seats allotted to a given party list in a given state, those mandates are subtracted which were directly won by that party in the constituencies of that particular state. The remaining seats are distributed to the party's state list according to rank position on that list.

9) Should the number of mandates won by a given party in a given state surpass that of the number of mandates allotted by step 7, those mandates—surplus mandates (*Überhangmandate*)—are kept by that party. The other parties are *not* compensated for those surplus mandates, contrary to the situation in most of the ten states of the Federal Republic.

This system of personalized PR, whatever elements of majority rule it may entail, is nevertheless a system of strict PR. Whatever distortions in the relationship of votes and mandates do exist, are due to just two factors which have had a differential impact over the years: 1) the operation of the five percent clause, and 2) the well-known property of the d'Hondt calculating algorithm to work in favor of the larger parties (Nohlen 1978, pp. 300-301).

THE WEST GERMAN "ELECTORAL MIRACLE"— MYTH OR REALITY?

The international impact of what had happened in Nazi Germany between 1933 and 1945 was such that concerns with the development of the young West German democracy in the 1950s were monumental; even now they have not completely receded. When West Germany seemed, for a long time, like the alternate model to the disruptiveness of the political process in the Weimar Republic, this was particularly due to its astounding process of consolidation and concentration in the electoral and party areas. From 1949 to 1961, the number of parties represented in the Bundestag decreased from eleven to three; the joint share of the popular vote of CDU/CSU, SPD, and FDP rose from 72.1 percent to 94.3 percent, and reached a climactic 99.1 percent in 1972 and 1976 (see Table

15.2; also Dishaw 1971). It seemed that it was not overstating the case when this development was termed "das deutsche Wahlwunder" (the German electoral miracle; see Nohlen 1978, p. '307).

Nevertheless, in all fairness to the beneficial effect of the electoral system, especially the five percent clause, on this development, it was certainly but one, and probably, not, by far, the most important contributing factor. The absence of major ideological, religious, language, and other cleavages, the fast integration of the one large minority group West Germany possessed after the war—the refugees—the enormous economic recovery, and the existence of impressive political actors, the most noteworthy being Konrad Adenauer, plus the clear-cut orientation towards the West, jointly made West Germany a reasonably stable and operational democratic polity of the Western kind. The extent to which these factors were relevant is well signified by the fact that the one major new cleavage in West German politics—the old versus new politics cleavage (Baker, Dalton, and Hildebrandt 1981) has rather easily been translated into the new party of the Greens which at the second general election they participated in (in 1983) jumped the five percent hurdle with a 5.6 percent share of the second vote.

Table 15.2 Number of Parties in the Bundestag Since 1949, and the Percent share of CDU/CSU, SPD, and FDP of the Total Vote

Year of General Election	Turnout Percent	Number of Parties in the Bundestag	Percent-Share of Valid Votes (Second Ballot) of CDU/ CSU + SPD + FDP
1949	78.3	11[1]	72.1
1953	85.8	6[2]	83.5
1957	87.8	4[3]	89.7
1961	87.7	3	94.3
1965	86.8	3	96.4
1969	86.7	3	94.6
1972	91.1	3	99.1
1976	90.7	3	99.1
1980	88.6	3	98.0
1983	89.1	4	94.0

[1]In addition, there were two independent candidates elected into the Bundestag. CDU and CSU, as for all other elections, are counted as one party. [2]Of those, the Center Party, which had only been admitted in North-Rhine-Westphalia, gained representation in the Bundestag because the CDU did not put up a candidate in one safe constituency and asked their voters to vote for the Center Party candidate. [3]Of those, the German Party (DP) gained representation in the Bundestag because the CDU did not put up candidates in six safe constituencies and asked their voters to vote for the DP candidates.

Instead of dwelling too much on the seemingly integrative effects of the West German electoral system, it appears desirable to look at some of the expectations and problems connected with that particular variety of the additional-member system. For the purpose of this chapter, four such aspects of the West German electoral system are singled out: (1) the relationship between members of parliament and their constituency, (2) the impact of the electoral law on the relationship between the central party and its local organizations, (3) the two-ballot system, and (4) the surplus mandates.

One of the reasons leading the parliamentary council to propose this particular version of personalized PR was the expectation that the single-member constituency system would build and strengthen the ties between the members of parliament and the citizens. This is not the place to discuss, in any detail, the different theories and notions of political representation. One empirical study in West Germany of this relationship (Farah 1981), which was designed in the tradition of the Miller-Stokes representation study (Miller and Stokes 1963), clearly shows that, with regard to issue cleavages and agenda priorities, the overall link between constituency and deputy is practically nonexistent, if not even negative (Farah 1981, pp. 167–86). The important distinction between directly elected deputies and those elected via a party list leads—as expected—to a slightly stronger, positive relationship between various elements of the constituency—(directly elected) deputy relationship. Thus, a conclusion would seem to be warranted that the particular "deputy type mix" of the West German electoral system produces quite different deputy orientations towards constituency representation. On the other hand, Nohlen (1978, pp. 305–306) argues that the number of double candidacies—in a constituency as well as on a party list—in the 1970s has increased to a point where it no longer appears meaningful to make the distinction between the two.

Looking at this from the citizen perspective, the problem is somewhat mellowed by the fact that a majority of West German voters in 1970 endorsed the Burkean notion of representation, giving the deputies a free hand (Farah 1981, pp. 239–49). (This notion, incidentally, is institutionalized in article 38 of the West German constitution.) This endorsement has not weakened over time, as data from a 1983 survey indicates, showing two-thirds of the population preferring that the deputy, in a conflict between party and himself, should follow his own way (Forschungsgruppe Wahlen 1983, p. 239).

Whatever hopes there may have been that citizens become familiar with, and develop attachments to, "their" deputies were not borne out. Empirical studies can testify to the lack of familiarity and interest of voters with constituency candidate and deputy names, although this varies somewhat with the type (urban-rural) of constituency (Kaase 1965; Zentralarchiv 1979, p. 126). This does not come as a surprise, taking into account the fact that the average West German constituency has about one hundred and seventy thousand voters. Thus, the initial expectations in designing the personalized PR system with respect to citizen-deputy ties have certainly not materialized, despite obvious efforts by the deputies to establish firm roots in their constituencies (Farah 1981, pp. 191–92).

The second aspect, to be discussed briefly, is the relationship between the central and local party organization, and the extent to which it is influenced by the electoral law. Taking into account the concerns democratic theorists have voiced regarding the oligarchic tendencies in parties, the electoral law has had a beneficial effect in strengthening the position of the local party organization in nominating candidates. Local parties have the right to nominate constituency candidates, and can even override vetoes by the state party organization (Nohlen 1978, pp. 301–304). The list system, on the other hand, enables the central party organizations to assure the election of minority candidates, women, and specialists into the Bundestag (Nohlen 1978, pp. 304–306).

The two-ballot element of the electoral system has been regarded as a particularly intelligent feature, because it is supposed to highlight the direct voter influence on the selection of deputies. Unfortunately, surveys have repeatedly shown that even at the height of any given campaign, less than half of the voters know the precise meaning of the two ballots; to this, the misleading name of the ballot decisive for the compositon of the Bundestag as "Zweitstimme" (second vote) contributes substantially (Spiegel 1983, p. 37; Zentralarchiv 1979, p. 47; Zentralarchiv 1981, pp. 237–38). Shortly after an election, even this percentage drops, to roughly one-fifth of the voting population (Spiegel 1983, p. 37).

This, in itself, may not seem like a major problem, as long as voters do not vote in large numbers for different parties with their two ballots. Since, without exception, West German governments were and—with just one exception—had to be coalition governments, and the distance between government and opposition in terms of popular vote is notoriously small, ballot splitting becomes an increasing concern. The first, but smaller, point to be made is that, if voters split their votes without understanding the logic of the two ballots, they make "wrong" choices. The second, much graver, concern can only arise because of a deficiency in the electoral system.

The basic point here is that the system allows for surplus mandates (*Überhangmandate*) in the states without compensation for the other, disadvantaged, parties. Thus, if two parties in a coalition advise their supporters to strategically split their ballots between the two partners, or if one large party were to formally split into two parties, then a large number of surplus mandates could be artificially created (Meyer 1973, pp. 240–46). This effect has been noted by Unkelbach as early as 1956, and has been termed "Ultraproporzeffekt" (Unkelbach 1956, p. 130).

The percentage of split-ballot voting has consistently increased between 1961 (4.1 percent of the voters, excluding mail ballot voting) and 1983 (10.9 percent). Split-ballot voting is disproportionately high among FDP and "Green" voters; in 1980, less than half of those voting FDP with their second ballot also voted FDP with their first ballot (Statistisches Bundesamt 1981, p. 24). In both 1980 and

1983, the SPD gained one surplus mandate in Schleswig-Holstein, plus, in 1983, one in Bremen. This may not sound terribly impressive, but it points to a definite deficiency, a fault in the present electoral system that could be used for a manipulation of the electoral outcome because it allows for different weights of individual voters.

CONCLUSIONS

By and large, the West German electoral system of personalized PR, or additional-member system, has not given rise to major problems. On the contrary, many observers have attributed a large impact—too large an impact, for that—of that system on the German "electoral miracle" of the development of a stable three-party system even under conditions of PR (with the five percent clause). Unfortunately, miracles hardly ever happen, and even the most superficial inspection will quickly demonstrate that it was the unique interaction of factors, including the electoral law, that can be held responsible for the outcome of a stable three-party system without grave socio-political antagonisms. The entry of the Greens may or may not signal an end to that concentration process. Nevertheless, the West German electoral system has shown several desirable properties in comparison to other systems. Its five percent clause definitely prohibits esoteric parties from getting disproportionate momentum and encouragement through fast parliamentary representation. Other regulations at least enhance the chance for stronger deputy-constituency ties, and strengthen the role of the local party organizations in candidate nominations. The list system enables parties to establish parliamentary representation of disadvantaged groups and experts. The system does not permit substantial differences in vote-seat relations. Still, as with all electoral systems, it cannot compensate for, and eradicate all, the deficiencies otherwise innate in the political culture, the political institutions, and the political process of any given polity.

16

"Additional-Member" Electoral Systems

William P. Irvine

The single-member plurality electoral system—the "British model"—is increasingly under challenge in Western democracies. The types of discontent are quite disparate, and arise from a variety of perceived defects in the operation of plurality systems. These defects stem from quite different social conditions, and give rise to a variety of electoral forms being proposed as potential correctives.

A significant class of these defects has to do with the diminished legitimacy of electoral outcomes under plurality election rules. The factors that undermine legitimacy are of at least two kinds. First, the parliamentary outcomes may bear only a very tenuous relationship to the pattern of votes cast. The plurality electoral system harshly penalizes second parties whose vote is most evenly distributed across the country. This was most evident in the 1983 national election in the United Kingdom. There, the most glaring deficiency of the electoral system lay in the fact that the Social Democratic/Liberal Alliance, in its first national election, received the support of twenty-six percent of the British electorate but only twenty-three seats in the House of Commons—a paltry 3.5 percent. Occasionally, this effect becomes so exaggerated as to give the largest proportion of parliamentary seats to the party with the second largest proportion of the votes. This happened in Canada in 1979.

There have been other manifestations of weakness in the electoral system. A plurality system does not reflect dynamic change in the electorate with acceptable accuracy. In the United Kingdom case, again, one must note that the Conservative party fell slightly from forty-four percent of the vote in 1979 to forty-two percent of the vote in 1983, yet its share of the seats in Parliament *increased* substantially from fifty-three percent to sixty-one percent. The effect on the Labour party was less distorted. Its share of seats fell from forty-two to thirty-two percent of the House on a nine percentage point decline in the vote. As noted above, the largest deficit in seats compared to votes was reserved for the Social Democratic/Liberal Alliance.

The plurality electoral system may also fail to represent significant minorities. The moderate Roman Catholics in the SDLP in Northern Ireland, organized in the Social Democratic Labour Party, got eighteen percent of the vote in Northern Ireland but only one of its seventeen seats (six percent). Sinn Féin also captured but one seat, with thirteen percent of the vote. Of the minor parties in Northern Ireland, it was the more moderate, the SDLP, that was most badly represented, and the more extremist Sinn Féin and Democratic Unionist parties that were the least assailed by the electoral system. (All three smaller parties were underrepresented.)

This is similar to the type of result that has brought the plurality system into question in Canada. There, total underrepresentation or overrepresentation, while present, are not so glaring. In the 1980 federal election, each party's share of seats was within ten percentage points of its share of the national vote. What *was* striking, however, was the extreme regional imbalance in the recruitment of those seats. In that same 1980 election, the Liberal party got *no* seats in the three westernmost provinces—the site of the major oil and gas production in the country—despite winning more than twenty percent of the vote in those provinces. The major opposition party, the Progressive Conservative party, was almost as badly afflicted in Quebec, gaining only one of seventy-five seats from that province, despite winning more than twelve percent of the vote.

Whichever of these defects, representational unfairness, insensitivity to dynamic trends, or the exclusion of important political minorities, is taken to be the most important, will determine, in part, what kind of change is judged to be desirable. Any kind of change will involve movement to some form of proportional electoral system, but there are many subvarieties in this category. The three main ones are list systems, single transferable vote systems, and additional-member systems. All can achieve a close correspondence between the distribution of votes cast and the distribution of parliamentary seats. In this sense, all are fully proportional. All share the same operating philosophy, though they may compromise on different ways to apply it.

A fully proportional system works on the philosophy that "a vote is a vote" no matter *where* it is cast in the country, *nor for whom* it is cast. That is to say, everyone's vote should have the same weight in contributing to the election of a member of parliament. In practice, this means that each party should have approximately the same vote:seat ratio. This clearly did not obtain in the United Kingdom in 1983. The Conservative party got one seat for every 32,777 votes cast for it; the Social Democratic party got one for every 338,860 votes, more than ten times as much. A fully proportional system would have "charged" every party the same vote "price" for a seat. In addition, it would have charged the same party the same price everywhere in the country. Canada's plurality system certainly does not do this. In the 1980 federal election, the Liberal party would get one seat in Quebec for every 26,985 votes it attracted in that province. It received 268,262 votes in British Columbia. In Quebec, that would have been worth ten seats, but it wasn't worth any in British Columbia. That would not happen in any proportional electoral system.

Many of the forms of fully proportional electoral systems are reviewed in other chapters in this book. All but one involve holding elections in constituencies that elect more than one representative to the parliament. The constituency may vary in size from the whole country, as in the Netherlands or Israel, to as small as the three-person constituencies found in many single transferable vote systems. Only one fully proportional system builds on the single-member constituency found in Great Britain, the United States, and Canada, among other countries. This is the "additional-member" system now established in the Federal Republic of Germany. The name derives from the fact that the system uses additional members to compensate for the distortions inevitably deriving from a system of single-member constituencies.

In all of these systems, constituencies can be allocated according to population. The additional members simply represent a different and larger group of the population from the constituencies. In a federal state, they may represent states, provinces, or *Länder*. In a unitary state, they could represent other large groupings: perhaps ancient counties or duchies, perhaps modern regions or economic areas. Whatever the basis for the groupings, each would return a number of representatives proportionate to its population.

For purposes of illustration, I will use an example derived from the system I proposed for Canada (Irvine 1981, Chapter 4). In that proposal, voters would cast a single vote, choosing among candidates (whose party affiliation, if any, would be identified on the ballot). In this way, the actual practice of voting would be unchanged from what is currently done in Canada. This is a prime advantage for the "additional-member" system when change is proposed for a country with a long tradition of plurality elections.

What would change would be the way the votes were treated by the authorities after they had been cast. To simplify the presentation, I will discuss here a "country" of only three provinces. Two of them, Quebec and Alberta, are dominated by a single party; one, Ontario, is more competitive.[1] The election results are taken from the 1979 federal election, and the number of constituencies in each province is proportional to the 1971 population, the distribution in force at the time of that election. The allocation of seats by province is illustrated in Table 16.1. There are somewhat fewer "provincial seats" (which the additional members will hold) than traditional constituencies. As we shall see later, the ratio of constituency to provincial members could be variable. The essential point, however, is that both the the number of constituency representatives and the number of provincial representatives can be, as nearly as practicable, proportional to the provincial populations.

The actual distribution of seats among the parties in 1979 in those provinces

Table 16.1 Allocating "Additional Members"
Among Three Canadian Provinces, 1979

Province	Actual	Constit. Membs.	Proposed Prov. Membs.	Total
Quebec	75	50	44	94
Ontario	95	63	56	119
Alberta	21	14	12	26

Source: excerpted from Irvine 1981. Table C-2. Note: Constit.
Membs. = Constituency Members. Prov. Membs. = Provincial Members.

is reported in Table 16.2. The inevitable distortions engendered by the single-member plurality system are immediately evident. The Liberal party elected no members of parliament from Alberta, despite winning twenty-two percent of the vote. The Progressive Conservative party elected two (of seventy-five) members from Quebec on thirteen percent of the vote. Even in a more electorally competitive province, the seat results were far from proportional to the distribution of votes. The Liberal party was treated quite fairly: thirty-four percent of the seats for thirty-six percent of the vote. The Progressive Conservative party was overly rewarded with sixty percent of the seats for forty-one percent of the vote, and the New Democratic party was heavily penalized. Their twenty-one percent of the Ontario vote could get them only six percent of that province's constituencies.

Table 16.2 shows how the seats would be allocated in an additional-member system. I have distributed the constituency members in the same way that they were distributed in the election. The additional members are distributed among the parties in each province in such a way as to offset the distortion at the constituency level. Each province's legislative entitlement is the *sum* of its constituency members and its provincial members. Each party's share of that entitlement in that province is the proportion of that sum equal to its proportion of votes in that province. From the number of seats to which a party would be entitled is subtracted the number of constituencies that it won in the single-member contests. The remainder (if positive) is the number of provincial representatives to be allocated to each party. The effect of this operation is to substantially equalize the vote "price" for any seat among the parties, and among the provinces within any party. This is illustrated in Table 16.3.

In 1979, the single-member plurality system resulted in large discrepancies in translating votes into seats in Canada. The year was not at all atypical. Over the three provinces considered here by way of example, the votes:seats ratio for the Progressive Conservative Party varied from just under twenty-seven thousand votes for an Alberta seat to two hundred sixteen thousand votes for a Quebec seat. The Liberal party got *no* seats for one hundred eighty-eight thousand votes in Alberta, but one for every twenty-nine thousand votes in Quebec. The

Table 16.2 Results of the 1979 Canadian General Election

A. Actual Outcomes

	Proportion of Seats				Proportion of Votes			
	Lib.	P.C.	NDP	Other	Lib.	P.C.	NDP	Other
Quebec	89	3	0	8	62	13	5	20
Ontario	34	60	6	0	36	42	21	1
Alberta	0	100	0	0	22	66	10	2

B. Possible Outcomes in the "additional-member" system of Table 16.1

		Percent of Vote	Total Seats	less	Constit. Membs.	equals	Prov. Reps.
Quebec:	Lib.	62	58		45		13
	P.C.	14	13		1		12
	NDP	5	5		0		5
	Others	20	18		4		14
Ontario:	Lib.	36	44		21		23
	P.C.	42	50		38		12
	NDP	21	25		4		21
	Others*	1	0		0		0
Alberta:	Lib.	22	6		0		6
	P.C.	66	17		14		3
	NDP	10	3		0		3
	Others*	2	0		0		0

Legend: Lib.–Liberal Party of Canada
P.C.–Progressive Conservative Party of Canada
NDP–New Democratic Party of Canada

*"Other" parties get no additional members because they represent a scattering of small parties, none of which is entitled to a seat. The realtively sizable vote for them is in aggregate.

Source: Actual results are taken from Appendix B of Howard R. Penniman (ed.) *Canada at the Polls, 1979 and 1980* (Washington, D.C.: American Enterprise Institute for Public Policy Research, 1981). Hypothetical results are taken from William P. Irvine *op. cit* Appendix C and table C-2.

additional-member system is much more even-handed in its effects, substantially equalizing the vote "price" for any seat. Liberal and Progressive Conservative ratios vary in a three thousand vote range over the three provinces. The NDP ratio is slightly larger (seven thousand votes) but still much smaller than under the present electoral system. The variance in the ratios across the parties in any province is similarly reduced.

The importance of this in a regionally divided polity, like Canada's, is immediately apparent. Canadian parties generally have avoided highly regionally

Table 16.3 Votes Obtained for Each Seat Won in
Selected Canadian Provinces, 1979, by Electoral System

	Actual Plurality System				Additional Member System			
Province	Lib.	P.C.	NDP	Other	Lib.	P.C.	NDP	Other
Quebec	29,485	216,100	a	105,469	34,061	33,246	32,698	35,156
Ontario	47,185	30,399	145,530	b	34,316	34,654	34,927	b
Alberta	c	26,647	d	e	31,382	32,917	28,079	e

a. No seats won for 163, 492 votes. b. No seats won for 27,170 votes. c. No seats won for 188,295 votes. d. No seats won for 84,236 votes. e. No seats won for 21,058 votes.

focused appeals to the electorate, but could not do so completely. In the first place, Canadian parties do not have, in their legislative caucuses, a sufficient number of members able to interpret the views of particular regions on matters of public policy and to try to fashion acceptable compromises. In the second place, parties must be sensitive to the different "productivity" of votes won in different regions. It would be quite rational for the Progressive Conservative party to adopt a policy (on support for suburban householders, for example) that promised to gain one vote in Ontario even at the cost of losing up to six votes in Quebec. Similarly, it would be quite rational for the Liberal party to adopt a gas and petroleum pricing policy that would gain one vote in Ontario, even at the expense of four votes in Alberta. No Canadian party has been quite this crass, and the science of psephology is nowhere near this exact. The incentives are there, nonetheless, and the policy examples cited, though no doubt the result of more complex processes of policymaking, are by no means hypothetical. Both the incentives of the political market and the social solidarity incentives of managing a party caucus, exert influence in the same direction. Which, if either, is actually decisive is an interesting theoretical point, but is immaterial to whether or not regionalism is heightened in the country.

One could imagine similar effects at work in other countries where an additional-member system might be tried. In the United Kingdom, the Conservative caucus would obtain more recruits from Wales, Scotland, and the industrial Midlands. The Labour party would draw more from the south of England.[2] Both caucuses would be more representative of the society than either is at present. It is important to stress that this representativeness would, in no way, be artificial. The caucus would reflect the distribution of the party's electorate and not of the total electorate.

The additional-member system would address other disabilities of the single-member plurality system as well. The most popular party in the country would gain the largest number of seats in the parliament. No party would be massively underrepresented. To the extent that voters demanded *fairness* from their electoral system, they would see an additional-member system operating fairly. Dynamic change would be faithfully represented as well. From the 1974 to 1979 elections, in Canada, the Liberal party's vote declined by three percentage points and the Progressive Conservative party's increased by less than one point. Their representation in the House of Commons was much more volatile. The Liberal presence declined from fifty-three percent of the House to forty percent. The Progressive Conservatives went from thirty-six percent of the House in 1974 to forty-eight percent in 1979.

The tendency of an additional-member system to accurately reproduce, but not to exaggerate, dynamic changes in the electorate has interesting implications for the operation of a political-economic cycle. It may be that, with any fully proportional system, policy will be framed with more long-run considerations in view. As compared to a plurality system, additional-member systems produce seat changes of much less amplitude for any given vote shift. There is, therefore, much less incentive to attempt to produce short-run economic booms to be followed by postelection cutbacks. Much more research is needed to establish this point. Still, the fragments of evidence are encouraging. In looking for evidence of a partisan-inspired economic cycle (indicated by faster growth in real disposable income in election than in nonelection years), Edward Tufte found eight countries where such a cycle was *not* in evidence. All were PR systems and included Austria, Denmark, the Federal Republic of Germany, Italy, and the Netherlands (Tufte 1978, p. 12).

With all these advantages—fair representation, faithful reproduction of shifts of voter sentiment, and representation of the regional distribution of party voters, why is the additional-member system not high on the political agenda of a country like Canada? There are two reasons. To many, in the public as well as among the politicians, these advantages are purchased at too high a price—the price of having to form governments where no party has a majority in the legislature. Occasionally, these fears harken back to the earliest criticisms of PR. A PR electoral system, it is said, could result in policymaking immobility that would harm the legitimacy of the political process much more than does the representational failures of the plurality electoral system.

Even if immobility seems to be an exaggerated fear, politicians resist the additional-member system. We may posit that politicians strive to maximize the range of discretion within which they operate. Having to negotiate their policies with one or more other parties is seen to take all the enjoyment out of office-holding. It is quite true that the Canadian or the British governing parties could no longer function as elected dictatorships for four or five years. This is probably more of a disadvantage to the politician than to the citizen or to the commentator on politics. If it is the case that the new international economic order will impose considerable demands on political elites, it is probable that governments will have to proceed more by consultation and consensus than by command. The political task may well become less enjoyable, but it is unavoidable. An electoral system which compels such a policymaking style is probably an advantage rather than an encumbrance.

How would the additional members be chosen to fill the seats allocated to each party? The West German system uses a rank-ordered list of nominees named before each election, with the additional members selected from that list. Who would name such a list? In a country like Canada, where the government is seen as overly centralized, it could not be the central party apparatus. To leave the naming of the party list to the party leader would be to open too widely the door for cronyism, and would diminish the prospects of gaining legitimacy for the central government in the various regions of the country. A better alternative would be to have the list for any province named by the party organization in that province. This would have the additional advantage of providing an incentive to the parties to establish themselves organizationally in all regions of the country.

The prospect of election from a list is often another motive for rejection of the additional-member system by current members of parliament. They perceive the system as giving the additional members privileged entry to the House of Commons and freeing them from the onerous political work in which constituency members must engage. This objection is a common one, and was expressed by no less a person than former Progressive Conservative prime minister C. Joseph Clark (1980):

> I think that my Party is at fault for our failure in the province of Quebec and we will not become appreciably stronger by being able to have some people sitting there without doing the hard work that sinks roots in individual constituencies and results in election. I think you have to earn your way in politics as elsewhere. I think that the present electoral system ensures that the people who are sitting in the House of Commons are people who have a direct connection back to a particular constituency, a particular section of the people of Canada.

These claims strike one as much exaggerated. In a parliamentary system, back-bench members of parliament do work very hard, but their election is usually beyond the reach of their own efforts. It depends, instead, on the standing of the party and the party leader (Irvine 1982). Ironically, in the additional-member system, it may come to depend crucially on the efforts of the list members. One may be confident that the constituency representatives would exert pressure in the caucus to make sure that these members played their role.

The additional-member system would thus be an indispensable asset in overcoming feelings of regional alienation, bringing both symbolic and practical improvements. No longer would any region feel, after an election, that a government had been elected in which it had no influence. Moreover, with a list system of electing the additional members, the representatives would, over time, gain sufficient expertise in policy and in policy-influencing to actually be effective in advancing the interests of their regions. Much of what gets done in a parliamentary system is done behind closed doors and is not easily amenable to research. If research were possible, I suspect that small group theory would be a most useful guide. The need to maintain harmony in the caucus would, as mentioned above, would be a powerful influence on the senior members elected from the list. The expertise and longevity of the "list-elected" cabinet ministers would give them considerable influence in the cabinet room.

The additional-member system, as noted earlier, would significantly strengthen the political parties in regions where they do unwarrantedly badly in terms of seats. Moreover, the system changes the political calculus animating the politicians. Votes *do* become equally weighty in all regions so that parties need not shun opportunities to gain small footholds.

A list system for choosing the additional members could also be helpful in overcoming particular feelings of alienation or underrepresentation. Through creative use of list making, a party could seek to appeal to particular groups. Women, or aboriginal peoples, or a particular ethnic minority might be given prime positions on a particular list. In this way, a party could signify its commitment to the group. This may be another way where a party, pursuing its self-interest, could serve the interest of the country by helping to overcome feelings that the governmental institutions are foreign to members of the group in question. By providing parties with both the motivation and the manpower to establish themselves throughout the country, such a reform would restore a party system's capacity to act as a nation-binding force.

Much resistance to the additional-member system derives from these two fears of its propensity to parliaments with no majority party and its giving some members of parliament privileged access not given to other members. Both these concerns are easily disputed but neither can be as easily allayed. Some steps are possible. The avoidance of minority government can, in part, be built into the design of an additional-member system.

Important in this is the relative number of Additional Members and Constituency Representatives. The more that the latter outnumber the former by, the less effectively proportional is the total system and the less, therefore, the chance of minority government *ceteris paribus*. One scholar has recommended that Canada adopt an additional-member system with one additional member for each million population (for thirteen to twenty-two additional members for the post-1945 period) (Dobell 1981). Such a system would not have produced, over that period, appreciably more minority governments than were produced by the existing single-member plurality system. Unfortunately, it offsets caucus underrepresentation in a party's weak areas by only a modest number of representatives—possibly too few to assume the governmental and political roles needed of such members. Nor does it equalize the weight of votes across the parties or across the provinces.

Another way to avoid parliaments in which no party has a majority would be to modify the "operating philosophy" of the additional-member system. Rather than insist that votes be equally weighty no matter where they are cast nor for what party they are cast, one could abandon this last requirement. Now, one party (one of the major ones, in practice) would need fewer votes to return a member of parliament than would another party (one of the minor ones). Within each party, votes would be approximately equally productive. Such an additional-member system was recommended for Canada by a federal inquiry (Task Force on Canadian Unity 1979, pp. 104–106). Very briefly, the Canadian Parliament was to be enlarged by creating sixty additional seats. After each election, each party would obtain a share of those seats equal to its share of the national vote, regardless of the number of constituencies it had won. The parties would nominate lists of candidates in each province for these seats. Each party would then allocate its total number of additional members among its various lists, electing members in such a way as to equalize the vote:seat ratio for that party across all provinces. It is a descriptively complex system, but one easily calculable (Irvine 1981, appendix B).

There are many other discretionary features of an additional-member system. Among these are the number of ballots a voter would cast, whether or not a person could simultaneously be a candidate in a constituency and on a list, whether those elected from lists should be so elected only a fixed number of times, the precise formula for achieving proportionality, and so on. None of these affect the dynamics of the system as significantly as the ratio of additional members to constituency members or the mode of nomination to the list.

In conclusion, the additional-member system offers an effective response to many of the forces disruptive of political systems. It is especially useful as a response to the exacerbation of regionalism which can occur in a single-member plurality system. The additional-member system restructures political incentives to encourage political parties to continue to frame broad national appeals. In addition, it offers a more faithful reproduction of popular preferences, and of shifts in those preferences over time. While the system does raise the probability of national parliaments with no majority party, even the plurality system is hardly proof against this in a regionally divided country. The additional-member system can also be designed to minimize this tendency. This should not be carried to excessive lengths, however. The malaise in many states stems from the representational failures of electoral institutions. It is this failure that reform seeks to dispel, and its ability to do so should not be excessively compromised.

NOTES

1. For treatment of all of Canada, see Irvine 1981, Appendix C.

2. In reporting the election results, the *Economist* (1983, p. 13) noted that "in all southern England from Kent to Cornwall over 1m[illion] Labour voters elected just one MP."

17

A Note on Variable-Size Legislatures to Achieve Proportional Representation

Steven J. Brams
Peter C. Fishburn

Is it possible to ensure PR in multiple-winner elections—to some legislative body or other assembly—in a way that avoids the nonmonotonicity of STV (see our discussion in Chapter 14 of this volume)? We would like to introduce, without much elaboration, a new voting system that we call *adjusted district voting*, based on the following assumptions:

1) There is a jurisdiction divided into equal-size districts, each of which elects a single representative to a legislature.

2) There are two main factions in the jurisdiction, one majority and one minority, whose size can be determined. For example, if the factions are represented by political parties, their respective sizes could be determined by the votes that each party's candidates, summed across all districts, receive in the jurisdiction.

3) The legislature consists of all representatives who win in the districts *plus* the largest vote-getters among the losers, necessary to achieve PR, if it is not realized in the district elections. Typically, this "adjustment" would involve adding minority-faction candidates, who lose in the district races, to the legislature, so that it mirrors the majority-minority breakdown in the electorate as closely as possible.

4) The size of the legislature would be *variable*, with a lower bound equal to the number of districts (if no adjustment is necessary to achieve PR) and an upper bound equal to twice the number of districts (if a nearly fifty percent minority wins no district seats).

Adjusted approval voting, we discovered after formulating it, is in fact used in Puerto Rico (Still 1984) and has been proposed by the Hansard Society (1976) for use in Great Britain. It is one of a class of what are variously called add-on, additional-member, and topping-up systems, probably the best known of which is West Germany's (variations can be found in Denmark, Iceland, and Sweden). In the German Bundestag, half the seats are decided in single-member district contests, with the other half determined from second votes cast for parties that are used, after the district results are factored in, to achieve PR on the basis of the second party votes. These and related voting systems are discussed in, among other places, Bogdanor (1981), Gudgin and Taylor (1979), Irvine (1979), Lakeman (1974), Lijphart (1982), and Taylor and Johnston (1979).

As an example of adjuisted district voting, suppose there are eight districts in a jurisdiction. If there is an eighty-percent majority and a twenty-percent minority in the jurisdiction, the majority is likely to win all the seats unless there is an extreme concentration of the minority in one or two districts.

Suppose the minority wins no seats. Then its two biggest vote-getters would be given two "extra" seats to provide it with representation of twenty percent in a body of ten members, exactly its proportion in the electorate.

Suppose the minority wins one seat, which would provide it with representation of about thirteen percent in a body of eight members. If it were given an extra seat, its representation would rise to about twenty-two percent in a body of nine members, which would be closer to its proportion in the electorate. However, assume that the addition of extra seats can never make the minority's proportion in the legislature exceed its proportion in the electorate.

Clearly, the minority would benefit by winning no seats and then being granted two extra seats to bring its proportion up to exactly twenty percent. To prevent a minority from benefiting by *losing* in district elections, assume the following constraint: the allocation of extra seats to the minority can never give it a greater proportion in the legislature than it would obtain had it won in more district elections.

How would this constraint work in our example? If the minority won no seats in the district elections, then the addition of two extra seats would give it $2/10$ representation in the legislature, exactly its proportion in the electorate. But two paragraphs above we showed that if the minority had won exactly one seat, it would *not* be entitled to an extra seat—and $2/9$ representation in the legislature—because this proportion exceeds its twenty percent proportion in the electorate. Hence, its representation would remain at $1/8$ if it won in exactly one district.

Because $2/10 > 1/8$, the constraint prevents the minority from gaining two extra seats if it wins no district seats initially. Instead, it would be entitled in this case to only one extra seat because the next-highest ratio below $2/10$ is $1/9$, and $1/9 < 1/8$, as the constraint specifies.

But $1/9$ = eleven percent is only about half the minority's proportion in the electorate. In fact, we prove in the general case that the constraint may prevent a minority from receiving up to about half of the extra seats it would be entitled to on the basis of its population proportion were the constraint *not* operative and it could therefore get up to this proportion in the legislature (Brams and Fishburn, 1983a).

The constraint may be interpreted as a kind of "strategyproofness" feature of adjusted district voting: it makes it unprofitable for a minority party to deliberately lose in a district election to do better after the adjustment that gives it extra seats. But strategyproofness, in precluding any possible advantage that might accrue to the minority from throwing a district election, has a price. As our example demonstrates, it may severely restrict the ability of adjusted district voting to satisfy PR. Thus, we have an *impossibility result*: under adjusted district voting, one cannot guarantee a close correspondence between a party's proportion in the electorate and its representation in the legislature if one insists on the strategyproofness constraint. Dropping it allows one to approximate PR but may give an incentive to the minority party to lose in certain district contests in order to do better after the adjustment.

It is worth pointing out that the "second chance" for minority candidates under adjusted district voting would encourage them to run in the first place, because even if most or all of them are defeated in the district races, their biggest vote-getters would still get a chance at the (possibly) extra seats in the second stage. But these extra seats might be cut by up to a factor of two from the minority's proportion in the electorate should one want to motivate district races with the strategyproofness constraint. Indeed, Spafford (1980, p. 393), anticipating our impossibility result, recommended that only an (unspecified) fraction of the seats that the minority is entitled to be allotted to it in the adjustment phase to give it "some incentive to take the single-member contests seriously,... though that of course would mean giving up strict PR."

We cannot explore here a number of practical and theoretical issues. For example, what if there are more than two factions that should be represented in the legislature? Even if there are only two factions, what if one is an ethnic, linguistic, religious, or racial group that is not represented by a single political party and whose size cannot, therefore, be determined from the electoral returns? Will uncertainty about the final size of the legislature create problems?

It seems to us that adjusted district voting that results in a variable-size legislature may provide a simple mechanism for approximating PR without the non-monotonicity of STV. How good this approximation is depends not only on the size of the legislature but also on what rules one adopts in apportioning seats. Though specific to adjusted district voting, our results so far lead us to believe that rules that incorporate strategyproofness may be in fundamental conflict with rules that prescribe PR.

PART VI
OTHER ALTERNATIVES

18

The Double-Ballot System as a Weapon against Anti-System Parties*

Domenico Fisichella

The best example of the double-ballot system is France, which has had a long historical experience with this electoral system extending to the present time. The double-ballot was used during the Second Empire and between 1873 and 1936 (with the exception of the 1919 and the 1924 elections, which were held with a mixed system in an attempt to combine list voting and an absolute majority formula), and is again in use today: the Fifth Republic has reintroduced it starting from the National Assembly elections of 23–30 November 1958. However, many other countries have also used the double-ballot system: Spain in the period 1836–1870 (when the plurality system was introduced), and again in the period 1931–1936, combining the limited vote with a second ballot; Germany, in the period 1871–1919 for the *Reichstag* elections; Austria until 1919; Belgium until 1900; Italy until 1919; Norway until 1921; the Netherlands until 1918; and Switzerland until 1919. For Germany, Austria, Belgium, Italy, Norway, the Netherlands, and Switzerland, the abolition of the double ballot coincided with the introduction of proportional representation (PR).[1]

Under the double-ballot system, elections can take place in single-member or multimember constituencies, the latter being relatively uncommon. Double-ballot systems in multimember constituencies were used in Belgium, Spain, Switzerland, Norway (prior to 1906), and France (in 1873 and 1885). In the period 1882–1891, Italy was divided into multimember constituencies, each having from two to five seats. In constituencies with up to four seats, each voter had as many votes as there were deputies to be elected. In constituencies with five seats the limited vote was applied, with each voter entitled to four votes. Single-member

---

*Translated by Maurizio Ferrera.

constituencies were used in Germany, Austria, the Netherlands, Norway (from 1906 on), Italy (except for the years 1882–1891), and France (except for 1873 and 1885). The Fifth Republic uses single-member constituencies.

In single-member constituencies, success in first-round elections is normally dependent upon gaining an absolute majority of the valid votes in the constituency. Sometimes, however, a smaller *quorum* is sufficient. For example, when the double ballot was first introduced in France, election in the first round was conditional on gaining votes equal to one-eighth of the total number of registered voters. On the other hand, the absolute majority of the votes cast is sometimes also required to represent a given *quorum* of those registered to vote. This is the case in the Fifth Republic's electoral law: for election in the first round, this requires, besides the absolute majority of votes cast, that these votes also constitute no less than one-fourth of those registered to vote.

When no candidate obtains the prescribed majority, a second round is held, normally one or two weeks later. Admission to the second round may be regulated in different ways: (1) entry may be granted to the two candidates with the highest number of votes in the first round, or (2) granted to all candidates with a given percentage of votes in the first round; for instance, under present French provisions this percentage amounts to 12.5 percent of the electorate;[2] (3) candidates not presented in the first round may be inserted at the second to replace those who have withdrawn; and (4) all first-round candidates may be represented in the second round without exclusions.

ANTI-SYSTEM PARTIES AND THE MECHANICS OF ALLIANCES

How does the double-ballot system work? Double-ballot formulae diverge from the plurality system in that they have no sizable effect on the number of parties; they diverge from PR in that they display a marked manipulative and disproportional effect. However, it does not automatically follow from this that manipulation and disproportionality have the same features when stemming from the plurality system or from the double-ballot system.

Let us begin with an analysis of disproportionality. In which direction does the double-ballot system operate? Which parties (in a structured party system) will be underrepresented or overrepresented? More particularly, does this disproportionality work to the disadvantage of smaller parties? If this were the case, the double-ballot system would constitute a powerful deterrent against splinter groups and new parties, as does the plurality system.

Here we run into the first peculiarity of the double-ballot system, which is of the utmost importance: its effect on the distribution of seats differs according to the presence or absence of an anti-system party—perceived as such by the prevailing political culture—in the electoral competition. If there is such an anti-system party, it is the party that is primarily, and often very strongly, under-represented regardless of its electoral size—provided, of course, that its size does not approximate too closely the size of all other groupings together. (In this extreme case, we would not have a "prevailing" culture, but the political culture would be split into two antagonistic belief systems; I do not know any historical example of this kind under a double-ballot system.) A significant test is offered by the electoral and parliamentary fortunes of the French Communist party in the elections held with a double-ballot system: those of the 1928–1936 period and during the Fifth Republic. The following table presents the data in detail:

Year	Communist Votes (In Percent)	Communist Seats (In Percent)
1928	11.4	2.4
1932	8.4	2.0
1936	15.4	12.0
1958	18.9	2.2
1962	21.7	8.8
1967	22.5	15.5
1968	20.0	7.0
1973	21.4	14.9
1978	20.7	17.5
1981	16.1	8.9

Clearly, there is an oscillation in the extent of disproportionality which reflects the different political circumstances that influence party alliances in each election. But the general conclusion that emerges from the French experience is that its Communist party is always—and almost always to a marked extent—underrepresented under the double-ballot system.

My argument concerning the double-ballot system and the underrepresentation of anti-system parties is not based exclusively on the French experience. In some other countries of continental Europe before World War I, the behavior of Socialist parties was also perceived by the prevailing political culture as being contrary to the existing system. Where this was the case, and where the party system was structured, the double-ballot system penalized the Socialist vote in terms of representation.

In the German Empire, one cause of the underrepresentation of the Social Democrats was the failure to redistribute seats within the national territory in connection with the demographic increases of urban areas, which had the highest concentration of Socialist support. But this is only one of the reasons explaining this party's underrepresentation. Another explanation is the effect of the double-ballot system and the Socialists' attitude toward the political system (and vice versa). In the thirteen *Reichstag* elections held between 1871 and 1912, the Social Democratic party was constantly underrepresented. The following table shows the discrepancy between the percentage of votes and the percentage of seats obtained by the Social Democrats in the six elections (the last six elections held in the Empire) in which they surpassed the ten percent threshold of the popular vote:

Year	Social Democratic Votes (In Percent)	Social Democratic Seats (In Percent)
1890	19.7	8.8
1893	23.3	11.1
1898	27.2	14.1
1903	31.7	20.4
1907	29.0	10.8
1912	34.8	27.7

In the first quarter of the twentieth century, the Norwegian Labor party constituted the most radical sector of Scandinavian socialism. The strength of its revolutionary orientation was so marked that it was the only Socialist party to adhere almost en bloc to the Comintern. Given these conditions, the double-ballot system again constantly operated in the direction of an underrepresentation of this "alienated" party, as illustrated in the following table:

Year	Socialist Votes (In Percent)	Socialist Seats (In Percent)
1903	12.1	3.0
1906	16.3	8.1
1909	21.6	9.0
1912	26.3	18.7
1915	32.1	19.5
1918	30.8	14.3

Conversely, in cases where the Socialist parties were not perceived as being different from the others, these parties were treated as normal competitors by the double-ballot system. The fortunes of Belgian socialism are quite telling in this respect. This party was characterized by an early integration into the system and by an undogmatic orientation in its political relationships. It assumed the role of loyal opposition much more rapidly than the majority of the other Marxist parties. In the two elections in which it took part at the national level prior to the introduction of PR, the Belgian Socialist party was even overrepresented, albeit only slightly. In 1894 it obtained sixteen percent of the vote and 18.5 percent of the seats; in 1896–1898, with 17.5 percent of the votes it obtained eighteen percent of the seats.[3]

What happens to the other parties when an anti-system party is under-represented? Keeping in mind that an anti-system party is underrepresented even when it constitutes the relative majority in terms of votes (e.g. the German Socialists in 1890), and as long as it does not approach an absolute majority, we can say that the general tendency of the double-ballot system is to favor the strongest of the other competing parties. In particular, this has always been the case for the French Fifth Republic, Imperial Germany, and Norway, while the tendency is less clear for French elections during the period 1928–1936. As far as the smaller parties are concerned, disproportionality does not follow a linear trend. It depends to a large extent on the size of the underrepresented anti-system party and of the overrepresented loyal party, and also on the degrees of disproportionality for these two parties. If a strong anti-system party is severely underrepresented and at the same time the strongest of the loyal parties is only slightly overrepresented, there may be some overrepresentation of one or more smaller groupings.

The second important feature of the double-ballot system concerns the alliances that it encourages. The electoral formula often legally requires that access to the second round (if such a round is necessary) be reserved to the two candidates obtaining the most votes in the first round.[4] Even when access to the second round is free, the system still functions as a mechanism of reduction; it should be noted that, in this case, the two candidates participating in the second round are not necessarily those with the most votes in the first, but may well be other candidates, depending on the withdrawal agreement among parties during the interval between rounds. The experience of the Fifth Republic confirms this effect of reduction. Let me cite two examples: in the 1962 National Assembly election, the second round involved 369 constituencies; only 96 out of the 465 seats assigned to the metropolitan territory had been allocated in the first round. Of these 369 constituencies, as many as 228 were contested by two candidates only, 130 by three, and only 11 by four. In 1978, 68 seats out of 491 were allocated in the first round, while 409 seats were contested in the second round by only two candidates.

Whether as a matter of law or in practice, the double-ballot system is largely based on the withdrawal of some of the candidates. Consequently, a number of voters in each constituency find themselves without the candidate for whom they had voted in the first round. If these voters do not abstain, they are obliged to adapt and to cast their ballots for a party that was not their original choice. This is where the manipulation of the vote occurs. Now the complex game of alliances and bargains takes place in which all parties remaining in the competition strive to secure for themselves the vote of the ''orphaned'' electorate. Generally, this game is based on mutual appeals between homogeneous, or at least proximate, orientations, ideologies, and political interests. The expectation is, for instance, that a conservative is more likely to vote for a Christian Democrat than for a Radical, a Socialist is more likely to prefer a Radical than a Liberal and so forth. The pattern of agreements does not necessarily follow a coherent trend throughout the country; in some areas, for instance, Radicals may prefer to ally themselves with Socialists, and in other areas with Liberals. This has two important consequences.

The first consequence is that smaller parties may be overrepresented, as has sometimes been the case for the French Radicals. As a center party, it may well yield its votes to either the party to its left or the party to its right, but may also be accepted by both electorates jointly. This constitutes the strength of a small center party in a double-ballot system: it may bargain the withdrawal of a certain number of its candidates both to the advantage of its right and left neighbor in exchange for support in other constituencies, where, starting with a relatively modest number of votes, it may expect to be successful thanks to the possibility of gathering support from more than one direction. In this respect, the double-ballot system behaves quite differently from the plurality system.

We now come to the second consequence. Even an anti-system party may actively participate in the game of electoral alliances. With some specific objectives in mind—such as the fight against the majority, the imposition of a given socio-economic program, or the modification of foreign policy orientations—parties integrated in the system may consider it convenient to reach an electoral agreement with an "alienated" grouping, especially if it is a large one, and the anti-system party may well have an interest in getting out of its isolation. In this case, electoral agreements will be made and the usual process of agreed-upon withdrawals will follow. But very often—and this is the important point—the practice of alliances will not yield the expected electoral return for the anti-system party. Why is this so? Let us imagine that anti-system party A reaches an agreement of mutual support with party B in ten constituencies: party A commits itself to support party B's candidate in five constituencies and the latter party commits itself to support party A's candidate in the remaining constituencies. However, while the anti-system party's electorate tends to vote in a disciplined way for party B's candidate, the followers of party B display some reluctance to support party A's candidate; they prefer to abstain or even to vote for the adversary of the anti-system party. The French electoral results confirm such orientations. The Communist party's electoral alliances usually result in a loss: whether these were made in the "popular front" climate of the 1930s—which was certainly most favorable to the extreme Left's plans—or the result of partial agreements (with the Radicals and Socialists in 1962); whether they were the consequence of advance, comprehensive, and public agreements with other groupings (with the PSU and the Left Federation in 1967) or the prelude to a return to the government for the first time since the Liberation period (in 1981).

It must be added that, when in a constituency the anti-system party's candidate is opposed by two or three candidates, the "integrated" votes may disperse themselves, and hence the former's chances are improved. In 1962, for instance, the French Communists obtained only ten seats in two-candidate constituencies in the second round, while their remaining twenty-two seats (nine had already been won in the first round) resulted from a competition in "triangular" constituencies.

CONDITIONS FOR INTRODUCING THE DOUBLE-BALLOT SYSTEM

Both the historical evidence of various countries and the experience of contemporary France highlight the special capacity of the double-ballot system to reduce the parliamentary representation of alienated parties, whereas we do not have evidence of this kind for the plurality system. Indeed, the electoral formula which is worthiest of attention for the purpose of securing the underrepresentation of a strong anti-system party is the double-ballot system in single-member constituencies. However, if we are faced with the prospect of replacing PR with the double-ballot system, we have to go beyond historical evidence. We have to make sure of the existence of the conditions necessary for the functioning of this electoral formula in a direction that is consistent with the aim for which its adoption is recommended.

The first condition to be ascertained is the capacity of pro-system parties to form electoral alliances with each other. If these parties are unable to organize a system of alliances for selecting one common candidate to oppose the anti-system candidate in each constituency in the second round, the chances of underrepresenting the alienated grouping decrease as the number of constituencies contested by more than two candidates increases.[5] I regard parties as capable of concluding functional alliances if they have structured organizations with a considerable level of internal discipline and cohesion, but without being rigid and crystallized around ideological orientations.

A further condition involves the character of the electorate. As stated earlier, the double-ballot system gives birth to a vast system of electoral alliances. In order for these alliances to lead to the underrepresentation of the anti-system party, the integrated voters must (1) adhere to the game of withdrawals and supports bargained among candidates of the loyal parties, and (2) refuse to follow those pro-system parties that conclude electoral agreements with alienated groupings. How can we formulate reliable hypotheses about the voters' behavior in the case of an introduction of a double-ballot formula? This question is directly related to the notion of party identification. In the second round, in which, compared with the first, a limited number of candidates take part, many voters will no longer find the candidate of the party with which they identify themselves or for which they voted in the first round. Because the voters' behavior in the second round is obviously of crucial importance, we must look at the role of party identification from a new perspective.

First of all, the question of abstentionism deserves special attention. Behavioral studies frequently regard electoral apathy as the result of the absence of party identification: for those who vote, the absence or weakening of identification may lead to electoral volatility, and thus to a shift from one party to another; for those who do not vote, the failure to vote often stems from an absence of party identification. However, if elections take place with a double-ballot system, we must consider the opposite hypothesis, namely that the failure to vote may be the consequence of a high degree of identification. In other words, those who abstain may be strong identifiers who, unable to find the symbol of their party in the second round, prefer not to vote instead of "betraying" their party.

Why is it so important to ascertain whether the electorate is composed of individuals with an identification so marked that they are led to abstain? When in an extreme multiparty system there is a sizable anti-system party, the introduction of the double-ballot system often makes this party one of the "fixed" competitors in the second round (the more so as its electoral size increases). On the contrary, only one of the six or seven pro-system candidates present in the first round enters the second round. This means that, whereas the anti-system party's voters find their preferred symbol in both rounds, only the voters of one of the other parties will find their candidate in the second round. If party identification is so strong that it will lead to abstention when the preferred party is not on the second ballot, the introduction of the double-ballot system will have a negative effect mainly on the pro-system parties. This is why it is vitally necessary to measure the intensity and distribution of party identifications before adopting this formula.

In addition to party identification, what I call the "regime image" must also be ascertained. In order to increase its electoral appeal, an anti-system party may try to blur the integrated electorate's perception of the difference between pro-system and anti-system orientations. If the electorate is no longer able to distinguish clearly between the alienated and the loyal pattern of regime orientation, the introduction of the double-ballot system will not result in an adequate underrepresentation of the anti-system party—and it may even have the opposite effect. Hence, before the introduction of the double-ballot system, a careful assessment of the influence and scope of the alienated regime orientation in the political culture is in order.[6]

In conclusion, if the integrated parties are capable of and available for reciprocal alliances, if the electorate presents certain characteristics regarding party identification and regime image, and if the anti-system party's strength is below the critical level of about thirty-five percent of the votes, the introduction of the double-ballot system will result in an underrepresentation of the anti-system party. The exact degree of this underrepresentation also depends on the way in which the boundaries of the single-member constituencies are drawn.

NOTES

1. My discussion is restricted to the electoral systems for the lower houses. For a more detailed treatment of the arguments presented here and for bibliographical references, see Fisichella 1983.

2. This percentage was stipulated by the law of July 19, 1976. Initially it was five percent of the votes cast (ordinance of October 13, 1958), and subsequently ten percent of the registered voters (law of December 29, 1966).

3. The Belgian Chamber was normally elected in a staggered manner, one half being renewed every two years (as in 1896 and 1898), except when a dissolution required the renewal of the whole body (as in 1894).

4. This was the case in Italy, Germany, Austria, and the Netherlands. In Belgium, which was divided into multimember constituencies, only the strongest candidates competed in the second round: twice as many candidates as there were seats to be distributed in the constituency.

5. This may lead to the conclusion that the most functional formula is one which by law limits the second round to the two strongest candidates. I do not agree. Especially when there is a sizable anti-system party and a loyal party of equal or greater size, such a double-ballot system would, in practice, operate as a plurality system—which is not desirable. Hence, I think that the second round ought to be open, at least to all those candidates who have obtained a certain *quorum* in the first round. This makes it possible, by means of alliances and bargained withdrawals, to oppose the anti-system candidate in a certain number of constituencies with the loyal candidate of party A, in other constituencies with the candidate of party B, and in other of party C. Thus, the party system is not forced into a two-party format, which is unsuitable for political situations characterized by the presence of an anti-system party with considerable electoral strength. In other words, it is true that in order to assure an adequate underrepresentation of the anti-system party, the party's candidate must be opposed by *only one* loyal candidate in each constituency. But it is not necessary that all loyal candidates in the various constituencies belong to *only one party*, as would in fact happen very often if access to the second round were limited to the two strongest candidates of the first round. I emphasize, therefore, that in this paragraph I refer to the open variety of the double-ballot system.

6. The two principal methods for formulating reliable predictions about party identification and regime image in a prospective general election are opinion surveys and the introduction of the double-ballot system on an experimental basis in local elections.

19

Semi-Proportional and Proportional Representation Systems in the United States

Leon Weaver

It is unrealistic to discuss options in electoral systems in the abstract, in the sense of a search for an ideal or optimum system that will best suit any situation regardless of circumstances. Realistic discussion becomes possible, but not necessarily easy, when one contemplates concrete situations, because behaviors of electorates and parties do not always conform to theory-of-choice principles. This essay undertakes to summarize experiences in the United States with proportional (PR) and semi-proportional (SPR) systems from the standpoint of what light those experiences can shed on electoral-system design for situations in this country.

In choosing or designing an electoral system for a given legislative body (assuming a multiple-seat rather than single-seat election), there are certain issues which have to be addressed at the outset. These seem to fall into two broad catagories or questions:

1. What priorities or weights are given to the purposes or values which electoral systems are supposed to serve? For example: Representativeness? Governmental decisiveness? Political consequences (including, but not limited to, advantageous or disadvantageous effects on various groups)? What trade-offs between these values are we prepared to accept?[1] It seems reasonable to posit that the answers to such questions should vary with "the situation." For example, in a national government that might have to make quick decisions in wartime when the enemy is at the gates, one could reasonably opt for top priority for decisiveness; but in local government it seems that we could safely alter the weights in the direction of more representativeness (Weaver 1980b). From such considerations would flow answers to other questions, such as: How important is it to have a "working majority" in the legislative body?

2. What is the "situation" or factual context in the governmental unit in which the electoral system is to function? Most of the important variables can probably be summarized under two categories: a) the personality of the community (e.g., homogeneous or

heterogeneous; conflict-ridden or comparatively consensual; etc.) and b) other components of the electoral system and general political system which affect the way a given electoral arrangement would function (e.g., a partisan or nonpartisan ballot; competitive or noncompetitive parties; etc.).

Although political scientists do not know everything we need to know, close students of electoral systems know enough to take premises established by answers to questions such as those discussed above and proceed to design electoral systems which, within limits, will serve certain purposes and values.

BROAD CHOICES

The charter drafter or legislator confronted with the problem of devising an electoral system for filling several seats on the same representative body has three broad choices: electing members at-large (AL)[2] whereby each voter has a vote for each of several offices to be filled; electing from single-member districts (SMD) or wards; and a PR or SPR system. If a PR system is chosen, a further choice exists between two principal subtypes: the party list (PR/PL) and single transferable vote (PR/STV) methods. If an SPR system is chosen the choice presumably lies between the subtypes which have been used in this country: cumulative voting (CV) and limited voting (LV).[3] To this list might be added whatever "combined" systems which decisionmakers wish to consider; such systems are discussed further below.

AT-LARGE (AL) and SINGLE-MEMBER DISTRICTS (SMD) COMPARED

In order to provide a basis for the ensuing discussion, the pros and cons of AL and SMD systems are summarized here, but only briefly; they are dealt with in a substantial and relatively convenient literature (for example: Newland 1982; Zimmerman 1972, Chapter 4; and Hamilton 1978, Chapter 2).

At-Large (AL)

Pro:

1) Representatives elected AL tend more to "represent the whole city" rather than more parochial viewpoints to which district representatives are perceived as being more susceptible. 2) Also, districting and redistricting problems are avoided.

Con:

1) There is a "sweep effect" or tendency, in that any party, slate-making organization, ethnic group, etc. that can get a bare majority (or plurality in any election that permits plurality winners) will tend to win all or most of the seats at stake, in effect allowing "the majority to defeat the minority on all fronts" (Justice William O. Douglas, Kilgarlin v. Hill, 386 U.S. 120, 1967). 2) Bodies elected at-large tend to be white middle-class people residing in a few of the "better" sections of the city (Zimmerman 1972, pp. 66–68; Berkeley 1966; Davidson and Korbel 1981). 3) As a result, many AL systems are vulnerable to attack on constitutional grounds (O'Rourke 1982). The "sweep effect," however, may be mitigated by other features of the system, such as the nonpartisan ballot.

Single-Member Districts (SMD)

Pro:

1) In comparison with AL systems, SMD systems, especially if it is assumed that nominees for office are required to reside in their districts,[4] are generally believed to bring the representative "closer" to his constituents, not only geographically but also in terms of social distance and interest. 2) Representation of all geographic areas of the governmental unit concerned. 3) Improvement of the prospects of representation of minorities. 4) Perceptions of constituents, especially lower-class ones, that their representative is more accessible (Heilig 1983). 5) Beneficial effects on voter interest and participation as a result of a "head-to-head" contest between two individual candidates. 6) A tendency to encourage a two-party system, since minor parties would not have a chance to elect candidates proportionate to their numbers unless, which would not often be the case, their supporters were optimally distributed with reference to district lines.

Con:

Important disadvantages of SMD systems as perceived by their critics are: 1) The voter's influence and interest tends to be confined to the single representative from his district, who tends to represent the parochial interests of that district rather than the whole community. 2) The obscurities of district politics elude scrutiny by press and public, and facilitate the development of self-serving cliques (Zimmerman 1972, pp. 68–69, citing Childs). 3) The necessity of drawing district lines present well-nigh intractable problems to one seeking a rational basis for such decisions; no matter how they are drawn, some groups are advantaged and others are disadvantaged. Gerrymandering exacerbates, but does not create, this problem. 4) Although under most SMD systems minorities will fare better than under AL systems, in many situations SMD is a weak strategy for minorities because they will tend to be underrepresented as compared to their fraction of the votes cast as a result of their concentration in a few districts where they "over-win" (pile up large majorities), or in other districts will be unrepresented because, although accounting for a substantial fraction of the votes, they are thinly spread and so do not win any district seats. 5) The "head-to-head-contest" argument is more fallacious than valid, because genuine competition is the exception rather than the rule in most districts; this becomes more true as one goes down the scale from national to state to local, because the districts become smaller and hence more demographically homogeneous (Weaver 1980b: Everson and Parker 1983).

In short, a district election is an AL election with one seat awarded on a "winner-take-all" basis. Combined AL and SMD systems will blend these advantages and disadvantages to the extent that the combined systems provide for a majority of the representatives to be elected AL or by SMD.

PR AND SPR SYSTEMS COMPARED WITH AL AND SMD

PR and SPR systems avoid some of the disadvantages of AL and SMD, but at the cost of some unique disadvantages. The principal pros and cons may be summarized briefly as follows.

Pro:

PR and SPR systems avoid the "sweep" tendency in AL systems without most of the difficulties and disadvantages inherent in SMD systems. 1) The avoidance of the need for drawing district boundaries and its attendant problems, including but not limited to gerrymandering, is an important advantage. 2) Another is that more representative legislative bodies, which such systems tend to bring about, are believed by some to promote compromise and consensus rather than unmitigated majoritarianism (Everson et al. 1982, p. 31); to reduce political alienation (Zimmerman 1971, but see Hamilton 1969); and to ventilate social conflict (National Advisory Commission on Civil Disorders 1968; Campbell, Sahid, and Stang 1970). 3) Some of the "extremists" which AL and SMD systems tend to exclude from representative bodies (see the next paragraph) are some who would command a broad consensus as being legislators of "extreme" ability and virtue.

Con:

PR and SPR systems are, however, at least in the eyes of their critics, subject to the following disadvantages: 1) Election of representatives of parochial outlook oriented to particular groups rather than to geographic districts, including "extremists" who would have no chance in AL or SMD systems. 2) Weakening of the two-party system by facilitating the formation of minor parties. 3) Difficulty of the largest party or a coalition of parties in the legislature in finding a stable majority, and consequent indecisiveness in the legislature. 4) In addition, some SPR systems suffer from crudities and the possibilities of chancy effects as discussed further below. 5) PR/STV, compared to other systems, is more complicated for the election administrator, and arguably so for the voter. 6) PR/PL needs parties; enhances their role; and, in some forms, increases the power of party officials over nominations; in some lexicons these effects might be perceived as advantageous.

EXPERIENCE WITH PROPORTIONAL (PR) AND SEMI-PROPORTIONAL (SPR) SYSTEMS

Experience with PR and SPR systems in the United States has been quite limited from a quantitative standpoint, but this experience has some important lessons for electoral systems designers. This section undertakes to summarize that experience. The principal focus here will be on SPR systems because these have been less documented and are less well understood than the PR systems (Weaver 1984) but some references to PR systems will be necessary for the sake of context.

The numbers of PR and SPR systems constitute a very small sample when compared with the total number of electoral systems in the United States, most of which are of the SMD variety (all national, virtually all state, and many local legislative seats), or in the AL category, which are found mostly at the local level. Limiting our consideration to this century, uses of PR or SPR as alternatives to SMD and AL can be summarized as follows: All of the PR systems have been STV rather than PL systems.[5] PR/STV systems have been used in approximately two dozen cities for city councils and school boards (Childs 1952, Chapter 26; 1965, pp. 65–68; Bromage 1962, p. 16; Hermens 1941, Chapter 14; Weaver 1984). These cases might conceivably be counted as five dozen if one wished to count the school committees in Massachusetts PR cities and the New York community school boards as separate cases.

There has been only one use of CV in this country during the modern era:[6] for the lower house of the state legislature in Illinois, recently repealed by referendum after being in use for 110 years (Everson et al. 1982; Everson and Parker 1983).

Generalizations concerning use of LV are more difficult because of complications resulting from the existence of several variant forms: 1) the limited vote without limited nominations (LV without LN); 2) limited nominations (LN); 3) a combination of the two (LV/LN); and 4) the "fixed-ratio" (FR) system in use for state boards and commissions and for some city councils in Connecticut. Although no accurate count is available at this time, it is estimated that the number of such cases would be on the order of two hundred, mostly in Connecticut and Pennsylvania.

A further description of the variant forms is required at this point. In essence, LV without LN consists in specifying that the voter shall have fewer votes than there are seats to be filled. LN means that a party is allowed to nominate only a specified number of people which is less than the number of seats to be filled. Both of these features appear in some systems which are characterized here as LV/LN. In FR systems there is a specification in the statute or charter of the relationship between the numbers of representatives of the parties and the number of seats to be filled. For example, on a body with three positions, it might be specified that no more than two may be filled by members and nominees of any one party, with the remaining seat to be filled by a member and nominee of the next largest party. (Although this is the form that the Connecticut statute takes, conceivably this method could also be extended to minor parties). A crosscutting variable is whether an electoral system is partisan or nonpartisan as far as ballot form is concerned. If it is nonpartisan (with nominations by petition and perhaps a nonpartisan primary), only the LV-without-LN form would be available; Rome, New York, would be an example (Emmert 1983). However, LN and LV/LN require a partisan system.

The extent of the use in the United States of the various forms of LV during this century[7] can be summarized as follows:

Limited Voting Without Limited Nominations (LV without LN).

LV (without concomitant LN) has been used in Rome, New York (in a previous charter); in Hartford, Connecticut (under a previous charter); currently in some other Connecticut cities and towns;[8] and in Pennsylvania counties.[9] LV without LN was also recently introduced into intraparty affairs as a court-ordered remedy in the Conecuh (Alabama) county Democratic Executive Committee.[10]

Limited Nominations (LN).

LN (without concomitant LV) has been used sparingly, but also in important jurisdictions: in a previous Indianapolis charter;[11] in a one-time at-large election of the House of Representatives in Illinois;[12] and for at-large members of the council in Washington, D.C.[13]

Combined Limited Voting and Limited Nominations (LV/LN).

Combined LV/LN systems are probably the best-known examples of LV: at-large borough representatives on the New York City Council;[14] at-large members of the councils in Hartford and West Hartford, Connecticut;[15] and at-large members of the council in Philadelphia.[16]

Fixed Ratio (FR).

FR systems are found in Connecticut, where they are established by charter for some cities and towns, and by statute for others. FR also applies to state boards and commissions, both elective and appointive.[17]

ANALYSIS OF EXPERIENCES WITH PR AND SPR SYSTEMS

In seeking generalizations from experiences with PR and SPR systems in the United States, we need to be aware of several problems: 1) The experiences have been shaped by the particular circumstances which have formed the political context for the evolution, and in some cases demise, of these systems; under different circumstances the experiences might have been different. 2) There is a *ceteris paribus* problem posed by the difficulty of disentangling the effects of the electoral system from the effects of other concomitant features of the political system. 3) The record is incomplete in that the workings of some PR/STV systems and most LV systems are undocumented in important respects.

However, scanning the record to the extent to which it exists permits some generalizations, some fairly firm and uncontroversial, and some of an admittedly tentative and hypothetical nature which are put forward here in the hope that they will stimulate other investigators to test them. Whether a statement falls into one such category or the other should be clear from the context.

Proportional Representation (PR)

All of the PR systems were and are in local government. All were and are STV systems. Of the twenty-two such[18] systems for election of city councils (and school committees in Massachusetts cities), all have been abandoned with one exception: Cambridge, Massachusetts. In addition, thirty-two community school boards in New York City have been elected since 1970 by PR/STV. Although these numbers are miniscule in comparison with the frequency of other election systems used in this country, and contrary to the impression one might gain from some standard works (such as Bromage 1962, p. 16), acquaintance-ship with political life in present PR systems in Cambridge and New York City leaves no doubt that in these few situations PR is still alive and well, and there do not appear to be any substantial initiatives to eliminate it. The above statement may be suprising to some, and disagreed with by others, reflecting the extent to which the existing literature focuses on PR abandonments and does not give commensurate attention to the survivals (Weaver 1984).

The reasons for the abandonments appear to have had little if anything to do with PR's theoretical merits, such relatively exact reflection of various groups in the electorate on the legislative body (Hallett 1940; Wright 1980), or demerits (such as an alleged tendency to produce factionalism, unstable majorities, and indecision). Such reasons are to be found more in such factors as the enmity of majority party leaders to whom the nonpartisan ballot and loss of control over nominations may have been as important a consideration as the ballot form and counting rules; vulnerability of the PR system to local repeal referenda; and their attrition on the resources and zeal of reform groups which constituted the main base of PR support (Weaver 1984).

The survivals, on the other hand, seem to be accounted for largely by such factors as demographic and political mixes which place a premium on the virtues of PR (such as "representativeness" and a tendency to facilitate compromise); a strong citizen-support group in the case of Cambridge; and enactment by state legislation rather than local referendum in the case of the New York City school boards (Weaver 1984).

SPR Systems

SPR systems are in contrast with PR systems in that the former have shown a high survival rate. This phenomenon is especially remarkable in the case of LV in that, as compared to PR and CV, it is largely undocumented insofar as its specific effects are concerned.

Cumulative Voting (CV).

CV was adopted for the lower house of the Illinois legislature in the Constitution of 1870 in an effort to diminish sectionalism and bitterness following the Civil War by affording minority Republicans in the southern part of the state and minority Democrats in the northern part opportunities for representation which they would not have had in an SMD system. Subsequent experience and research validated that this result was achieved, but at the cost of some unintended consequences, such as noncompetitiveness in general elections in many districts because the majority party would nominate only two and the minority party only one candidate. To some critics, this behavior smacked of interparty collusion, and was hardly offset by the tendency of such a system to generate vigorous competition in party primaries, to which CV was also applied.[19]

The principal reason why CV lasted so long in Illinois was that it was based on a bargain between the major parties and was an expression of a "live-and-let-live" approach to political competition, in contrast with a spirit of gamesmanship inherent in "winner-take-all" systems. Its demise is best understood as resulting from the confluence of some particular and perhaps unique historical developments.

Although the voters of the state decisively voted to keep CV in 1970 (in a separate proposition in a referendum on a new constitution), in 1980 they also decisively voted to abolish it in favor of SMD. The change of the results is accounted for by the 1980 proposal to abolish CV being linked to a proposal to decrease the size of the lower house, a proposal which had its genesis in the public outcry when the lower house voted pay raises for its members which were substantially higher than those for other state officials. In the conservative political climate of the 1980 general election, the overblown argument that the proposal would reduce state government costs overshadowed the issue of CV versus SMD.

The consensus of considerable scholarly research on this system is that, despite the crudeness of the method, it achieved near proportional representation as far as the two major parties were concerned. This effect was accomplished by trade-offs which some people consider unfortunate, such as numerous (approximately half) of the general elections being noncompetitive (only three candidates nominated); and lesser working majorities and less party discipline in the legislative body than would be the case in an SMD system.

Although the differences in results produced by the CV system and the SMD system which replaces it will probably not be as great as both proponents and opponents of CV have claimed, there probably will be important differences, as pointed out by Everson and Parker (1983, p. 33):

> The style, substance and "feel" of the House undoubtedly will change. It will probably become more orderly and dignified like the Senate...What may be gained or lost as a result of greater party homogeneity and cohesion is difficult to predict. Whether the public policy of the state will be significantly altered can be doubted. In that sense, the [amendment] was more of a ripple than a wave. Illinois' unique experiment in representation has been ended for reasons which seem, in retrospect, to be insubstantial.

An important question remains unanswered: whether the consequences of CV in Illinois are inherent[20] in the CV principle or were specific to that particular application of the principle; and whether those consequences would be different in kind or degree if the principle were applied with a different methodology in a different political culture. For example, it is doubtful if such negative consequences would be the same if the method were applied in a situation including a nonpartisan ballot; a political culture embodying low or no party involvement; and nomination by petition (perhaps without a primary, perhaps with a nonpartisan primary in the event people nominated exceeded twice the number of seats).

Limited Voting (LV).

Assessment of the experiences with LV in the United States must be carried out within the serious limitations posed by the state of the literature. Probably the greatest irony encountered by this investigator is the relative dearth of empirical literature concerning the practical workings of LV systems; in contrast to PR and CV, LV systems have been more widely adopted and have shown greater capability to survive, but they have been written about very little as compared to CV in Illinois, and to PR/STV.

The principal reasons for LV adoptions appear to be: 1) A desire to avoid exclusion or near exclusion of the minority party from the legislative body which results in many AL and SMD systems; in some cases, as Featherman (1980) has persuasively shown, the *appearance* of minority party representation apparently was more important to the adopters than the reality, as far as efficacy is concerned, although there may be important values other than effective minority party participation in legislative decisionmaking. 2) Simplicity; the method is simpler than CV, and much simpler than PR/STV.

The simplicity carries with it an important trade-off: crudeness. Whether the relationship between seats to be filled and the lesser number of votes given the voter is reasonable depends on the division of voters between parties, "slates," factions, etc., and may vary over time[21] if political alignments and voter divisions change. Whether the crudeness results in a reasonably close approach to proportionality in the system as a whole (as in the case of CV in Illinois) must await empirical research yet to be done. The test of proportionality will presumably turn on whether the relationship between number of seats to be filled and votes given the voter is congruent with political cleavages. The fact that minority party representation in the better-known systems, such as Philadelphia, New York, and Washington D.C., are less than proportional to their share of the vote is not inherent in the LV principle, but rather results from a half-hearted application of the principle (only to at-large members of the council, whose numbers are exceeded by district representatives).

The principal reasons for the survival of LV systems appear to be that 1) they are based on interparty bargains (in contrast to the PR/STV systems) and 2) are expressions of a "live-and-let-live" political culture that accords with the values of the electorates involved. This sentiment is given only minimal expression in systems where LV is used to allow only underrepresentation of the minority as an alternative to exclusion or near exclusion from the legislative body; but such an attitude is sometimes given exaggerated expression in systems which consistently, and apparently by intent of the designers of the system, *overrepresent* a minority.

It is cogently argued (Featherman 1980, p. 20) from Pennsylvania data that "the values of limited voting are apparently sufficiently meager, even under the best circumstances, as to raise concerns as to whether it is worth utilizing." Assuming, for the sake of argument, that this statement is correct with regard to the Pennsylvania jurisdiction examined, it leaves us with the familiar question: are the negative consequences of LV in Pennsylvania inherent in the LV principle or are they specific to the particular applications of the LV principle in that state? Tantalizing glimpses of LV systems in Connecticut and in Rome, New York (in a nonpartisan system under a previous charter as described by Emmert 1983) lead this writer to suspect that LV systems can be designed to incorporate many capabilities and values, if the designers can agree on them, to an extent unrealized in most extant examples of LV, subject, of course, to limitations and trade-offs which may be inherent in choices the designers make. If this is true, then empirical research to define and test the possibilities and the limits of LV should have a high priority on the research agenda.

Comparisons

The foregoing discussion of experiences in the United States with PR and SPR systems permits some comparisons between PR and SPR systems, and between CV and LV.

SPR Compared with PR.

There is no question that, from the standpoint of pure decision theory, PR is considerably superior to the SPR methods, which embody only a crude proportionality dependent on the relationship between the cleavage in voting strengths at the polls and the number of votes exercised by each voter, as provided by the designers of the electoral system. Indeed, from the standpoint of pure game theory, the SPR systems are vulnerable to strategic voting to the point where majority-minority relationships in votes can occasionally be reversed in the allocation of seats (Brams 1975; Newland 1982, pp. 32–33, 35–37, 55–56; Bogdanor 1981, pp. 103–104). However, while these possible negative effects would have to be given considerable weight if SPR were proposed for use in a body small enough to permit the communication and discipline necessary for strategic voting, these objections do not seem to be nearly as weighty when SPR methods are applied in electorates large enough to render strategic voting difficult and perhaps impossible. In such electorates, it appears that the superiority of PR over SPR in the seats:votes relationship may be only marginal. For example, Newman and Rogers (1953) found that, in a Cambridge PR election, the same candidates usually would have been elected if the voters' first choices had been treated as unranked approvals, as is the case with LV. Everson et al. (1982) found that CV in Illinois produced a seats:votes relationship close to proportionality, although occasional anomalies at the district level were observed. These considerations suggest that, in situations where there is considerable resistance to PR methods, whether justified or not, it would be reasonable to accept CV or LV, assuming knowledgeable application of the methods, because of their simplicity as compared to PR/STV, at least as painted by its critics. Isn't approximate proportionality close enough?

CV and LV Compared.

From the standpoint of acceptance and survival, LV in this country has demonstrated its superiority to CV, but this consideration is hardly dispositive. The Illinois application of CV was but one case; whether the dissatisfactions it encountered there were specific to that application or generic is a question that must await further study. Additional empirical studies of LV in its variant forms are also needed for more definitive judgments concerning it. In the meantime, people who have to make a choice between CV and LV will have to make it mainly on the basis of the theory-of-choice and pragmatic considerations discussed further below.

CUSTOM-TAILORING AN ELECTORAL SYSTEM

To return to the theme with which we started, and which is the central preoccupation of this volume: How should we choose or design an electoral system? From what has been said above it must be apparent by now that this writer believes that the answer to that question must be sought not in a quest for an ideal or optimum system which is best for any situation regardless of circumstances, but in research-validated techniques which enable us to custom-tailor a system composed of features which, in a particular set of conditions, conduce toward results in line with our values.

Following this line of thinking results in an attitude of acceptance of a fairly broad range of electoral systems *provided* they fit "the situation"; and a realization that choices between systems involve compromises and trade-offs between various values. A brief explication of this position is best served by examples:

1. *The home town.* Population: four thousand. Homogeneous population. Little or no political competition. Nonpartisan ballot and political culture. A community where local government serves primarily as a "caretaker" because there are virtually no issues and little or no social conflict. An AL system is acceptable, and probably preferable. Why not? Since people in one part of town are much like people in the other parts, districting would seem to be superfluous, and so would a PR or SPR system.

2. *The dormitory suburb.* Population: forty thousand. Considerable social stratification by neighborhoods, but the range in SES is narrow and there is no substantial racial or ethnic conflict because practically everybody is a WASP. Rapid growth. Consequently, politics is dominated by the politics of development (planning, zoning, etc.). The present partisan ballot is being replaced in a new Home Rule charter by a nonpartisan ballot. Under the present partisan AL system the minority party, which normally polls forty to forty-five percent of the vote, virtually never elects a council member. It is estimated that with a nonpartisan ballot, party involvement will be low, but probably not lowest on the scale of Adrian's (1959) typology. A proposed SMD system has districts

that conform well to existing neighborhoods, that are reasonably compact, and that contain social mixes which should result in a council considerably more representative of geographical areas, social groups, and the minority party than the present one. Therefore, why not accept the SMD system?

3. *Minimetropolis.* Population: One hundred thousand. Wide variations in socioeconomic status. Considerable conflict; cleavages concern racial, ethnic, religious, school, and residential-development issues. Dynamic population changes. Changing neighborhoods. Economic decline for industry, but increase for think-tanks and high-tech enterprises. An AL system combined with primaries would result in a council dominated by the largest ethnic group, one committed to traditionalist and conservative instincts, and one which would probably carry out policies which would exacerbate social conflict. These effects might be somewhat mitigated by a district system, but because of the geographic distribution of group strengths the reform political organization and its minority-group supporters would be seriously underrepresented. In such a situation the reasonable alternatives seem to dwindle down to some kind of PR or SPR system, perhaps in multiseat districts.

4. *Maximetropolis.* Population: 1 million and up. Conditions somewhat similar to Minimetropolis, but more varied and more complex. Same conclusion.

In short, if an AL or SMD system, or some combination of them, will result in a legislative body that is reasonably representative of the principal social and political groups, they would be acceptable, and perhaps preferable. The rub is that in many situations (more than many proponents of AL or SMD systems seem to recognize or acknowledge) an AL or SMD system demonstrably will not meet this condition.

If a PR or SPR system is considered, which should it be? Again, "it depends on the situation." The superiority of PR/STV from the standpoint of the theory of choice is demonstrable, at least in this writer's opinion, and sufficiently so that the advantages outweigh the disadvantages as perceived by the critics (such as a more complex task for the voter and for counting officials). Such criticisms are usually exaggerated and sometimes self-serving. However, this is hardly the end of the matter. Historical experience suggests strongly that, unless a PR/STV system can develop a strong and self-renewing constituency, it will not survive. As for PR/PL, the inattention to and disinterest in it in this country is a puzzle. Perhaps the reason is that such support as has existed for PR systems has been almost exclusively channeled into PR/STV.

If a SPR approach is considered, should it be CV or LV? Experience suggests that each is subject to limitations, trade-offs (Newland 1982, pp. 35–37, 55–56, 59, 79, 85), and sometimes unintended consequences (Brams 1975, pp. 116–121; Everson and Parker 1983; Bogdanor 1981, pp. 103–104); but these possibly can be minimized by careful design. On theory-of-choice grounds, Newland (1982, pp. 36, 56, 59) recommends LV in its single nontransferable vote (SNTV) form, but if the voter is given two or more votes, he recommends CV. Appraisal of experience in the United States leads to a more guarded judgment. The experience in Illinois with CV suggests that, in a partisan election system, public perceptions of the system lead to dissatisfaction in substantial parts of the electorate when party leaders' strategies, for whatever reasons, result in uncontested general elections. Whether this problem can be countered or minimized by design features is an interesting question; the problem may be minimized or nonexistent in nonpartisan systems. The experience with LV tends to suggest its superiority to CV on three grounds: 1) the greater simplicity for the voter and election officials; 2) its flexibility in terms of availability of several subtypes; and 3) its record of greater acceptance and survival. This judgment, however, must be considered as only tentative until empirical studies can be carried out on LV in its variant forms.

Instead of preoccupation with debates in the abstract concerning such issues as proportional versus nonproportional systems in general, we need to give more attention to methods for compensating for the recognized weaknesses in any given system by designing in countervailing tendencies or by combining two or more components which tend to compensate for each other.[22]

CONCLUDING COMMENTS

Although the experiences analyzed in this chapter suggest guidelines for the designer of electoral systems, the guidelines will not emancipate the designer from an issue or dilemma that lies at the core of the idea of representative government itself: the tension between *representing* and *governing*.

The opponents of PR and SPR fear that, in some situations, representing will be maximized at the expense of governing; proponents believe that acceptable trade-offs between the two are possible and desirable. At issue are different weights given to different models of politics: (1) decisive government, which is facilitated by a "working majority" in the legislature and which, in turn, may be dependent on overrepresentation of the majority or, in plurality systems, a plurality (Weaver 1980b); or (2) as representative a body as possible, which places a premium on interparty or interbloc bargaining, compromise, and consensus (Everson et al. 1082, p. 31). "You pays your money and you takes your choice."

In the judgment of this writer, the relative merits or weights which might reasonably be given to these positions vary with "the situation," the case for proportionality becoming stronger as one approaches the local level because the kinds of decisions made there make the adverse consequences of delays and compromises (if they occur) less serious and because citizens' perceptions of government in general seem to be affected by their experiences with local government (Heilig 1983).

NOTES

1. The first two values (representativeness and decisiveness) are usually discussed as if they are always (rather than sometimes) competitive. Yet, there must be cases where making government

more representative would also make it more decisive, as in the case where there is a majority consensus in the electorate which is frustrated by an unrepresentative electoral system.

2. There are several variants or subtypes of the AL system: 1) the "place" system, wherein a candidate competes only for a designated seat rather than against all candidates for all vacant seats; it is therefore an election for a single place. 2) Nomination by districts, but elections at-large. 3) Residence requirements (for a district "place," although the election is still at-large). 4) The "unmodified" AL system, also sometimes termed the "general-ticket," "block vote," or "9X" system (assuming there are nine places to be filled) (Lakeman 1974, Chapter 2; Heisel 1982; Straetz 1958). A multiseat district may also be regarded as a variant of the AL system. Historically, the "place" system was developed to render ineffective resort by minorities to the "single-shot" (or "bullet") ballot whereby only one first-choice candidate would be supported lest votes for other candidates defeat him (Young 1965; Davidson and Korbel 1981).

3. The limited vote (LV) and cumulative vote (CV) represent attempts to prevent the "sweep effect" in AL systems, without the methods of PR/PL or PR/STV. LV in principle requires the voter to vote for fewer candidates than there are seats to be filled. A cumulative vote (CV) system gives the voter as many votes as there are seats to be filled and permits him to concentrate all of them on one candidate or otherwise allocate them in accordance with his preferences. The single nontransferable vote (SNTV) may be considered a variant of LV (Newland 1982, pp. 34–37, 54–55), but it will be discussed only tangentially here because there are no documented instances of its use in this country. Concerning SPR systems generally, see Newland (1982) and Lakeman (1974, pp. 80–89). Readers who wish to consult short descriptions of PR/STV methodology are referred to Zimmerman (1972, pp.78–79), Lakeman (1974, Chapters 6, 7 and 8), and Newland (1982, Chapter 7).

4. Not the case universally—e.g., MPs in Great Britain, but practically universally in this country by virtue of strong custom in the case of United States Senators and Representatives in Congress, and de jure in most state and local systems.

5. However, the representation systems for the Senate and House of Representatives in Puerto Rico are essentially PR/PL systems since they provide that, in the event a party elects more than two-thirds of either house (from a combined SMD and AL system), the underrepresented parties shall have their delegations increased until their proportion in the legislature approximates their proportion of the vote for governor. Puerto Rico Constitution, Art. III, Sec. 7. Cintron-Garcia v. Romero-Barcelo.

6. Some nineteenth century examples can be found in New York (Weaver 1980a, p. 45, note 13).

7. LV was also used in Boston during the nineteenth century (Weaver 1980a, p. 45, note 11).

8. Connecticut Law Review 1969, p. 200; Connecticut Public Expenditure Council 1981. For Connecticut case law, see note 17.

9. Pennsylvania Statutes Annotated, Title 16, Sec. 501 and 3501; Kaelin v. Warden.

10. Gray v. Robson; Evergreen [Alabama] Courant, August 5, 1982. p. 1.

11. Indianapolis Municipal Code (1951) Sec. 2-101 (in effect through 1967).

12. Andrews 1966; People v. Carpentier.

13. District of Columbia Self Government and Governmental Reorganization Act, P.L. 93-198, 93rd. Cong. 87 Stat. 744 (1973), Secs. 401 (b) (2) and 401 (d) (3); Hechinger v. Martin.

14. New York City Charter, Ch. 2, Sec. 22 (1963); Zimmerman 1969, p. 17; Blaikie v. Power; Andrews v. Koch. At-large borough representatives have been eliminated in New York as a result of court decisions finding that part of the system unconstitutional, not on grounds that involved the limited-vote principle, but on the grounds that allocation of two seats to each borough regardless of population violated the one person–one vote principle (New York Times, May 28, 1983, p. 27).

15. Connecticut General Statutes Annotated, Title 9 (Elections), Sec. 167a; Connecticut Public Expenditure Council 1968, 1981; Littlefield 1965. For Connecticut case law, see note 17.

16. Philadelphia Home Rule Charter (1951), Sec. 2-100 and 101; Zimmerman (1969, p. 18); Featherman (1980).

17. The "Minority Representation" statute: Connecticut General Statutes Annotated, Title 9 (Elections), Sec. 167a. Statutory provisions regarding specific offices are: 9-197 (assessors); 9-199

(boards of tax review); 9-204 (boards of education); 9-188 (boards of selectmen). Connecticut Law Review (1969, p. 197); Littlefield (1965, p. 386); Connecticut Public Expenditure Council (1981). There is a substantial body of case law on FR and other aspects of minority representation in Connecticut: Anderson v. Ludgin. Blanco v. Gangloff. Hoblitzelle v. Frechette. Lo Frisco v. Schaffer. Montano v. Lee. State ex. rel. Chapman v. Tinker.

18. With the exception of New York, these were all council-manager cities and were only a little over one percent of council-manager cities (Weaver 1985).

19. Except where otherwise noted, this section on CV is based on Everson et al. (1982, pp. 7–8, 23–33); and Everson and Parker (1983, pp. 14–17).

20. It is suggested by Blair (1960, pp. 130–34) that they are not.

21. This problem seems susceptible of solution if election system designers have the will to find a way. The outlines of such a way are suggested as follows: Provide for a commission analogous to a reapportionment commission to meet periodically, such as once a decade, to carry out the essentially ministerial function of adjusting the proportions between seats to be filled and votes which the voter may cast, using as the criterion the relationship between votes cast for the winning and runner-up candidates for chief executive (or some other contest). Moving averages also might be incorporated into the arrangement.

22. Examples would be: 1) Combined SMD and AL systems; these are widely used in local government in this country, but it is a weak approach; each subsystem has the deficiencies already noted, and these cancel out only slightly. 2) Combined SMD and PR/PL systems, as exemplified in the lower house in West Germany and in Puerto Rico; limitations of this approach are given by Newland (1982, pp. 57–59). 3) If in a PR/PL system no party or coalition has a majority, it is given a "premium" in the form of extra seats if, in the case of a coalition, its constituent parties present the electorate with a common program before the election (Barzini 1982). 4) A rule such as has been suggested by Hermens (1976, p. 51) which would establish an upper limit to the size of the permissible legislative majority of a party to compensate for the tendency of a majority party to be overrepresented in an AL or SMD system. This suggestion essentially calls for the application of the FR variant of LV to a legislature elected by SMD, whereas LV/FR applications in Connecticut are in AL systems.

CASES

Combined System in Puerto Rico
Cintron-Garcia v. Romero-Barcelo 671 F. 2d 1 (1982)
Limited Voting
Alabama. Gray v. Robson U.S. District Court for the Southern District of Alabama, Southern Division, CA 82-0491-H (1982)
Connecticut. Anderson v. Ludgin 400 A. 2d 712 (1970). Blanco v. Gangloff 265 A. 2d 502 (1970). LoFrisco v. Schaffer 341 F. Supp. 743 (1972). Judgment affirmed 93 S. Ct. 313 (1972); 409 U.S. 972; 34 L. Ed. 2d 236. Montano v. Lee 401 F. 2d 214 (1968); 208 F. Supp. 871 (1968); 384 F. 2d 172 (1967)
District of Columbia. Hechinger v. Martin 411 F. Supp. 650 (1976)
Illinois. People v. Carpentier 30 Ill. 2d 590; 198 N.E. 2d 517 (1964)
New York. Andrews v. Koch 528 Fed. Supp. 248 (1981). Blaikie v. Power 375 U.S. 439 (1964); 11 L. Ed. 2d 471; 84 S. Ct. 507; 913 NE 2d 55 (1963); 13 N.Y. 2d 134; 243 NYS 2d 185. Appeal dismissed (Memorandum) 375 U.S. 439 (1964); 11 L. Ed. 2d 84; S. Ct. 507
Pennsylvania. Kaelin v. Warden 334 F. Supp. 602 (1971)

20

Trying to Have the Best of Both Worlds: Semi-Proportional and Mixed Systems*

Arend Lijphart

Among the many controversies and disagreements in the field of electoral systems, the main one divides the advocates of proportional representation (PR) from the partisans of the plurality method. Each camp is firmly convinced of the superior merits of its electoral system. This state of affairs prompts the following question which I shall attempt to answer in this chapter: Are there any electoral systems halfway between plurality and PR or combining some of the features of plurality with some of those of PR, which provide the advantages of both systems? Is it possible to find an electoral system that has the best of both worlds? If the answer should be yes, the disagreement between plurality and PR proponents would be effectively settled. And, of course, we would have found the "ideal" electoral system. My answer, unfortunately, will be a qualified no.

There are two types of electoral systems that may be said to aim at having the best of both the PR and plurality worlds: semi-proportional and mixed systems. Semi-proportional systems entail the conceptualization of plurality and PR as the two extreme points of a continuum; the assumption is that the semi-proportional systems can be located somewhere in the middle of this continuum. Hence semi-proportional systems can also be called semi-plurality systems. Mixed systems do not involve the assumption of an underlying PR–plurality continuum but simply try to combine the most desirable features of each. I shall define the term "mixed" later, but I should point out right away that this category does not include the West German additional-member system, which is sometimes erroneously described as mixed, but which is mainly a PR system (see

---

*This chapter is, to a large extent, based on Lijphart (1984) and Lijphart, Lopez Pintor, and Sone (1984).

Chapter 15 in this volume). My examples will be taken from legislative elections at the national level.

In my evaluation of the semi-proportional and mixed systems, I shall concentrate on the primary advantages of PR and plurality and on a few of their secondary advantages. The main advantage that plurality advocates cite for their system is that it encourages a two-party system—which, in turn, makes stable one-party governments in parliamentary regimes possible. Although plurality is neither a necessary nor a sufficient condition for two-party systems—Austria has a two-party system without plurality and Canada does not have a strict two-party system in spite of its plurality rule—the logical and empirical links are indeed strong. The secondary advantages of plurality are its great simplicity, the fact that it allows a vote for individual candidates instead of party lists (a characteristic shared, of course, with the single transferable vote form of PR), and that it permits close contact between each representative and his or her constituents. Especially the last advantage presupposes that the plurality method is applied in single-member districts—which is usually the case for national elections. The overriding advantage that PR partisans see in PR is that it yields more or less proportional results. This is regarded as a value in and of itself, but it is also considered to be especially important because it allows minority representation.

SEMI-PROPORTIONAL SYSTEMS: THE LIMITED VOTE AND SNTV

Of the various systems that have been described as semi-proportional (see Lakeman 1974, pp. 82–91), only one type is empirically important: the limited vote, including as a special subtype the single nontransferable vote or SNTV. The only other semi-proportional method worth mentioning is the cumulative vote, but it has never been used at the national level and was recently abolished in Illinois, long its major showcase.

The limited vote resembles the plurality method in two important respects: the voters cast their votes for individual candidates, and the candidates who receive the largest numbers of votes are the winners. The main difference is that the limited vote, as its name suggests, limits the voter to fewer votes than there are seats at stake in the district, whereas the plurality method gives each voter exactly as many votes as the numbers of district seats. The single nontransferable vote (SNTV) is a special case of the limited vote in which each voter has only one vote in a district electing two or more representatives. The second difference between limited and plurality voting is a logical corollary of the first: the plurality method can be applied both in single-member and in multimember districts, whereas the limited vote requires multimember districts. Moreover, at the national level plurality is in fact most often used in single-member districts. The most important difference is that the limited vote, unlike plurality, facilitates minority representation to some extent. In this respect, the limited vote resembles PR rather than plurality.

The limited vote and SNTV have been used only rarely for national elections. The best-known historical example consists of a few constituencies in British general elections in the late nineteenth century: twelve three-member districts in which each voter had two votes and one four-member district with three votes per voter (Bogdanor 1981, pp. 101–104). The two contemporary national-level examples are the SNTV elections of the Japanese House of Representatives and the limited vote elections of the Spanish upper house, the Senate (Stockwin 1983; Martinez Cuadrado 1983). Most of the Japanese SNTV districts are three-member, four-member, and five-member districts, in which each voter has one vote. Of the 511 representatives, 510 are elected in this manner; one is elected in a single-member district, which is necessarily a plurality instead of an SNTV district. Of the 239 Spanish senators, 197 are elected by the limited vote in four-member districts, in which each voter has three votes, and in a few three-member districts with two votes for each voter. The other 42 senators are chosen by plurality in single-member or two-member districts or indirectly elected by the regional assemblies.

How well do the limited vote and SNTV perform in terms of the respective advantages of plurality and PR listed earlier? Let us first look at the criterion of minority representation. How high a threshold does a minority party have to surmount in order to win a seat in a district? There are two thresholds to be considered: the threshold of representation and the threshold of exclusion (Rae, Hanby, and Loosemore 1971; Lijphart and Gibberd 1977). The threshold of exclusion is the percentage of the vote that will guarantee the winning of a seat even under the most unfavorable circumstances. For instance, in a four-member SNTV district, the least favorable situation for a minority party is to face one large majority party with four candidates who each receive exactly equal shares of the majority supporters' votes. However, if the minority has only one candidate who receives slightly more than twenty percent of the votes, the minority candidate is assured of election; because the four majority candidates have to share the remaining votes, totaling slightly less than eighty percent, they cannot have more than twenty percent each. Hence the threshold of exclusion in this case is twenty percent.

In the Japanese SNTV system, the threshold of exclusion is twenty-five percent in the three-member districts, twenty percent in the four-member districts, and 16.7 percent for the five-member districts. In Spain, the three-member and four-member districts have thresholds of 40.0 and 42.9 percent respectively. Relatively small parties can obviously not benefit much from the Spanish system. Their chances are enhanced when each voter has only one vote—that is, in SNTV systems—and in large districts. In fact, small parties have about equally good chances under SNTV as under STV, which is a PR system, because the SNTV threshold of exclusion is virtually identical with the so-called Droop quota of votes that entitles a candidate to be declared elected under STV.

It is also possible, of course, that a minority party wins a seat with fewer votes than the threshold of exclusion. The threshold of representation is the vote percentage that may be sufficient to win a seat under the most favorable conditions. The limited vote and SNTV have the unusual property that the latter threshold is almost zero. For instance, if all but two of the voters in a three-member SNTV district concentrate their votes on one candidate, two other candidates can be elected with one vote each. This example shows that SNTV entails special problems for the larger parties, and hence some special advantages for the smaller ones.

The small parties can follow a simple strategy: they should nominate as many candidates as each voter has votes and ask their voters to support these candidates. The larger parties face two problems. First, they have to decide how many candidates they can safely nominate. Nominating too few candidates is unwise because a party can obviously not win more seats than it has candidates in a district. Nominating too many candidates runs the risk of splitting the majority's votes and consequently losing one or more seats. Secondly, nominating the "correct" number of candidates is not enough: the party also has to instruct its voters to distribute their votes as equally as possible among its candidates. In the 1980 elections in Japan, thirty-two seats were lost as a result of undernomination, overnomination, and unequal vote distribution. Significantly, thirty of these thirty-two seats were lost by the largest party, the Liberal Democrats. In the Spanish Senate elections of 1982, no party attempted to nominate more candidates in any district than the number of votes at the disposal of each voter. A more aggressive strategy could have resulted in the winning of all of a district's seats by the strongest party in thirty-one of the fifty limited vote districts.

How proportional were the 1980 Japanese and 1982 Spanish election results? In Japan, the Liberal Democrats were overrepresented and most of the smaller parties somewhat underrepresented by the SNTV system—but not more so than would have been the case under STV. When the effects of malapportionment, favoring the Liberal Democrats, and unequal voter turnout are controlled, the conclusion does not change: SNTV yields results that are not significantly different from STV. In Spain, as expected, the overrepresentation of the largest party, the Socialists, was much more pronounced, and STV would have given much more proportional results. Here again, the pattern does not change when malapportionment and voter turnout are controlled. The election result closely resembled that of a plurality election: the two largest parties, Socialists and Popular Alliance, were overrepresented; the third party, the Union of the Democratic Center, was severely underrepresented; but two even smaller but geographically concentrated parties, the Catalan and Basque Nationalists, obtained fairly good results. (For a more detailed analysis of these two elections, see Lijphart, Lopez Pintor, and Sone 1984.)

This pattern also demonstrates that there is an inverse relationship between the primary advantages of PR and plurality which the different forms of the limited vote may be able to provide. SNTV is about as proportional as STV, but it also does as little to promote a two-party system as STV. The Spanish limited vote system helps the largest parties, but it is quite unproportional and discriminates against minorities except the regionally concentrated ones. Only one, less significant, combination of advantages can be attributed to SNTV: it can yield about the same degree of proportionality as STV, but it has the same simplicity as plurality—one vote cast for one candidate—and does not require STV's more complicated ranking of candidates.

MIXED SYSTEMS: PLURALITY WITH SPECIAL MINORITY PROVISIONS

The mixed systems start out with the basic rule of plurality—the voters cast as many votes as there are seats in the district for individual candidates, and the candidates with the largest vote totals are elected—and then add further rules in-order to obtain a fair representation of minorities. There are two types of additional rules for minority representation: (1) the establishment of electoral districts reserved for minority voters, as exemplified by New Zealand, Cyprus, and Zimbabwe, and (2) the requirement that the voters cast their votes for ethnically balanced slates of candidates, as in Lebanon (Lijphart 1984).

The first type of mixed system entails districts that are defined not only in terms of geography, as is usually the case in plurality systems, but also in terms of ethnic group membership. For instance, four of New Zealand's ninety-two single-member districts consist of the Maori voters in four areas of the country (McRobie 1978). The 1960 election in Cyprus was held in separate Greek and Turkish districts in six areas, that is, in a total of twelve both geographically and ethnically defined areas (Nuscheler 1969). In Zimbabwe's 1980 election, blacks elected eighty representatives in eight multimember districts, and whites voted in twenty single-member districts; this last example is imperfect, because the eight black districts used PR, but the principle of delimiting districts by both geographical and ethnic criteria is the same as in New Zealand and Cyprus (Gregory 1981).

If these districts contain equal populations, a proportional representation of the minority is assured, while at the same time the plurality rule does not have to be violated. Hence, these mixed systems appear to offer an excellent combination of the advantages of PR and plurality. However, the requirement of separate ethnic voter registers entails two serious problems. The first is that it may be difficult to decide which ethnic groups do, and which groups do not, deserve to be recognized as "official" minorities. One of the advantages of regular PR is that it allows the representation of any minority that wishes to be represented without a prior official determination as to which minorities should be singled out for special treatment. The second problem is that, after the ethnic groups have been officially designated, it may be hard to assign individual voters to the ethnic districts. Moreover, the very principle of registering individuals according to their ethnicity may be controversial, or even completely unacceptable, to many citizens.

A partial solution to the second problem was found in New Zealand in 1975, when the Maori districts were made optional. Maoris were given the choice of remaining on the separate Maori voter register or to put their names on the general electoral register and to vote in a regular district. This kind of solution eases the problem of labeling individuals according to ethnic affiliation against their wishes, but it does not solve the problem of making the invidious distinction between groups entitled to and barred from special minority representation.

A different solution to the second problem has been found in religiously divided Lebanon. One part of the Lebanese solution is to establish some geographical districts with largely homogeneous populations. The 1960 electoral law set up ten districts of this kind electing about one-fourth of the legislators. In each of these districts, only members of the district's dominant sect can be candidates: Maronites in four districts. Shi'a Moslems in three, Sunnis in two and Greek Orthodox candidates in one. The more important part of the Lebanese electoral system concerns the election of representatives in heterogeneous districts according to a predetermined proportional sectarian ratio. For instance, in the four-member Akkar district, two seats are reserved for Sunni Moslems, one for a Maronite, and one for a Greek Orthodox representative. The ballots normally contain two or more proportionally constituted slates as well as individual candidates. In the Akkar district, the slates must consist of two Sunni, one Maronite, and one Greek Orthodox candidate. Most voters cast their votes for one of these slates, but they may also select candidates from different slates or from the independents as long as they do so according to the predetermined 2:1:1 sectarian ratio for the district (Baaklini 1976, pp. 145–47).

The advantage of the Lebanese system is that it does not require separate voter rolls. The only prerequisites are a determination of the sectarian composition of each district, based on census data or estimates, and clear identification of the group affiliation of each candidate. A serious weakness, however, is that it violates the basic principle of representation: being the representative of a certain group means not just belonging to that group but being chosen by the group. This also entails an important practical drawback. As Pierre Rondot (1966, pp. 132–33) points out, each legislator elected in one of the larger heterogeneous districts "is above all the representative of members of communities other than his own...To be elected as a deputy, a man must be a compromise candidate. The typical champions of each community run the risk...of being passed over in favor of tamer individuals." As a result, the deputies are not the true spokesmen for the sects, and the Lebanese legislature has not been a very effective representative body.

Of the various examples of mixed systems, only the New Zealand plurality method with optional ethnic districts comes close to the ideal of combining the advantage of maintaining a two-party system with the advantage of minority representation. The replacement of plurality by PR in New Zealand would, in all probability, result in a multiparty system and a break in the pattern of one-party majority cabinets. The one clear disadvantage is that even optional districts require discrimination in favor of a particular group or groups, in contrast with regular PR, which treats all minorities equally. The New Zealand system also offers the advantages of simplicity and a close link between representatives and represented since all districts are single-member districts. The latter advantage cannot be claimed for the Cypriot and Lebanese systems which have used mainly multimember plurality districts. And, as we have seen, these two systems have some other serious faults as well.

CONCLUSION

This survey of semi-proportional and mixed systems used for the election of several national legislatures has shown that there is no perfect compromise between PR and plurality. The model that comes relatively close to this ideal is New Zealand's plurality system with optional ethnic districts. In evaluating the applicability of this model to other countries, the crucial question is whether one is willing to designate one or more officially recognized minorities, to institute special nongeographical districts reserved for these minorities, and to compile voter registers on the basis of ethnic or other group affiliation.

All of the other systems that have been discussed in this chapter fail the test of combining the advantages of PR and plurality much more clearly than the New Zealand model. The next best system is probably SNTV, as used in Japan, which has the plurality method's advantages of simplicity (in contrast with STV) and voting for individual candidates (in contrast with list PR). But, as far as its effect on the number of parties in the party system is concerned, it behaves much more like PR than like plurality. In the choice of an electoral system, it is unfortunately impossible to have the best of both worlds.

PART VII
PROSPECTS FOR
ELECTORAL REFORM

21
Changes and
Choices in Electoral Systems
Dieter Nohlen

In this chapter, I shall discuss the question of choice in the context of social development and institutional change in Western democracies. Taking socio-political conditions into account, one must—from the very beginning—refute the assumption that electoral systems may be constructed deliberately and changed freely, that a great number of options exist under which national legislatures may choose. In my view, this impression is wrong and the public debate on electoral systems is used by politicians and academics alike in order to feign a freedom of choice that really does not exist.

Let's have a look at the international reform map (Table 21.1). It shows that, in most countries, those reforms which included basic changes took place some fifty years ago; since then, the basic type of the electoral system has remained unchanged in most cases; and almost all those countries are still using the principle of representation (i.e. either the majority/plurality system or the system of proportional representation (PR); for this distinction, see Chapter 8 in this volume) that was introduced during the first quarter of the twentieth century. The few deviant cases can be explained primarily in terms of deep-rooted ruptures in the historical and political development in those countries in question. The countries in which fascism rose to power, or in which democratic government was temporarily abolished, had to choose their electoral system for a second time at a later date; they usually went back to the system they had opted for in the past. After World War II, Italy, Austria, and the Federal Republic of Germany reintroduced PR, which had been in force in those countries after 1919. After long decades of authoritarian regimes, Spain and Portugal abandoned their traditional electoral systems (plurality systems with limited votes) and introduced systems of PR at the time of the transition to democratic rule in the 1970s. France, too, is a special case, because the far-reaching electoral reform of 1958 (reintroduction of the majority system with two ballots) was preceded by the collapse of the Fourth Republic and implemented in the specific situation of a *pouvoir constituant*, which in turn arose out of a deep political and social crisis.

In all other countries, electoral reforms have remained within the realm of the established principle of representation. In five countries, Belgium, Denmark, Finland, Luxembourg, and Switzerland, the reforms did not affect the structure of the electoral system. In most other cases, the reforms aimed at a higher degree of proportionality, which was achieved, for example, by a reform in the distribution of constituencies (Iceland) or by changing the formula of translating votes into seats (for example, by introducing the Sainte-Laguë highest average formula instead of the d'Hondt formula, by changing the denominator in the quota formula, or by modifying the formula of allocating the remaining seats). Changes of this kind took place in Greece in 1977, in Iceland in 1959, in Italy in 1956, in Norway in 1953, and in Sweden in 1949. Reforms that went in the opposite direction, that were intended against the splinter parties and that led to a reduction in the degree of proportionality, were successfully introduced in the Federal Republic of Germany in 1953 and again in 1956, in Greece in 1974, in Ireland in 1936, in 1947, and in 1969, in the Netherlands in 1921 and in 1923, and in Sweden in 1971. These effects were achieved primarily by the means of a redistribution of the constituencies, by changes in the procedures of allocating the remaining seats, and, above all, by the introduction of legal thresholds of representation (in the Federal Republic of Germany, in Sweden, and in Spain in 1977).

Assessing the evidence presented so far, we can conclude that the principles of representation have remained unchanged in most countries throughout the last fifty years. Fundamental changes are rare and arise only in extraordinary historical situations. Some room for reform exists, however, within the established basic two types of electoral systems which, in fact, have been used in various countries. The historical evidence, therefore, allows us to conclude that there is only very limited room for changes in electoral systems—quite a contrast to the conventional wisdom of most analysts that one may choose freely among different elements of electoral systems and that there is ample space for "choosing an electoral system." Those discussions of reform which center exclusively around the more general and abstract questions and which span the possible range for reform from the majority/plurality system to PR, suggest a freedom of choice that obviously does not exist. Those debates are purely academic—a reminder especially for those scholars who sustain this general debate, motivated by their belief in social engineering. If, however, the debate should not remain a purely academic exercise, the arguments should be put into their historical context, starting by analyzing the existing electoral systems in the various countries, by taking into account the different national contexts, and by realizing that the options for change are usually limited by the existing principle of representation and its historically strong perseverance.

Table 21.1 Reforms in the Electoral Systems in Eighteen European Countries

Country	Last change of the principle of representation	Basic type currently in force	Reform within the established principle of representation	Intention of the reforms	Number of elections since the introduction of the principle of representation currently in force
Austria	1919/1945	PR	1971	New distribution of the constituencies.	12
Belgium	1919	PR	none	—	20
Denmark	1920	PR	none	—	26
Federal Republic of Germany	1919/1949	PR	1953 1956	Less proportionality. Raising of the threshold of representation.	10
Finland	1906	PR	(1935, 1955)	(Affecting candidacy only.)	29
France	1958	Majority rule	1966	Against splinter parties (ten percent for participation in second ballot).	7

219

Table 21.1 (*Cont.*)

Country	Last change of the principle of representation	Basic type currently in force	Reform within the established principle of representation	Intention of the reforms	Number of elections since the introduction of the principle of representation currently in force
Great Britain		Majority rule	1832, 1884/85, 1918, 1948	Introduction of the plurality system in single-member constituencies.	
Greece	1951	PR	1974, 1977, among others	1974: Increase. 1977: Reduction of disproportionalities.	7
Iceland	1942*	PR	1959	More proportionality/new distribution of the constituencies.	14
Ireland	1923	PR	1936, 1947, 1969	Less proportionality by increase of number of constituencies.	20
Italy	1919/1946	PR	1956	More proportionality by reform of the divisor.	10

220

Luxembourg	1919	PR	none	—	16
Netherlands	1917	PR	1921, 1923	Less proportionality. Reform of the allocation of the remaining seats.	18
Norway	1919	PR	1953	More proportionality/reform of the divisor procedure.	16
Portugal	1975	PR	none	—	5
Spain	1976	PR	none	—	3
Sweden	1909	PR	1949, 1971	1949: More proportionality. 1971: Threshold of representation against splinter parties.	24
Switzerland	1919	PR	none	—	18

*In order to reduce disproportionalities, six out of forty members of the Althing were elected on the Land level as early as 1915.
Sources: Nohlen 1978, 1981.

What are the causes for this kind of stability in the history of electoral systems? In addressing this question, I will once again tackle the issue of "choice" and discuss the areas of reform one should concentrate on. Generally speaking, we can start with the following hypothesis: The electoral systems in the Western democracies were not invented theoretically, constructed artificially at the drawing boards of social or political scientists, and then put into practice; to the contrary, most electoral systems were developed historically in a rather long evolutionary process. This is true even for the British electoral system, the "first-past-the-post" system in single-member constituencies, which is often regarded as a model.[1] And it is true with regard to the many systems of PR which exist today. Historically, the introduction of PR came about in most countries by a process of adapting a theoretical concept, that of representing all political forces in proportion to their numerical strength, to specific historical conditions and by developing a particular system of PR which would suit those national, as well as socio-political, preconditions. The many systems of PR differ accordingly, reflecting the whole range of possible variations without affecting the principle of representation itself. Elsewhere, I have shown in detail that empirical electoral systems are usually the result of compromises between opposing political forces at a certain point in time (Nohlen 1978, 1981).

The more recent electoral legislation in Spain is a good example to illustrate this fact: In the process of transition to democracy, the political right, under the leadership of Fraga Iribarne (an outspoken advocate of the British electoral system) opted for a plurality system, whereas the democratic opposition (supported principally by regionalist forces) demanded a system of PR for the first democratic election to the Cortes. The Suárez administration was caught in the middle of both positions, but it opted for the principle of PR in accordance with its strategy of consociationalism, and with its intention to integrate the opposition forces into the political system. In order to break the resistance of the political right in the Franquist Cortes, the administration of Suárez was prepared to compromise and to accept the introduction of the so-called "correctivos" which were intended to prevent the fragmentation of the party system. While the selection of the components of the electoral system, especially those "correctivos" (the d'Hondt formula and a three percent threshold of representation), was hardly convincing in systematic terms,[2] in its entirety the electoral system was acceptable politically for the opposing political forces. That is to say that the acceptance of the Spanish electoral system was not determined by its technical adequacy or by its theoretical consistency, but that it was based on the political compromise of those single components.

While the historical and political constellations under which systems of PR were implemented have been quite different in the various countries, the historical outcome was quite similar as far as the principle of representation is concerned, for the introduction of those systems of PR which proved "stable" and remained unchanged, was triggered by a common cause. Their introduction took place in a time of fundamental change, social as well as political; it occurred in the context of the democratization of voting rights and of the introduction of universal suffrage; and it was connected with the rise of the labor parties and the restructuring of the traditional party systems (conservatives versus liberals). The subsequent period has been interpreted as a time of frozen cleavages and party systems (Lipset and Rokkan 1967). Under those conditions, the change of the principle of representation and the introduction of PR served not only the interests of the new rising political parties against which the (restricted) suffrage and/or the existing electoral system had been discriminating in the past, but it also served the interest of the weaker ones among the older, established parties which were threatened of being eliminated by the rise of the newly formed political forces. Kohl (1982, p. 497) has quite correctly pointed out the functional ambivalence of the principle of PR for those minorities on the rise as well as for those on the defense, a quality which has facilitated the compromise of the socio-political forces in a system of PR. The introduction of the principle of representation currently in force in those countries we have reviewed, was thus brought about in periods of deep socio-political upheaval, where it suited best the political interests of the socio-political forces. No other comparable political change has taken place in the Western democracies since the beginning of the age of mass politics. Since it was exactly in this period that the electoral reforms were implemented, we have to rely on the empirical material of those historical cases that were structured by a wide array of causal relationships in the past, but that do not correspond anymore to today's socio-political circumstances, for the purpose of analyzing the structural effects of different electoral systems on the political system, the party system, and the political process. The historical contingency has to be stressed, not only as far as the analysis of specific historical cases is concerned, but also in relation to theoretical conclusions derived from the experiences of the electoral reform of those past times and with regard to the ''choices'' available today.

Furthermore, the behavioral pattern of political parties seems to have changed regarding their assessment of the advantages and disadvantages of electoral systems. Disadvantages are usually criticized by those political parties negatively affected by them. They form the stimuli for the public debate on electoral systems. Since advantages and disadvantages are not structurally determined and do not always favor the same political parties—their consequences may vary with the changes in the distribution of votes—political parties that used to be discriminated against, readily accept the situational change and utilize these advantages without putting into practice the reform plans they propagated when they formed the opposition. France under Mitterrand is a good example of this change in attitude. In Greece and in Spain, the Socialists similarly stopped their demands for electoral reform when they took office. Because parliamentary majorities are usually achieved by the disproportional effects of the electoral system,[3] those political parties in power which have gained their parliamentary majority by the mechanics of the electoral system and which have profited from what Rae (1967) calls "manufactured" majorities, will not be interested in electoral reforms. Furthermore, in view of the integration of the socialist parties into capitalist society, the alternation of the parliamentary majority between bourgeois and socialist parties no longer has the destabilizing or revolutionary impact that it was supposed, or feared, to trigger at the time when the parties of the working class began their rise.

In many countries a number of other reasons have contributed to the durability of the established set of rules governing the electoral process. In eleven of the eighteen countries under discussion, for example, the principle of representation is written into the constitution. Its reform, therefore, requires a qualified majority which in turn usually requires an agreement between the government and opposition parties—another factor that rather effectively limits the possibilities to fundamentally change the existing electoral system. Theoretically, the alternatives available within systems of PR are now restricted to reforms of mechanics and technical details; politically, those reform options have to be accepted by all major political forces, because one has to keep in mind that only those reforms that will not diminish the chances of the major parliamentary parties, can realistically be expected to be passed by parliaments.

NOTES

1. Before 1832, two-member constituencies were the rule. After the great reform, small-sized constituencies were formed. It was only with the reform of 1884–1885 that mainly single-member constituencies were introduced. There still remained twenty-five multimember constituencies, the number of which was reduced in 1918. Since 1950, the country has been uniformly divided into single-member constituencies.

2. The reform was motivated by the assumption that the d'Hondt formula would favor the major political parties, which is not true in such general terms. It is much more important that the formula of translating votes into seats is applied many times, i.e. in a great number of constituencies. The latter factor is mainly responsible for favoring the major parties and for the disproportional effect of the electoral system. In the special case of Spain, the three percent threshold of representation can only be applied in the two largest constituencies of Barcelona and Madrid, since in all other cases the size of the constituencies (the number of seats allocated per district) automatically leads to a higher threshold.

3. Here I follow Rae's (1967) analysis. Rae's findings concerning the frequency of so-called "manufactured" majorities were confirmed for the elections since 1967 in Nohlen (1983).

22

Reflections on the Electoral Debate in Britain

David E. Butler

The British electoral system can be traced back continuously to the Middle Ages. Since the thirteenth century, communities have been required to send one or two members to Westminster on the basis of first-past-the-post voting. In the course of the nineteenth century, the system was put on an orderly basis. Two-member seats were virtually eliminated; the secret ballot was introduced; the franchise was standardized and gradually extended to the whole population; and corrupt practices were stamped out.

But the system of majority voting was untouched by these reforms. The moves for proportional representation (PR), so successful on the continent, never took strong root in Britain. In 1867, John Stuart Mill advocated a very crude and impractical version of the single transferable vote and there were small experiments with the limited vote in multimember seats, and with the cumulative vote in local elections. But first-past-the-post was not seriously challenged.

It is true that, in 1910, a little-noticed Royal Commission advocated PR, while in 1917, the Speakers Conference on Electoral Reform supported the alternative vote. But there was negligible public debate. In 1918, at a bad moment in the war, the House of Commons did narrowly support the alternative vote, but the House of Lords, in a wrecking move, insisted on PR; there was no stir when, taking the line of least resistance, the government let things continue as they were.

In the 1920s, PR might have been brought in, as it was in Belgium in the 1890s, as a means of saving the waning Liberal party, crushed between the Conservatives who had taken over the representation of business and the growing Labour party, successfully asserting its claim to be the party of the working classes.

But the Liberals were not agreed on any one specific alternative to first-past-the-post and did not give priority to electoral reform until it was too late. In 1930, the minority Labour government, needing Liberal support, did agree to the alternative vote: but after the Bill had passed the House of Commons, it was mangled in the House of Lords, and in August 1931 the government fell before it could press home the changes.

For the next forty years, the two-party duopoly of Conservative and Labour stood firmly in the way of electoral reform. Each party liked a system that gave it full power for half the time rather than a potential share of power all the time. After 1935 no party won fifty percent of the votes—yet every election but one produced a clear majority. Change could only come from a government that owed its absolute power to the existing system. Change was not even discussed in the period from 1950 to 1970 when Conservative and Labour shared ninety-three percent of all votes cast in parliamentary contests and provided ninety-eight percent of all MPs.

But in the last decade, electoral reform has returned to the national agenda. There were several reasons for this:

1. In the elections of 1974, the Liberal party won almost twenty percent of the votes but only two percent of the seats. This was so much more flagrant an injustice than before that others, in addition to the Liberals, were stirred to question the system.

2. In October 1974, Labour won a clear majority although supported by only thirty-nine percent of the voters (and only twenty-nine percent of the registered electorate). Some Conservatives suddenly realized the threat to true conservatism posed by an electoral system that could, on this basis, put in office a party committed to a "fundamental and irreversible shift in the structure of power." A significant number of influential Tories recognized that PR offered the most respectable of constitutional safeguards against revolutionary changes being legitimately enacted by a minority party.

3. Growing troubles in Northern Ireland required consensual solutions. First-past-the-post contests had a polarizing effect. Conservative and Labour governments each arranged for elections to an assembly in Belfast by single transferable vote, in order to secure the representation of minorities and, above all, to get some moderates elected.

4. As a member of the European Community, the United Kingdom was committed to take part in direct elections to the European Parliament, ultimately on a common electoral system (which would necessarily mean a proportional system).

5. In 1977, the Labour government, which had lost its Commons majority through by-election defeats, felt forced to make a pact with the Liberals. Their terms for keeping Labour in office included government support for PR in European elections. Although the Commons rejected it, Mr. Callaghan's government did actually advocate a regional list system of voting.

6. In reaction to the 1974 elections, the Hansard Society set up a prestigious committee under Lord Blake to explore electoral systems. Its well-publicized report favored a variant of the West German additional-member system. For good or ill, people critical of the first-past-the-post arrangements had two seriously advocated and well worked-out alternatives, the additional-member system and the single transferable vote. There was also the regional list system, as favored by Labour in 1978 and by the European Parlia-

ment in 1982. The cause of electoral reform was not necessarily favored by this multiplicity of choice but no one could say that first-past-the-post lacked any serious alternative.

7. In the early 1980s, the political scene in Britain changed. As the Conservative and Labour parties seemed to polarize to right and left, the new Social Democratic Party, in Alliance with the Liberals, made great advances, winning sensationally in by-elections and rising high in the opinion polls. The Alliance put electoral reform in the forefront of their consensual policies. They set up a joint constitutional commission which came down in favor of a version of the single transferable vote. Although Alliance support fluctuated wildly, it continued strong enough to foster discussion of hung parliaments, coalition governments, and electoral reform.

8. The development of a three-party situation patently weakened the case for first-past-the-post. In the two-party situation of 1950–1970, it was arguable that this system worked fairly as between the two majority parties. Give or take one percent, a majority in votes would produce a majority in seats. The Cube Law, first enunciated in 1910 (if votes are divided in the ratio A:B, seats will be divided in the ratio $A^3:B^3$) held good, more or less, for elections from 1931 to 1970. In the 1970s the number of marginal seats fell and the Cube Law seemed to be replaced by a Square Law (if votes are divided in the ratio A:B, seats will be divided in the ratio $A^2:B^2$): instead of eighteen seats changing hands for each one percent swing between Conservative and Labour, only twelve seats were now likely to move. But the system still looked regular, as between the two big parties; each had about the same number of seats at risk to any given rightward or leftward movement of votes. The position of a third party, however, was very different: the Liberals got very few seats for their votes when they were relatively weak (in February 1974, twenty percent of the national vote elected only two percent of MPs to the House of Commons). But when third-party strength increased, the results could still be very disproportionate. Early in 1983 it was calculated that, given uniform movements from the 1979 votes, a three-way tie in popular support (thirty-three percent each) would return 290 Labour MPs, 260 Conservatives, but only 80 from the Liberal/SDP Alliance. The results of the June 1983 elections indicated such arithmetic. The Conservatives with 42.4 percent of the vote secured 397 seats (61.1 percent); Labour with 27.6 percent secured 209 seats (32.2 percent); the Alliance with 25.4 percent secured 23 seats (3.5 percent). The disproportionate treatment of the Alliance came from the evenness of their support: 546 (86 percent) of their candidates were near (± 10 percent) to their average 25.4 percent vote. They came in second or a strong third almost everywhere. Conservative and Labour strength being more bunched was much more effectively distributed from the point of view of winning seats. Only 194 (31 percent) Conservatives were so near to their 42.4 percent average; only 134 (21 percent) of Labour candidates were so near to their 27.6 percent average. First-past-the-post translates votes into seats with an unacceptable capriciousness when three or more parties are in serious contention—and this has become more and more widely appreciated.

One cause of the decline of the Cube Law has been a growing geographic polarizing in the distribution of party support. In 1955 Scotland was evenly divided between Conservative and Labour. Labour held a number of rural seats and the Conservatives had at least a third of the representation in big cities. By 1974, the situation was transformed. Conservatives' representation in the cities was halted and Labour had no agricultural MPs. Voters in the North of England and Scotland had, in nineteen years, swung to the left while the Midlands and South had swung to the right. Between 1955 and 1979 the Conservative share of MPs elected north of a line from the Mersey to the Trent fell from forty-seven percent to thirty-two percent. Among those elected south of that line Conservative representation rose from fifty-seven percent to sixty-eight percent.

9. Britain's decline in the international league table became apparent in a period that saw four alternations of government. None of the switches from Conservative to Labour and back again in 1964, 1970, 1974, and 1979 did anything obvious to stop the slide, but they did make voters more skeptical about the virtues of their favored parties or the ability of any government to change the course of events. However, the discontinuities in detailed policies for industry—tax allowances, regional incentives, nationalization and the like—made the compromises and continuities that have gone with coalition government in many European countries seem more attractive. Powerful figures in the Confederation of British Industry became converts to PR in the hope that it would lead to more broad-based and uninterrupted policies which would facilitate long-term planning.

However, although for all these reasons, the question of PR has returned to the British political agenda, it would be wrong to exaggerate its appeal. A largely uncomprehending public regularly told the pollsters that they would favor it, but the bulk of the established parties were firmly opposed. A mere handful of Labour MPs were willing to support a change that would deny them the chance of a clear parliamentary majority to push through their policies. Rather more Conservatives, including several Cabinet ministers, saw virtue in the reform, as a defense against socialism, but Mrs. Thatcher was implacably opposed, believing in the clear choice traditionally offered by first-past-the-post.

The case for the status quo, as most of us would have deployed it in the 1950s and 1960s, is that the system has worked well in making elections give unequivocal decisions. The electorate voted; one party got a clear majority; a few years later, at the end of the Parliament, the electorate could pass judgment on its performance. If things had gone wrong, there were no coalition partners to blame; the government party was unequivocally responsible for what had happened. Moreover, Britain was such a consensual nation, without serious religious, racial, or regional divisions, that two tolerant parties could encompass the needs of almost everyone. Indeed, on a Downsian linear model, since the extreme right and the extreme left presented no threat, it was to the interest of each party to edge towards the center and steal votes from its main opponent. While this happened, the arbitrary electoral system could be seen as fostering harmony and moderation.

A further argument much used in favor of the system (though one which impressed the elected more than the electors) is the supposed link between the MP and his constituency. All members act as welfare officers and ambassadors for the locality they represent. They sort out grievances and lobby ministers. They seek to win gratitude and loyalty by helping those whose votes they want. It is seldom so romantic a relationship as is claimed by the MP who inflates his ego by speaking about "my constituents" and "what my people want." But citizens do know that they have one particular MP to turn to, and MPs do feel an obligation to what they regard as their personal territory in a way that can be lacking in some proportional systems.

But many who defended the status quo in the 1960s have been moved by one or more of the developments listed above. The capricious outcomes of first-past-the-post voting in a three-party situation, the pressure of international examples, and the awareness of the national costs of traditional adversary politics have combined to worry a lot of those who recently automatically accepted the system. The convinced supporters of any one specific alternative are few in number but the feeling that change may be desirable is now widespread. Change will not come easily, for it can only be enacted by a parliamentary majority that owes its election to the existing system. One or more hung parliaments seem an almost essential preliminary to getting enough people in key position committed to reform. But writing as a veteran observer of the problem, yet without any deep convictions about what system would be best for Britain, it seems to me unlikely that first-past-the-post voting for the Westminster Parliament will last to the end of the century.

23
Transnational Problems of a Uniform Procedure for European Elections
Karlheinz Reif

A FEDERALIST STRATEGY FOR PIECEMEAL CONSTITUTIONAL ENGINEERING

The European Community (EC) is a common subsystem of ten nation states. The nation state is still the most important arena of politics in Western Europe. Elections to the European Parliament (EP) are nine (1979) or ten (1984) simultaneous national second-order elections.[1]

Reform of electoral procedures is, in any democratic political system, a matter of "domestic high politics,"[2] potentially affecting the balance of power between political parties. This observation is not only valid for reform in the first-order electoral arena, but it is also valid most of the time for electoral reform in second-order political arenas, like local, regional, or European elections.

Parties in government at the time of an electoral reform will attempt to secure built-in advantages for themselves in the electoral regulations to be newly established, or, in any case, attempt to prevent systematic disadvantages for themselves, unless the respective mechanisms come under severe pressure of being perceived as illegitimate by the relevant public.[3]

It is thus highly improbable that a governing party easily agrees to sacrificing established built-in advantages in the electoral procedures of a second-order political arena, particularly if such a sacrifice would contribute to the delegitimization of the same mechanisms in the electoral procedure for the chief political arena of the respective system.

This is why attempts to introduce a common and uniform electoral procedure for direct elections to the European Parliament were doomed to fail in the past, even if draft treaties since 1953 and treaties in force since 1957 prescribed it. This chapter briefly summarizes the history of direct elections to the EP and of attempts to arrive at a uniform procedure for such elections, paying particular attention to (a) the role of foreign "models" in the domestic debate on electoral system reforms and (b) to the significance of electoral procedures for second-order elections for the party system of a given country as a whole, as well as (c) for the dynamics of second-order electoral system reform debates in the first-order political arena. Finally, (d) the relevance of a uniform European electoral procedure for the development of the political system of the EC will be assessed.

In 1949, the clear rejection of any federal-supranational structure for the Council of Europe by the United Kingdom relieved the other West European nations of the need to precisely define their own attitudes. Forty-five years later, the EP proposal for an "Act adopting certain provisions relating to a uniform electoral procedure for the election of Members of the European Parliament" ran aground because of a British "no" which again relieved the other member states of the EC of the need to publicly explain their own attitudes.

The growth of density of relations among West European countries[4] is characterized, after the 1949 failure of federalist hopes, by a variable mixture of federal-supranational and confederal-intergovernmental elements on the basis of more or less hope for the fulfillment of neo-functionalist spillover prophecies. When the EDC/EPC failed in 1954, the federalists became aware of the fact that an immediate merger of sovereignty even of "the six" was not possible, and they developed a new strategy. It consisted of defending the already established federal-supranational elements within the institutional system of what was the European Coal and Steel Community at the time and of persistently striving for their strengthening and supplementation by additional such elements until the federal component would finally reach an unambiguous prevalence.[5]

The Assembly, being an as unambiguously supranational as unmistakably powerless institution, was an important focus of their attention. Its powers were to be extended and its members were to be elected by direct universal suffrage on the basis of a uniform electoral procedure in all member states of the community.

THE HISTORY OF DIRECT ELECTIONS AND THE IDEA OF A UNIFORM ELECTORAL PROCEDURE

While article 21 of the ECSC treaty of Paris in 1951 had left the method of selection of the members of the Assembly to the discretion of the member states,[6] article 13 of the 1953 draft treaty for an EPC stipulated that "the members of the Assembly are elected by universal, equal, direct, and secret suffrage of men and women. A *law of the Community* will fix the principles of electoral procedure." Together with the EDC treaty to which it was closely linked, this treaty never came into force. Since the establishment of the EEC and of the EAC by the treaties of Rome in 1957, article 138 EECT, article 108 of EACT, and article 21 of ECSCT used identical wording: "...the Assembly shall draw up proposals for elections by direct universal suffrage in accordance with a uniform procedure in all Member States."[7]

After some modest extension between 1970 and 1975 of the budgetary powers of the Assembly, which called itself "European Parliament" since 1959, the principle of direct elections was put into practice on June 7 and 10, 1979. A 1982 attempt by the EP to have the second European elections on June 14 and 17, 1984, held "in accordance with a uniform procedure" failed because of British opposition.

From 1958 to 1969, the history of the Community was marked by the sharp and total rejection of federal-supranational structures by the French President of the Republic, Charles de Gaulle, who was also strongly opposed to any extension of the EC to Great Britain. The principle of majority decision in the Council of Ministers (article 148 EECT) was replaced by the "Luxembourg Compromise" of 1966, giving each member state a right to veto. The role of the Commission which had handled its tasks in a clearly supranational spirit was cut back. The marginality of the EP was cemented. Direct elections were out of the question even if every one of France's partners declared to be prepared to put them into practice.

Shortly after the change of government in France and Germany (from de Gaulle to Pompidou and from Kiesinger to Brandt), the summit of The Hague in December 1969 infused considerable new dynamics into the Community,[8] but with respect to direct elections, the communiqué simply stated "The question...will be further examined by the Council." France was still opposed.

This suddenly changed, when in 1974 for the first time a non-Gaullist with well-known pro-European convictions, Valéry Giscard d'Estaing, had been elected President of the Fifth Republic[9] by including the remainders of the anti-Gaullist pro-European centre parties into his presidential and governmental coalition, thus beating the candidate of the Union of the Left, François Mitterrand, by a very narrow margin. At the Paris Summit of December 1974 it was France who proposed to hold direct elections "as soon as possible."[10]

Meanwhile, however, the EC had been enlarged by the UK, Denmark, and Ireland. At the moment when French opposition to direct elections were overcome, it was the British and the Danes who barred the road. They clearly preferred a confederal-intergovernmental Community to a federal-supranational one. Their resistance could be gradually vanquished after the British "re-negotiations" and "EC-Referendum" of June 1975. On September 20, 1976, the Council adopted an "Act concerning the election of the representatives of the Assembly by direct universal suffrage." Article 7 laid down that "...the Assembly shall draw up proposals for a uniform electoral procedure...pending the entry into force of a uniform electoral procedure...the electoral procedure shall be governed in each Member State by its national provision." The procedure of the 1979[11] first European elections was, thus, left to the discretion of the member states in the perspective, however, of a uniform procedure for the (near?) future (see Table 23.1).

Table 23.1 Major Characteristics of National Voting Procedures for Domestic and 1979/81 European Parliamentary Elections and of the European Parliament 1982 Draft Proposal

	B		DK		D		F		GR		IRL		I		L		NL		UK		EP
	N	E	N	E	N	E	N	E	N	E	N	E	N	E	N	E	N	E	N	E	E
ELECTORAL SYSTEM																					
majority	–	–	–	–	(X)	–	X	–	–	–	–	–	–	–	–	–	–	–	X	X	–
PR	X	X	X	X	X	X	–	X	X	X	X	X	X	X	X	X	X	X	–	–	X
ELECTORAL DISTRICTS																					
1 national district	–	–	–	X	–	X	–	X	–	X	–	–	–	–	–	X	–	X	–	–	X
plural member distr.	X	X	X	X	X	(X)	–	–	X	–	X	X	X	X	X	X	X	X	–	–	–
single member distr.	–	–	–	–	(X)	–	X	–	–	–	–	–	–	–	–	–	–	–	X	X	–
PREFERENCE VOTING																					
no preference	–	–	–	–	X	X	X	–	X	–	–	–	–	–	–	–	–	–	–	–	○ ○
pr. within list	X	X	X	X	X	–	–	X	–	X	–	–	X	X	–	–	X	X	–	–	–
pr. across lists	–	–	–	–	–	–	–	–	–	–	–	–	–	–	X	X	–	–	–	–	–
individual choice	–	–	–	–	(X)	–	X	–	–	–	X	X	–	–	–	–	–	–	X	X	–
FINAL DISTRIBUTION																					
national level	–	–	X	X	X	X	X	–	X	X	–	–	X	X	X	X	X	X	–	–	X
lower level	X	(X)	–	–	X	(X)	X	–	(X)	–	X	X	X	(X)	X	(X)	–	–	X	X	–
DISTRIBUTION MODE																					
d'Hondt	X	X	–	–	X	X	X	–	X	–	–	–	X	–	X	X	–	–	–	–	X
Hare+d'Hondt	–	–	–	–	–	–	–	–	–	–	–	–	–	–	–	–	X	X	–	–	–
Hagenb.-Bischoff	–	–	–	–	–	–	–	–	–	–	–	–	–	–	X	X	–	–	–	–	–
High. rem. Imperiali	–	–	–	–	–	–	–	–	–	–	–	–	X	–	–	–	–	–	–	–	–
High. rem. Hare	–	–	–	–	–	–	–	–	X	–	–	–	–	X	–	–	–	–	–	–	–
Mod. Sainte-Laguë	–	–	–	X	–	–	–	–	–	–	X	–	–	–	–	–	–	–	–	–	–
reinforced PR	–	–	–	–	–	–	–	–	–	–	–	–	–	–	–	–	–	–	–	–	–
STV	–	–	–	–	–	–	–	–	–	–	X	X	–	–	–	–	–	–	–	–	–

234

sing. memb. plural.	—	—	—	—	—	—	—	—	—	—	—	—	—	X	—
sing. memb. majority	—	—	—	—	—	—	—	—	—	—	—	—	X	X	—
LEGAL THRESHOLD															
yes	—	—	—	(X)	—	—	—	—	—	—	—	—	—	—	( )
no	X	X	X	—	X	X	X	X	X	X	X	—	X	X	( )
REPLACEMENT OF MP															
next on list	—	X	X	X	(X)	—	X	X	—	X	—	—	—	—	—
substitute	X	X	—	—	X	X	—	—	X	X	—	—	—	X	X
by-election	—	—	(X)	—	(X)	—	—	—	—	—	X	X	—	X	X
MIN. VOTING AGE															
18	X	X	X	X	X	X	X	X	X	X	X	X	X	X	X
20	—	—	—	—	—	X	X	—	—	—	—	—	—	—	—
MIN. ELIGIBILITY AGE															
18	—	X	X	X	X	—	—	—	—	—	—	—	—	—	—
21	X	—	—	—	—	X	X	X	X	—	X	X	—	X	X
23	—	—	—	X	X	—	—	—	—	X	—	—	—	—	—
25	X	—	—	—	—	—	—	—	X	—	—	—	X	—	—
26	—	—	—	—	—	—	—	X	—	—	—	—	—	—	—
VOTER'S RESIDENCE															
in nation	X	X	X	X	X	X	X	X	X	X	X	X	X	X	X
outs. n., within EC	—	X	(X)	X	(X)	X	X	X	—	X	(X)	X	X	(X)	X
outs. EC	—	(X)	—	(X)	(X)	X	X	X	—	X	—	(X)	—	(X)	(X)
other EC citiz. in nat.	—	—	—	—	—	—	—	—	—	—	—	—	(X)	(X)	(X)
OBLIGATION TO VOTE															
yes	X	X	—	—	—	—	(X)	(X)	X	X	—	—	—	—	—
no	—	X	X	X	X	X	X	(—) (—)	—	X	X	X	X	X	X
ABSENTEE VOTING															
by mail	—	X	X	X	—	X	(X)	—	—	—	—	—	X	X	X
by proxy	(X) (X)	—	—	X	X	(X)	X	—	—	—	—	—	—	X	X

235

Table 23.1 (*Cont.*)

	B		DK		D		F		GR		IRL		I		L		NL		UK		EP
	N	E	N	E	N	E	N	E	N	E	N	E	N	E	N	E	N	E	N	E	E
none	X	X	—	—	—	—	—	—	—	—	—	—	X	X	X	X	X	—	—	—	—
ELECTION DAY																					
Sunday	X	X	—	—	X	X	X	X	X	X	—	—	X	X	X	X	—	—	—	—	( )
Monday	—	—	—	—	—	—	—	—	—	—	—	—	X	—	—	—	—	—	—	—	( )
Tuesday	—	—	—	X	—	—	—	—	—	—	—	—	—	—	—	—	—	—	—	—	—
Wednesday	—	—	—	—	—	—	—	—	—	—	—	—	—	—	—	—	—	X	—	—	—
Thursday	—	—	—	—	—	—	—	—	—	—	X	X	—	—	—	—	—	—	X	X	—

Note: x means: applies. — means: does not apply. (X) means: applies in a limited way. ( ) means: framework.
Sources: Nohlen (1978); Hand, Georgel, and Sasse (1979); Sasse et al. (1981); Reif (1984); Avril et al. (1980); Seitlinger (1982).

THE NATIONAL REGULATIONS FOR THE 1979 FIRST EUROPEAN ELECTIONS

Although there was some discussion about details in almost every Member State (Huber 1979; Herman and Hagger 1980), changes compared with procedures for national parliamentary elections were put forward only in Belgium, Germany, France, and the UK. In none of the countries used to PR was this system seriously questioned. In both countries that use a plurality/majority system in single-member constituencies as the principal device for their national parliamentary elections, France and the UK, the government presented a European elections bill based on PR. But *only in France did a procedure eventually enter into force, which drastically abandoned the national tradition* of the Fifth Republic. While the double-ballot majority formula has been controversial among French political parties ever since its reintroduction in 1958, there was no controversy in the National Assembly about the choice of PR for the EP election, after the Communists and the Gaullists had given up their hostility to direct elections.

The Communists and Socialists are traditionally adherents of PR, and so are the minor parties (PRS and CDS) in President Giscard's party alliance, the UDF. President Giscard had publicly speculated about a possible return to PR for National Assembly elections. The Gaullist RPR, on the other hand, is absolutely opposed to changing the system for national elections from which they have enjoyed considerable profits since 1958. For the European elections, however, they insisted on PR with the entire country, including the overseas *départements* and territories, as a single constituency, because this would most unambiguously guarantee the "unity and indivisibility of the Republic." Giscard, on the other hand, thought that PR would provide a chance to contribute to the internal tensions within the oppositional Union of the Left, since there would be no need for electoral alliances in a second ballot. For the same reason he hoped to attract voters from his Gaullist rival within the governing coalition: opinion polls had revealed the Gaullist electorate to be much more "European" than the Gaullist party, for years.[12] By introducing a five percent threshold like in Germany, easily accepted by the parties in the National Assembly,[13] excessive fractionalization was effectively prevented: the "small lists," although accumulating twelve percent of the vote, could not obtain a single seat.[14]

Depending upon Liberal tolerance in the House, the British Labour government recommended a regional list system for European elections in the UK, which was rejected by a large Labour and Conservative majority in the Commons. It would have meant a considerable breakthrough for the opponents of the first-past-the-post system, which could not have been without repercussions on Westminster electoral regulations.[15]

The only aspect of serious discussion in the Federal Republic of Germany was the number of multimember constituencies.[16] Should there be several constituencies consisting of one or more *Länder*, as the CDU preferred, or should the entire republic form one single constituency, as the governing SPD wanted? As suggested by the also governing FDP, the choice was left to the discretion of each party presenting lists. Although the Liberals themselves presented one federal list, they wanted to avoid the danger of both Christian democratic parties running in the entire country[17] and thereby threatening the FDP to remain under the five percent barrier.[18]

Controversial in Belgium was not the electoral system but only the delineation of constituencies. This issue, however, was particularly delicate, being not yet decided for national elections within the framework of ongoing state reform. In the end, there were two electoral colleges, one Flemish and one Walloon, but three constituencies, the citizens of bilingual Brussels region being offered to opt individually for one of the two colleges and the choice among its lists. The delineation of the Brussels region arrived at, though clearly prejudicing future national solutions, was declared to be provisional and, therefore, encountered no opposition in Parliament.[19]

Summarizing, we retain that the degree of uniformity between the national procedures for the 1979 first European elections was higher than that between procedures for national parliamentary elections (cf. Table 23.1), mainly because Germany had dropped the single-member plurality component of the *Bundestag* system, and because France had switched to PR entirely. The accession of Greece to the EC on January 1, 1981, directly electing its MEPs on October 18 of the same year, still increased this tendency towards more uniformity. But this very process made Great Britain's[20] "deviation" stand out even more clearly.[21]

It is, thus, not surprising that all of the other Member States explicitly or implicitly assumed it to be logical for Britain to renounce its pecularities and join the crowd. Nobody, however, insisted more than the British Liberals, who had not been allowed to send one single Member to Strasbourg although they had received thirteen percent of the vote on June 7, 1979. They are eagerly supported by their friends within the European Liberal Democrats (ELD) transnational party federation, since it was the British electoral system that had caused the ELD's drop from rank 3 to rank 5 in the EP behind the European Democrats (Conservative) and the Communists and Allies.

The British political scientist Michael Steed (1981), also president of the Liberal Party Organization at the time of the 1979 European elections, has simulated the result of these elections on the basis of the votes actually cast, using "the most common procedure" of those in force by 1979, i.e. PR with distribution of seats at the national level[22] according to the d'Hondt method[23] without any legal threshold, and without *apparentement*.[24] Table 23.2 shows the result of such a stimulation extended to Greece and containing some minor modifications with respect to assigning individual national parties to European party families.[25]

Steed (1981, p.308) underlines the "massive overrepresentation of the British

Table 23.2 The Distribution of Seats After a "Most Common Procedures" Simulation Based on Votes Cast 1979/1981 as Compared to the Actual 1979/81 Distribution. (The first column under each party label shows the actual 1979/81 number of seats. The second column shows the differences through the simulation.)

	Extreme Left	Commu-nists	Social-ists	Ecolo-gists	Liberals (ELD)	Christ.-Dem. EPP	Progr.-Dem. DEP	Conser-vat. ED	others	Total
B			7 −1	0 +1	4 –	10 –			3 –	24
DK		1 −1	4 +1		3 –		1 –	3 –	4 –	16
D			35 −1	0 +2	4 –	42 −1				81
F	0 +2	19 −2	22 −2	0 +3	17 –	8 −1	15 −2	0 +1	0 +1	81
GR		4 –	10 +1			8 –			2 −1	24
IRL			4 −1		1 –	4 +1	5 –		1 –	15
I	2 −1	24 +1	13 −1	3 –	5 –	30 +1			4 –	81
L			1 –		2 –	3 –				6
NL			9 –		4 –	10 –			2 –	25
UK			18 +9		0 +10		1 –	61 −20	1 +1	81
EC	2 +1	48 −2	123 +5	3 +6	40 +10	115 0	22 −2	64 −19	17 +1	434

Note: − means: no change

Source: Author's calculations on the basis of Reif and Schmitt (1980); Reif (1984); Steed (1981); and EP-Bulletin: List of Members (1979, 1981, 1983). For further details, see note 25.

239

Conservatives, and the total exclusion of two significant political forces—the British Liberals and the Ecologists''—by the procedures actually used.

It is, therefore, not astonishing that it was the ELD group in the EP that, immediately after the first direct elections, concentrated heavily on the task of drafting a uniform electoral procedure as laid down in the treaties and 1976 act, in order to put the national governments represented in the Council under pressure, not the least of whom were the British. For the Euro-Liberals, a uniform electoral procedure is not only a matter of federalist principles—to which many of them, indeed, adhere—but a question of concrete power within the EP.[26]

THE 1982 EUROPEAN PARLIAMENT DRAFT ACT FOR A "MORE UNIFORM PROCEDURE"

Neither the Euro-Liberals, who have their particular interests, nor the "Federalists" of other party groups in the EP,[27] nor the officers of the Directorate General for Research and Documentation of the EP Secretariat General, whose job is the provision of expertise, nor the team of academics working on the uniform procedure problem at the European University Institute in Florence (Sasse et al. 1981) aspired to a maximalist solution of total cross-national identity of procedures. All of them hoped to arrive at something more than mere incantation of the fundamental principles of "universal, free, equal, direct, and secret." But they were prepared to be pragmatic enough to be confined to an interim partial solution for 1984, as long as there would be hope for the process of harmonization to go on, and, perhaps, for bridging the gap between Britain and the others right away.

There were, on the other hand, numerous MEPs in the Socialist group, among the French Communists, British Conservatives, French Gaullists, and Danes of all sorts, who rejected these endeavors, either on the grounds of anti-federalist conviction, or because they considered other efforts much more important in view of the real political and economic problems the Community and its Member States were confronted with.[28]

The Sub-Committee on "Uniform Electoral Procedures" of the Political Affairs Committee was established immediately after the 1979 election. The Belgian Liberal Jean Rey, former President of the Commission, was elected president; the French Christian Democrat Jean Seitlinger, Secretary General of the European People's Party, was designed Rapporteur. The fact that his *rapport* was only adopted after seven consecutive revisions had been presented and not before March 10, 1982 (the twenty-ninth anniversary of the EPC draft treaty), shows the difficulties of arriving at a majority in favor under the cross pressures of conflicting "European strategies," varying national peculiarities, and, before all, numerous attempts by individual national parties to secure or defend particular privileges. The draft act was approved by 158 votes to 76, with 77 declared abstentions. Forty-five of the 60 British members of the European Democratic Group (Conservative) and 12 of the 17 British members of the Socialist Group voted against.

From the start, the Seitlinger report presents two models for a general solution, besides an inventory of needs for regulation and actual regulations of the different Member States. Both solutions were based on PR and, thus, required a change of principle in Great Britain. And both offered ways to meet the British halfway by maintaining considerable degrees of personalizing the vote within the framework of PR. Model A was a copy of the German *Bundestag* mixed system of electing part of the representatives in single-member constituencies by plurality and securing proportional distribution of seats by differential call upon additional lists. Model B was a PR regional list system with distribution of seats at the national level.

Model A was preferred for a long time, both in the Sub-Committee and in the Political Affairs Committee. At an indicative vote taken on 27 October 1981 in the PAC, 21 approved it with 3 against and 3 abstentions. Nevertheless, it failed in the end, because with fixed numbers of MEPs given, the problem of *Überhangmandate* appears insoluble.[29] A possible solution requires a rather big quota of "additional" list seats, and, consequently, a rather limited number of single-member districts, thus reducing the personalization effect and the attractiveness of the model as a compromise for adherents of the single-member formula. Model B was adopted, having been pushed jointly by the ELD parliamentary leader Martin Bangemann and another German MEP, the Christian Democrat from Bavaria, Reinhold Bocklet, prescribing constituencies of between three and fifteen seats, the number and size of which was—within these limits—left to national discretion. The number of seats of each individual constituency was to be fixed by Member State provisions, but seats were to be distributed among parties at the national level according to the d'Hondt method.[30]

Although this model provides a general framework, the flexibility left for detailed national decisions was considerable. Member States were to decide whether they wanted to adopt a legal threshold,[31] whether they wanted to prescribe preferential voting, as well as whether they wanted to permit *apparantement*. In addition, there was a general clause for taking account of "special geographical or ethnic factors recognised by the constitution of a Member State."

But even such a flexible proposal was not adopted by the Council. A press release of February 21/22, 1983 simply stated that the Council would continue its work toward a uniform procedure for the elections of 1989. The deliberations of the Council, of the Committee of Permanent Representatives and its work groups are not open to the public. Nevertheless, one or the other detail came to be known.

DOMESTIC BALANCE OF POWER AND
EC CONSTITUTIONAL DEVELOPMENT

The European Parliament's thrust for a more uniform electoral procedure failed because the Thatcher government refused to give up the first-past-the-post system. It cannot be excluded that this refusal was facilitated by strong and successful efforts of other Member States to even further reduce the degree of uniformity which the proposal contained: While the EP-draft had a time span of two days for the elections (from Sunday to Monday), Denmark, Ireland, the Netherlands, and the UK reestablished the 1979 time span of four days (from Thursday to Sunday). While the EP draft required France to be divided up into several constituencies (between six and twenty-seven), the Ministers in the Council again conceded to France to form a single constituency. This enables Germany to retain the option between one Federal or several *Länder* lists. Ireland, insisting on the principle of residence,[32] and Greece, insisting on the principle of nationality,[33] could not agree on a compatible criterion for the franchise.

In view of this very low degree of uniformity among PR countries with respect to other aspects of a procedure, Britain seems to have seen no reason to betray her sacred tradition. At least, this is the official justification, which became known by hearsay.

The real reason, of course, was to prevent pressure by the Liberals and Social Democrats for change of the Westminster electoral system to become even stronger through a Euro-election precedent. The results of the June 9, 1983, British general election cannot but drastically magnify the dimensions of the problem: A PR system would have translated into the power distribution among parliamentary parties the facts that Margaret Thatcher's Conservatives had lost votes and that the gap between Labour and the Liberal-SDP Alliance was reduced to a negligible 2.3 percent.[34]

It is obviously the crucial variable determining chances for a more uniform electoral procedure for European elections in the future, whether the legitimacy of the first-past-the-post system for Westminster elections will remain stable or not in the eyes of the British public.

The causes of the 1982/83 failure to arrive at a common system reflects the decrease of the EC system's capabilities to arrive at any decision in any somewhat more sensitive policy area. This is particularly evident in the area of constitutional policy-making. Here, not only the sacrifice of elements of national sovereignty is at stake, but, in addition, the balance of power between political forces within the national bureaucratic and party systems of the Member States.

Constitutional progress in the EC seems to depend on a favorable "transnational constellation of domestic political constellations." Particularly changes in national government—often simultaneous changes in several Member States— have made important constitutional breakthroughs possible in the past. The federalist-supranationally inspired attempt to increase "integration" by quickly harmonizing electoral procedures was in vain, this time. But on the backdrop of a cross-national and over-time comparison, there is still no need to despair.

Most democratic federal states of today have had a uniform, federally regulated electoral procedure for the (lower chamber of the) federal parliament from their beginning.[35] But the EC is not—or not yet—a federal state, of course. On the other hand, Switzerland, independent since 1291, did not adopt a uniform electoral procedure until 1848–50. The electoral procedure of Canada, founded in 1867, did not become more or less uniform in important respects before the First World War. And the United States, finally, dates the relative uniformity of its electoral procedures to the 1960s—almost two centuries after its foundation.

NOTES

1. First-order elections determine the distribution of power among parties in the most important institution of a political system: presidential elections in a presidential system, parliamentary elections in a parliamentary, cabinet government, or prime ministerial government system. Second-order elections are all other general elections in the respective system: parliamentary by-elections, mid-term congressional elections, cantonal, regional, municipal elections, European elections, etc. See Reif (1978, 1983, 1984); Reif and Schmitt (1980).

2. For the concepts of "high politics" and "low politics" in international relations, see Haas (1967) and Hoffmann (1966). Similar criteria of "relevance for the power distribution among political forces" may be applied to matters of domestic politics and policy-making

3. Such processes of delegitimization of restrictive mechanisms played an important role in the extension of the suffrage to all men and, later, to all women during the late nineteenth and early twentieth centuries.

4. I prefer this term to "European integration."

5. This strategy was fairly successful with respect to the role of the Court of Justice, and rather unsuccessful with respect to the rule of the Commission or to majority decision-making in the Council. The federalist hope of strengthening supranational institutions by including the UK in the EC proved to be totally wrong.

6. In practice, there were only members designated by their national parliaments from among their own members.

7. The EP drew up such proposals in 1960, 1975, and 1982, but not before 1982 was there any serious attempt to arrive at a more uniform procedure.

8. The goal of a "European Economic and Monetary Union" to be established before 1980 was defined; the foundation of "European Political Cooperation" was laid; and the French resistance to membership of the UK, Denmark, Ireland, and Norway was overcome.

9. This change of government in France took place more or less simultaneously with the change from Brandt to Schmidt in Germany and from Heath to Wilson in Britain.

10. See Reif (1980) for the domestic political motives of Giscard's policy.

11. The first direct elections were originally scheduled for 1978, but they had to be postponed because Belgium and the UK had not completed the necessary legal and organizational preparations on time.

12. See Rabier (1977). The German model of "personalized PR" plays an important role in the French electoral reform debate (Weill-Raynal 1966, 1973; Goguel 1982), as well as in the EP, British, and Canadian debates (see the chapters by Butler and Irvine in this book). Nevertheless, the French did not adopt it for either the European or the Corsican regional elections of 1982, nor for

the municipal elections in 1983. The five percent threshold, on the other hand, was adopted for the European as well as for the municipal elections.

13. The small UDF parties were not enthusiastic about it. The UDF parliamentary leader Chinaud of the middle-sized Republican Party had even proposed a ten percent threshold, which would have seriously threatened any representation in the EP for the CDS and PRS (Reif 1980).

14. "Europe-Ecologie" had 4.4 percent, and the common list of the two Trotzkyist parties had three percent.

15. For details, see the White paper "Direct Elections to the European Assembly" (Cmnd. 6758); Reif (1984); and Herman and Hagger (1980).

16. Of the three main characteristics of the *Bundestag* system (PR with d'Hondt, five percent clause, and single-member district plurality system for about fifty percent of the seats) only the first two were retained, although the CDU gave consideration to the mixed system at one point (Reif 1980).

17. The CSU is traditionally confined to Bavaria; the CDU covers all other *Länder* except Bavaria.

18. The Greens, not represented in the *Bundestag* at the time, brought the case against the five percent threshold before the Constitutional Court—without success (Reif 1984).

19. Both Liberal parties, PVV and PRLW, as well as the Communist PCB/BKP abstained, because they had unsuccessfully advocated *apparentement* at the national level, hoping that this would give them better representation (Claeys, de Graeve-Lismont, and Loeb-Mayer 1980; Reif 1984).

20. Only Great Britain proper is "deviant." Northern Ireland had already voted by STV in 1979. The single member for Greenland within the Danish contingent was elected by plurality (Reif 1984).

21. One must not forget that there was an intense electoral reform debate in Germany during the end of the 1950s as well as during the end of the 1960s, with many advocates of the adoption of the "English model." Both times it was started when a CDU/CSU-FDP coalition broke up. Both times the aim was to get rid of the FDP; the CDU/CSU and SDP even formed a great coalition for that purpose in 1966. Both times the cause of failure was the prospect of a new coalition including the FDP—in 1961 with the CDU/CSU and in 1969 with the SDP (Conradt 1970; Bredthauer 1973; Schütt 1973). The situation would look quite different in the present EC if Germany had adopted the "English model': three of the big ED countries (with sixty-six percent of the population) would have a pure single-member national tradition.

22. With the exception of West Berlin, Greenland, and Northern Ireland, but including Belgium and Ireland.

23. Thus slightly favoring the large parties in Italy (and, later, Greece), and completely changing the British result.

24. Resulting in one extra seat for the Social Democrats, taken from the Danish SFP.

25. Leaving the Italian Radicals with the Ecologists, the SFP with the Communists, and giving the seat of the French list led by Malaud to the ED group, based on Malaud's declaration that the British Conservatives represented his own program best (interview with the author, May 1979). The SNP seat remains with the EDP. The Plaid Cymru seat is grouped with "others." SNP and PC are assumed to present one list.

26. For the strength of federalist tendencies in national parties and European party federations, see Reif, Cayrol, and Niedermayer (1980), and Niedermayer (1983).

27. Most Christian Democrats, but also some of the Socialists and Italian Communists. The well-known federalist Altiero Spinelli, former member of the EC commission, was elected on the PCI ticket as an *independente di sinistra*.

28. Most of the German SPD MEPs are to be found here.

29. The number of members of the *Bundestag* is enlarged when a party gets more direct seats than proportionally justified. These additional seats are called *Überhangmandate*. In some *Landtag* electoral rules, though not for the *Bundestag*, the other parties are compensated by additional seats from their lists (*Ausgleichsmandate*), in order to guarantee a proportional distribution of seats.

30. Such a combination of provisions presents considerable technical problems of adequate

representation of both regions and parties. For a method minimizing the discrepancy, see Steed and Reif (1982).

31. In the small Member States, there is a ''natural'' threshold of 4 percent (Netherlands), 4.17 percent (Belgium, Greece), 6.7 percent (Denmark, Ireland), and 16.7 percent (Luxembourg). Since there was no national distribution in Belgium and Ireland, the constituency threshold there was even higher than the national one.

32. The unpredictable effects of voting in the Republic by Irish citizens who are residents of Great Britain could threaten the balance of power in the Irish party system.

33. Greece would not accept a loosening of the linkage between Greeks residing (and voting) in other EC Member States and Greece.

34. The alliance of Liberals and the Social Democratic Party, founded in 1981, was supported by half of the British public in opinion polls before the Falklands war. Conservatives and Labour now hold 606 seats in the Commons. PR would have given 275 to the Conservatives, 180 to Labour, 165 to the Alliance, and 30 to others.

35. Germany since 1871, 1919, and 1949 after a confederal era from 1806 on, Australia since 1901, Austria since 1919, and India since 1950.

Bibliography

Adrian, C.R. 1959. "A Typology for Nonpartisan Elections." *Western Political Quarterly* 12: 449–58.

Andrews, J.H. 1966. "Illinois' At-Large Vote." *National Civic Review* 55: 253–57.

Aristotle. 1943. *Politics*. New York: Modern Library.

Avril, P., et al. 1980. "The Rules of the European Election Game." *European Journal of Political Research* 8: 133–44.

Baaklini, A.I. 1976. *Legislative and Political Development: Lebanon, 1842–1972*. Durham: Duke University Press.

Baker, K.L., R.J. Dalton, and K. Hildebrandt. 1981. *Germany Transformed: Political Culture and the New Politics*. Cambridge, Mass.: Harvard University Press.

Balinski, M.L., and H.P. Young. 1982. "Fair Representation in the European Parliament." *Journal of Common Market Studies* 20: 361–74.

Barzini, L. 1982. "Italy Debates Constitution but the Italians Carry On." *Wall Street Journal*, December 1, p. 29.

Batty, M. 1976. "A Political Theory of Planning and Design." GP 45, Department of Geography, University of Reading.

———. 1974. "Social Power in Plan Generation." *Town Planning Review* 45: 291–310.

Beard, C.A. 1913. *An Economic Interpretation of the Constitution of the United States*. New York: Macmillan.

Berkeley, G. 1966. "Flaws in At-Large Voting." *National Civic Review* 55: 370–73, 379.

Blair, G.S. 1960. *Cumulative Voting: An Effective Electoral Device in Illinois Politics*. Urbana: University of Illinois Press.

Bogdanor, V. 1981. *The People and the Party System: The Referendum and Electoral Reform in British Politics*. Cambridge, England: Cambridge University Press.

Bordley, R.F. 1983. "A Pragmatic Method for Evaluating Election Schemes through Simulation." *American Political Science Review* 77: 123–41.

Brams, S.J. 1982. "The AMS Nomination Procedure is Vulnerable to 'Truncation of Preferences'." *Notices of the American Mathematical Society* 29: 136–38.

———. 1975. *Game Theory and Politics*. New York: Free Press.

———, and P.C. Fishburn. 1983a. "Proportional Representation in Variable-Size Legislatures." Mimeographed.

———. 1983b. *Approval Voting*. Boston: Birkhäuser.

Bredthauer, R. 1973. *Das Wahlsystem als Objekt von Politik und Wissenschaft*. Meisenheim: Hain.

Bromage, A.W. 1962. *Political Representation in Metropolitan Agencies*. Ann Arbor: Institute of Public Administration, University of Michigan.

Camera dei Deputati. 1923. *Discussioni, Legislatura XXVI*. Rome.

———. 1919. *Discussioni, Legislatura XXV*. Rome.

Campbell, J.S., J.R. Sahid, and D.P. Stang. 1970. *A Staff Report to the National Commission on the Causes and Prevention of Violence*. Washington, D.C.: Government Printing Office.

Campbell, P. 1958. *French Electoral Systems and Elections Since 1789*. London: Faber and Faber.

———. 1951. "Remarques sur les effets de la loi électorale française du 9 mai 1951." *Revue Française de Science Politique* 1: 498–502.

Capitant, R. 1934. *La réforme du parlementarisme français.* Paris: Recueil Sirey.

Carstairs, À.M. 1980. *A Short History of Electoral Systems in Western Europe.* London: Allen and Unwin.

Chandler, J. A. 1982. "The Plurality Vote: A Reappraisal." *Political Studies* 30: 87–94.

Childs, R.S. 1965. *The First 50 Years.* New York: American Book-Stratford Press.

———. 1952. *Civic Victories.* New York: Harper.

Chubb, B. 1963. "Going About Persecuting Civil Servants. The Role of the Irish Parliamentary Representative." *Political Studies* 11: 272–86.

———. 1959. "Ireland 1957." In *Elections Abroad,* edited by D.E. Butler, pp. 181–226. London: Macmillan.

Claeys, P., E. de Graeve-Lismont, and N. Loeb-Mayer. 1980. *European or National? The 1979 Election in Belgium.* Leuven: Katholieke Universiteit.

Clark, C.J. 1980. "Address to the llth Annual Leadership Conference Sponsored by the Center for the Study of the Presidency." Ottawa. Mimeographed.

Cohan, A. S., R. D. McKinlay, and A. Mughan. 1975. "The Used Vote and Electoral Outcomes: The Irish General Election of 1973." *British Journal of Political Science* 5: 363–83.

Coleman, J. S. 1973. *The Mathematics of Collective Action.* London: Heinemann.

Connecticut Law Review. 1969. "Minority Representation on Local Legislative Bodies." *Connecticut Law Review* 2: 191–201.

Connecticut Public Expenditure Council. 1981. *Local Charter Provisions Re: Minority Representation on Legislative Body and Shared Legislative Authority.* Hartford, Conn.

———. 1968. "Minority Representation on Local Legislative Bodies?" *News and Views,* no. 82.

Conradt, D. P. 1970. "Electoral Law Politics in West Germany." *Political Studies* 18: 341–56.

Considérant, V. 1842. "La représentation nationale est un mensonge." *La Phalange,* June 17.

Converse, P. E. 1969. "Of Time and Partisan Stability." *Comparative Political Studies* 2: 139–71.

Craig, J. A. 1982. "Malta: Mintoff's Election Victory." *West European Politics* 5: 318–20.

Curtice, J., and M. Steed. 1982. "Electoral Choice and the Production of Government." *British Journal of Political Science* 12: 249–98.

Curtis, G. L. 1971. *Election Campaigning Japanese Style.* New York: Columbia University Press.

Dahl, R.A. 1956. *A Preface to Democratic Theory.* Chicago: University of Chicago Press.

Davidson, C., and G. Korbel. 1981. "At-Large Elections and Minority Representation: A Re-Examination of Historical and Contemporary Evidence." *Journal of Politics* 43: 982–1005.

Dishaw, F. 1971. "Bemerkungen zur Konkurrenz im deutschen Parteiensystem." In *Sozialwissenschaftliches Jahrbuch für Politik,* Vol. 2, edited by R. Wildenmann et al., pp. 61–71. Munich: Olzog.

Dixon, R. G., Jr. 1968. *Democratic Representation: Reapportionment in Law and Politics.* New York: Oxford University Press.

Dobell, W. M. 1981. "A Limited Corrective to Plurality Voting." *Canadian Public Policy* 7: 75–81.

Doron, G., and R. Kronick. 1977. "Single Transferable Vote: An Example of a Perverse Social Choice Function." *American Journal of Political Science* 21: 303–11.

Duhamel, O. 1983. "Pour une démocratie majoritaire et proportionnelle." *Le Monde*, March 4, p. 2.

Duverger, M. 1984. "'Duverger's Law': Thirty Years Later." In *Electoral Laws and Their Political Consequences*, edited by B. Grofman and A. Lijphart. New York: Agathon Press.

———. 1982. *La république des citoyens*. Paris: Ed. Ramsay.

———. 1980. *Institutions politiques et droit constitutionnel: Tome I, Les grands systèmes politiques*. 16th ed. Paris: Presses Universitaires de France.

———. 1956. "Esquisse d'une théorie de la représentation politique." In *L'évolution du droit public: mélanges en l'honneur d'Achille Mestre*, pp. 211–20. Paris: Sireyl.

———. 1954. *Political Parties: Their Organization and Activity in the Modern State*. New York: Wiley; London: Methuen.

Economist, The, 1983. "A Sense of Proportion," *The Economist*, June 18, pp. 13–15.

Emmert, R. 1983. "Limited Voting in a Nonpartisan Context: Rome, New York." Paper presented at the Annual Meeting of the American Political Science Association, Chicago, September 1–4.

Esmein, A., and H. Nézard. 1927. *Eléments de droit constitutionnel français et comparé*. Paris: Reculeil Sirey.

Everson, D. H., and J. A. Parker. 1983. "Legislative Elections: Reviving an Old Partnership." *Illinois Issues* 9: 14–17.

Everson, D. H., et al. 1982. *The Cutback Amendment*. Illinois Issues Special Report. Springfield: Sangamon State University.

Farah, B. G. 1981. "Political Representation in West Germany: The Institutionalization and Maintenance of Mass-Elite Linkages." Ph.D. dissertation, University of Michigan.

Featherman, S. 1980. "Limited Voting and Local Government: A View from the Politician's Seat." Paper presented at the Annual Meeting of the American Political Science Association, Washington, D.C., August 28–31.

Ferejohn, J.A. 1977. "On the Decline of Competition in Congressional Elections." *American Political Science Review* 71: 166–76.

Finer, S.E., ed. 1975. *Adversary Politics and Electoral Reform*. London: Wigram.

Fiorina, M. P. 1977. "The Case of the Vanishing Marginals: The Bureaucracy Did It." *American Political Science Review* 71: 177–81.

Fishburn, P. C. 1982. "Monotonicity Paradoxes in the Theory of Elections." *Discrete Applied Mathematics* 4: 119–34.

———. 1981. "An Analysis of Simple Voting Systems for Electing Committees." *SIAM Journal on Applied Mathematics* 41: 499–502.

———, and S. J. Brams. 1983a. "Manipulability of Voting by Sincere Truncation of Preferences." Mimeographed.

———. 1983b. "Paradoxes of Preferential Voting." *Mathematics Magazine* 56: 207–14.

Fisichella, D. 1983. *Elezioni e Democrazia: Un' Analisi Comparata*, 2nd ed. Bologna: Il Mulino.

Flora, P. 1983. *State, Economy and Society in Western Europe 1815–1975*. London: Macmillan.

———., and A. J. Heidenheimer, eds. 1981. *The Development of Welfare States in Europe and America.* New Brunswick: Transaction.

Forschungsgruppe Wahlen. 1983. "Politik in der Bundesrepublik, Februar 1983." Mannheim.

Gallagher, M. 1975. "Disproportionality in a Proportional Representation System: The Irish Experience." *Political Studies* 23: 501–13.

Gibbard, A. 1973. "Manipulation of Voting Schemes: A General Result." *Econometrica* 41: 587–601.

Gideonse, H. D. 1940. "Preface" to Hermens 1940.

Goguel, F. 1982. "Modes de scrutin et alternance politique." *Revue Politique et Parlementaire* 84: 13–25.

Gosnell, H. F. 1939. "A List System with Single Candidate Preference." *American Political Science Review* 33: 645–50.

Gregory, M. 1981. "Zimbabwe 1980: Politicisation through Armed Struggle and Electoral Mobilisation." *Journal of Commonwealth and Comparative Studies* 19: 62–94.

Grofman, B. 1982. "Reformers, Politicians, and the Courts: A Preliminary Look at U.S. Redistricting in the 1980s." *Political Geography Quarterly* 1: 303–316.

———. 1975. "A Review of Macro Election Systems." In *German Political Yearbook (Sozialwissenschaftliches Jahrbuch für Politik)*, Vol. 4, edited by R. Wildenmann, pp. 303–52. Munich: Gunter Olzog.

———, and A. Lijphart, eds. 1984. *Electoral Laws and Their Political Consequences.* New York: Agathon Press.

Gudgin, G., and P.J. Taylor. 1979. *Seats, Votes and the Spatial Organisation of Elections.* London: Pion.

———. 1976. "The Myth of Non-Partisan Cartography." *Urban Studies* 13: 13–25.

Haas, E.B. 1967. "The Uniting of Europe and the Uniting of Latin America." *Journal of Common Market Studies* 5: 315–43.

Hallett, G. H., Jr. 1940. *Proportional Representation: The Key to Democracy*, rev. ed. New York: National Municipal League.

———. Hamilton, H. D. 1978. *Electing the Cincinnati City Council.* Cincinnati: Stephen H. Wilder Foundation.

———. 1969. "Costs of Reform: Structural Change in City Governments May Not Resolve Alienation Problems." *National Civic Review* 58: 469–75.

Hansard Society. 1976. *The Report of the Hansard Society Commission on Electoral Reform.* London: Hansard Society for Parliamentary Government.

Hare, T. 1873. *The Election of Representatives, Parliamentary and Municipal*, 4th ed. London: Longman, Green.

Heilig, P. 1983. "District Representation and Satisfaction with City Government." Paper presented at the Annual Meeting of the American Political Science Association, Chicago, September 1–4.

Heisel, W. D. 1982. "Abandonment of Proportional Representation and the Impact of 9-X Voting in Cincinnati." Paper presented at the Annual Meeting of the American Political Science Association, Denver, September 2–5.

Herman, V., and M. Hagger, eds. 1980. *The Legislation of Direct Elections to the European Parliament.* Farnborough: Gower.

Hermens, F.A. 1976. "Electoral Systems and Political Systems: Recent Developments in Britain." *Parliamentary Affairs* 29: 47–59.

———. 1972a. *Democracy or Anarchy? A Study of Proportional Representation*, 2nd ed. New York: Johnson Reprint Corporation.

———. 1972b. "Sicherung, Ausbau und Verankerung des parlamentarischen Systems in der Bundesrepublik." in *Verfassung und Verfassungswirklichkeit*, Vol. 6, pp. 5–82. Cologne: Heymanns.

———. 1968a. *Verfassungslehre*, 2nd ed. Cologne: Westdeutscher Verlag.

———. 1968b. *La Democrazia Rappresentativa*. Florence: Vallecchi.

———. 1968c. "Besondere Stellungnahme." In *Zur Neugestaltung des Bundestagswahlrechts*, pp. 61–63. Bonn.

———. 1962. "Politische Parteien und politische Mässigung in den Vereinigten Staaten." In *Grundfragen der freiheitlichen Demokratie,"* pp. 59–74. Frankfurt: Diesterweg.

———. 1959a. *Introduction to Modern Politics*. Notre Dame: University of Notre Dame Press.

———. 1959b. "Totalitarian Power Structure and Russian Foreign Policy." *Journal of Politics* 21: 434–54.

———. 1958. *The Representaitve Republic*. Notre Dame: University of Notre Dame Press.

———. 1940. *Democracy and Proportional Representation*. Chicago: University of Chicago Press.

———. 1933. "Die antiparlamentarische Bewegung in Frankreich." *Zeitschrift für Politik* 22: 803–16.

Hermet, G., R. Rose, and A. Rouquié, eds. 1978. *Elections Without Choice*. London: Macmillan.

Hoag, C. G., and G. C. Hallett, Jr. 1926. *Proportional Representation*. New York: Macmillan.

Hoffmann, S. 1966. "Obstinate or Obsolete? The Fate of the Nation State and the Case of Western Europe." *Daedalus* 95: 862–915.

Huber, C. 1979. "Legislation for European Elections in the Nine." In *European Electoral Systems Handbook*, edited by G. Hand, J. Georgel, and C. Sasse, pp. 234–52. London: Butterworths.

Hume, E. 1982. "Plan to Ensure Congress Seat for Latino May Be Backfiring." *Los Angeles Times*, April 18, part II, pp. 1, 5.

Inter-Parliamentary Union. 1976. *Parliaments of the World*. London: Macmillan.

Irvine, W.P. 1982. "Does the Candidate Make a Difference? *Canadian Journal of Political Science* 15: 755–82.

———. 1981. *Does Canada Need a New Electoral System?*, 2nd ed. Kingston: Institute of Intergovernmental Relations, Queen's University.

———. 1979. *Does Canada Need a New Electoral System?* Kingston: Institute of Intergovernmental Relations, Queen's University.

Jackson, W. K. 1973. *New Zealand: Politics of Change*. Wellington: Read Education.

Johnston, R. J. 1983. "Texts, Actors and Higher Managers: Judges, Bureaucrats and the Political Organisation of Space." *Political Geography Quarterly* 2: 3–20.

———. 1982a. "Redistricting by Neutral Commissions: A Perspective from Britain." *Annals of the Association of American Geographers* 72: 457–70.

———. 1982b. "Political Geography and Political Power." In *Power, Voting and Voting Power*, edited by M.J. Holler, pp. 289–306. Vienna: Physica-Verlag.

———. 1979. *Political, Electoral and Spatial Systems: An Essay in Political Geography*. Oxford: Clarendon Press.

Kaack, H. 1971. *Geschichte und Struktur des Deutschen Parteiensystems.* Cologne: Westdeutscher Verlag.

Kaase, M. 1965. "Politiker und Wählerschaft." *Zeitwende* 36: 537–45.

Katz, R..S. 1984. "Intraparty Preference Voting." In *Electoral Laws and Their Political Consequences*, edited by B. Grofman and A. Lijphart. New York: Agathon Press.

———. 1981. "But How Many Candidates Should We Have in Donegal? Numbers of Candidates and Electoral Efficiency in Ireland." *British Journal of Political Science* 11: 117–22.

———. 1980. *A Theory of Parties and Electoral Systems.* Baltimore: Johns Hopkins University Press.

Kohl, J. 1982. "Zur langfristigen Entwicklung der politischen Partizipation in Westeuropa." In *Probleme politischer Partizipation im Modernisierungsprozess*, edited by P. Steinbach, pp. 473–503. Stuttgart: Klett-Cotta.

Laakso, M. 1979. "Should a Two-and-a-Half Law Replace the Cube Law in British Elections?" *British Journal of Political Science* 9: 355–62.

———, and R. Taagepera. 1979. " 'Effective' Number of Parties: A Measure with Application to West Europe." *Comparative Political Studies* 12: 3–27.

———. 1978. "Proportional Representation in Scandinavia: Implications for Finland." *Scandinavian Political Studies* 1: 43–60.

Lakeman, E. 1982. *Power to Elect: The Case for Proportional Representation.* London: Heinemann.

———. 1974. *How Democracies Vote: A Study of Electoral Systems*, 4th ed. London: Faber and Faber.

Laver, M. 1981. *The Politics of Private Desires.* London: Penguin.

———, and J. Underhill. 1982. "The Bargaining Advantages of Combining with Others." *British Journal of Political Science* 12: 27–42.

Leduc, A. 1945. "Gallic Trends: Will France Swing Toward Democratic Socialism?" *The New Leader*, October 20, pp. 9, 15.

Leibholz, G. 1929. *Das Wesen der Repräsentation unter besonderer Berücksichtigung des Repräsentativsystems.* Berlin: De Gruyter.

Liberal/SDP Alliance Commission on Constitutional Reform. 1982. *Electoral Reform: Fairer Voting in Natural Communities.* London: Poland St. Publications.

Lijphart, A. 1984. "Proportionality by Non-PR Methods: Ethnic Representation in Belgium, Cyprus, Lebanon, New Zealand, West Germany, and Zimbabwe." In *Electoral Laws and Their Political Consequences*, edited by B. Grofman and A. Lijphart. New York: Agathon Press.

———. 1982. "Comparative Perspectives on Fair Representation: The Plurality-Majority Rule, Geographical Districting, and Alternative Electoral Arrangements." In *Representation and Redistricting Issues*, edited by B. Grofman et al., pp. 143–59. Lexington, Mass.: Lexington Books.

———, and R.W. Gibberd. 1977. "Thresholds and Payoffs in List Systems of Proportional Representation." *European Journal of Political Research* 5: 219–44.

———, R. Lopez Pintor, and Y. Sone. 1984. "The Limited Vote and the Single Non-Transferable Vote: Lessons from the Japanese and Spanish Examples." In *Electoral Laws and Their Political Consequences*, edited by B. Grofman and A. Lijphart. New York: Agathon Press.

Lippmann, W. 1940. "Today and Tomorrow." *The Cleveland Plain Dealer*, October 3.

Lipset, S. M., and S. Rokkan, eds. 1967. *Party Systems and Voter Alignments*. New York: Free Press.

Littlefield, N. O. 1965. "Minority Representation Under C.G.S. 9-167a." *Connecticut Bar Journal* 39: 386–404.

Loosemore, J., and V. J. Hanby. 1971. "The Theoretical Limits of Maximum Distortion: Some Analytic Expressions for Electoral Systems." *British Journal of Political Science* 1: 467–77.

Mackenzie, W. J. M. 1958. *Free Elections*. London: Allen and Unwin.

Mackerras, M. 1980. *Elections 1980*. Sydney: Angus and Robertson.

Mackie, T. T., and R. Rose. 1982. *The International Almanac of Electoral History*, 2nd ed. New York: Facts on File.

Mair, P. 1982. "Redistricting and Gerrymandering: The Irish Experience of the Single Transferable Vote." Paper presented at the Annual Meeting of the American Political Science Association, Denver, September 2–5.

Martinez Cuadrado, M. 1983. "L'Espagne: Les systèmes électoraux de la nouvelle loi constitutionnelle espagnole du 5 janvier 1977." In *Les modes de scrutin des dix-huit pays libres de l'Europe occidentale: Leurs résultats et leurs effets comparés*, edited by J. Cadart, pp. 355–70. Paris: Presses Universitaires de France.

May, K.O. 1952. "A Set of Independent, Necessary and Sufficient Conditions for Simple Majority Decision." *Econometrica* 20: 680–84.

Mayhew, D. 1974. "Congressional Elections: The Case of the Vanishing Marginals." *Polity* 6: 295–351.

McNelly, T. 1982. "Limited Voting in Japanese Parliamentary Elections." Paper presented at the Annual Meeting of the American Political Science Association, Denver, September 2–5.

McRobie, A.D. 1978. "Ethnic Representation: The New Zealand Experience." In *Politics in New Zealand: A Reader*, edited by S. Levine, pp. 270–83. Sydney: Allen and Unwin.

Merrill, S., III. 1984. "A Comparison of Efficiency of Multicandidate Electoral Systems." *American Journal of Political Science* 28: 23–48.

Meyer, H. 1973. *Wahlsystem und Verfassungsordnung*. Frankfurt: Metzner.

Mill, J.S. 1862. *Considerations on Representative Government*. New York: Harper and Brothers.

Miller, W.E., and D.E. Stokes. 1963. "Constituency Influence in Congress." *American Political Science Review* 57: 45–56.

Milnor, A.J. 1969. *Elections and Political Stability*. Boston: Little, Brown.

Mirabeau, Comte de. 1834. "Sur la représentation illégale de la nation dans ces états actuels et sur la nécessité de convoquer une assemblée générale des trois ordres." In *Oeuvres de Mirabeau*, edited by M. Merilhon, Vol. I, pp. 3–21. Paris: Didier.

Misch, A. 1974. *Das Wahlsystem zwischen Theorie und Taktik: Zur Frage von Mehrheitswahl und Verhältniswahl in der Programmatik der Sozialdemokratie bis 1933*. Berlin: Duncker und Humblot.

National Advisory Commission on Civil Disorders. 1968. *Report of the National Advisory Commission on Civil Disorders*. Washington, D.C.: Government Printing Office.

Newland, R. A. 1982. *Comparative Electoral Systems*. London: Arthur McDougall Fund.

Newman, E. B., and M. S. Rogers. 1953. "PR Voting: An Analysis of the 1951 Cambridge City Elections." Mimeographed.

New York State Constitutional Convention Committee. 1938. "Proportional Representation for the State Legislature." In *Report of the New York State Constitutional Convention Committee.* New York.

New York Times, 1941. "P.R. and the Council." *New York Times,* November 14. ber 14.

Niedermayer, O. 1983. *Europäische Parteien? Zur grenzüberschreitenden Interaktion politischer Parteien im Rahmen der Europäischen Gemeinschaft.* Frankfurt: Campus.

Nohlen, D. 1983. *Elections and Electoral Systems.* Bonn: Friedrich-Ebert-Stiftung.

————. 1981. *Sistemas electorales del mundo.* Madrid: Centro de Estudios Constitucionales.

————. 1978. *Wahlsysteme der Welt–Daten und Analysen: Ein Handbuch.* Munich: Piper.

Nurmi, H. 1983. "Voting Procedures: A Summary Analysis." *British Journal of Political Science* 13: 181–208.

————. 1982. "On Taking Preferences Seriously." Mimeographed.

————. 1981. "On the Properties of Voting Systems." *Scandinavian Political Studies* 4: 19–32.

Nuscheler, F. 1969. "Zypern." In *Die Wahl der Parlamente und anderer Staatsorgane: Ein Handbuch,* edited by D. Sternberger and B. Vogel, pp. 1419–27. Berlin: De Gruyter.

O'Loughlin, J. 1982. "The Identification and Evaluation of Racial Gerrymandering." *Annals of the Association of American Geographers* 72: 165–84.

————. 1979. "District Size and Party Electoral Strength: A Comparison of Sixteen Democracies." *Environment and Planning A* 12: 247–62.

————, and A.-M. Taylor. 1982. "Choices in Redistricting and Electoral Outcomes: The Case of Mobile, Alabama." *Political Geography Quarterly* 1: 317–40.

O'Rourke, T. G. 1982. "Constitutional and Statutory Challenges to Local At-Large Elections." Paper presented at the Annual Meeting of the American Political Science Association, Denver, September 2–5.

Owen, G., and B. Grofman. 1982. "Collective Representation and the Seats-Votes Swing Relationship." Paper presented at the Annual Meeting of the American Association of Geographers, San Antonio, April 22–28.

Paddison, R. 1976. "Spatial Bias and Redistricting in Proportional Representation Election Systems: A Case Study of the Republic of Ireland." *Tijdschrift voor Economische en Sociale Geografie* 67: 230–40.

Parliamentary Library, Australia. 1983. *Federal Elections 1983.* Basic Paper No. 5, 1983. Canberra: Department of the Parliamentary Library, Parliament of the Commonwealth of Australia.

————. 1980. *Federal Elections, 18 October 1980: Analysis of the Outcome in the House of Representatives and in the Senate.* Basic Paper No. 9, 1980. Canberra: Department of the Parliamentary Library, Parliament of Australia.

Pasquino, G. 1979. "Suggerimenti scettici agli ingegneri elettorali." *Il Mulino* 265: 749–80.

Piesse, E. L. 1913. "Bibliography of Proportional Representation in Tasmania." *Papers and Proceedings of the Royal Society of Tasmania* 1913: 39–75.

Plott, C. 1967. "A Nation of Equilibrium and Its Possibility under Majority Rule." *American Economic Review* 57: 787–806.

Powell, G. B., Jr. 1982. *Contemporary Democracies: Participation, Stability and Violence.* Cambridge, Mass.: Harvard University Press.

Pulzer, P. 1983. "Germany." In *Democracy and Elections: Electoral Systems and Their Political Consequences,* edited by V. Bogdanor and D. Butler, pp. 84–109. Cambridge: Cambridge University Press.

Rabier, J.-R. 1977. "Les attitudes du public a l'égard de l'élection du Parlement européen au suffrage universel direct." *Revue d'Intégration Européenne* 1: 47–62.

Rae, D. W. 1971. *The Political Consequences of Electoral Laws,* 2nd ed. New Haven: Yale University Press.

———. 1967. *The Political Consequences of Electoral Laws.* New Haven: Yale University Press.

———, V. Hanby, and J. Loosemore. 1971. "Thresholds of Representation and Thresholds of Exclusion: An Analytic Note on Electoral Systems." *Comparative Political Studies* 3: 479–88.

Reif, K. 1984. *Ten European Elections 1979 and 1984.* Farnborough: Gower.

———. 1983. "Die Nebenwahlen: Einbussen der französischen Linken seit ihren Wahlsiegen 1981." *Zeitschrift für Parlamentsfragen* 14: 195–208.

———. 1980. "Primaries for '81? The 1979 European Elections in France." In *EES-Report VII.* Mannheim: European Electoral Studies.

———. 1978. "European Elections and National Electoral Cycles." Paper presented at the Annual Meeting of the American Political Science Association, New York, August 31–September 3.

———, R. Cayrol, and O. Niedermayer. 1980. "National Political Parties' Middle-Level Elites and European Integration." *European Journal of Political Research* 8: 91–112.

———, and H. Schmitt. 1980. "Nine Second-Order National Elections: A Conceptual Framework for the Analysis of European Election Results." *European Journal of Political Research* 8: 3–44, 145–62.

Riker, W. H. 1982a. *Liberalism Against Populism: A Confrontation Between the Theory of Democracy and the Theory of Social Choice.* San Francisco: Freeman.

———. 1982b. "The Two-Party System and Duverger's Law: An Essay on the History of Political Science." *American Political Science Review* 76: 753–66.

Rogaly, J. 1976. *Parliament for the People.* London: Temple Smith.

Rondot, P. 1966. "The Political Institutions of Lebanese Democracy." In *Politics in Lebanon,* edited by L. Binder, pp. 127–41. New York: Wiley.

Rose, R. 1976. *Northern Ireland: Time of Choice.* Washington, D.C.: American Enterprise Institute.

———. 1964. "Parties, Factions and Tendencies in Britain." *Political Studies* 12: 33–46.

———, and T. T. Mackie. 1983. "Incumbency in Government: Asset or Liability?" In *Western European Party Systems,* edited by H. Daalder and P. Mair, pp. 115–37. Beverly Hills: Sage.

———, and D. W. Urwin. 1969. "Social Cohesion, Political Parties and Strains in Regimes." *Comparative Political Studies* 2: 7–67.

Royal Commission on Systems of Election. 1910. *Report, Cd. 5163.* London.

Sacks, P. M. 1970. "Bailiwicks, Locality, and Religion: Three Elements in an Irish Dail Constituency Election." *Economic and Social Review* 1: 531–54.

Salvemini, G. 1927. *The Fascist Dictatorship in Italy.* New York: Holt.

Sartori, G. 1984. "The Influence of Electoral Systems: Faulty Laws or Faulty Method?" In *Electoral Laws and Their Political Consequences*, edited by B. Grofman and A. Lijphart. New York: Agathon Press.

Sasse, C., et al. 1981. *The European Parliament: Towards a Uniform Procedure for Direct Elections*. Florence: European University Institute.

Satterthwaite, M. A. 1975. "Strategy-Proofness and Arrow's Conditions: Existence and Correspondence Theorems for Voting Procedures and Social Welfare Functions." *Journal of Economic Theory* 10: 187–217.

Scarrow, H. 1982. "The Impact of Reapportionment on Party Representation in the State of New York." In *Representation and Redistricting Issues*, edited by B. Grofman et al., pp. 223–36. Lexington, Mass: Lexington Books.

Schattschneider, E. E. 1960. *The Semisovereign People: A Realist's View of Democracy in America*. Hinsdale, Ill.: Dryden.

Schütt, E. 1973. *Wahlsystemdiskussion und parlamentarische Demokratie*. Hamburg: Lüdke.

Seitlinger, J. 1982. "Report Drawn up on Behalf of the Political Affairs Committee on a Draft Uniform Electoral Procedure for the Election of Members of the European Parliament." EP-Document 1-988/81 (PE 64.569 fin.).

Shively, W. P. 1977. "Information Costs and the Partisan Life Cycle." Paper presented at the Annual Meeting of the American Political Science Association, Washington, D.C., September 1–4.

Sidney, J. B. 1981. "Single Ballot Non-Ranked Voting Systems for Committee Selection." Mimeographed.

Smith, J. H. 1973. "Aggregation of Preferences with Variable Electorate." *Econometrica* 41: 1027–41.

Société pour l'Etude de la Représentation Proportionnelle. 1888. *La représentation proportionnelle*. Paris: Pichon.

Spafford, D. 1980. Review of Irvine 1979. *Canadian Journal of Political Science* 13: 392–93.

Spiegel, Der. 1983. "In fremden Teichen." *Der Spiegel*, February 28, pp. 37–41.

Statistisches Bundesamt. 1981. *Wahl zum 9. Deutschen Bundestag am 5. Oktober 1980: Heft 8, Wahlbeteiligung und Stimmabgabe der Männer und Frauen nach dem Alter*. Stuttgart: Kohlhammer.

Steed, M. 1981. "Twelve into One: The Effect of Using Diverse Procedures for the First European Parliamentary Elections." In *Das Europa der Zweiten Generation*, edited by R. Bieber et al., pp. 287–310. Baden-Baden: Nomos.

———, and K. Reif. 1982. "Procedure for Allocation of Seats between Constituency Lists in the EP Electoral System." Report to the Commission of the European Communities, Brussels.

Sternberger, D., and B. Vogel, eds. 1969. *Die Wahl der Parlamente und anderer Staatsorgane: Ein Handbuch*. Berlin: De Bruyter.

Still, E. 1984. "Alternatives to Single Member Districts." In *Minority Vote Dilution*, edited by C. Davidson. Washington, D.C.: Joint Center for Political Studies.

Stockwin, J. A. A. 1983. "Japan." In *Democracy and Elections: Electoral Systems and Their Political Consequences*, edited by V. Bogdanor and D. Butler, pp. 209–27. Cambridge: Cambridge University Press.

Straetz, R. A. 1958. *PR Politics in Cincinnati*. New York: New York University Press.

Straffin, P. D., Jr. 1980. *Topics in the Theory of Voting*. Boston: Birkhäuser.

Taagepera, R. 1983. "Effect of District Magnitude on Party Representation." Unpublished paper.

——, and M. Laakso. 1980. "Proportionality Profiles of West European Electoral Systems." *European Journal of Political Research* 8: 423–46.

Task Force on Canadian Unity. 1979. *A Future Together*. Ottawa: Minister of Supply and Services.

Tasmania House of Assembly Select Committee on Electoral Reform. 1957. *Report of Select Committee with Minutes of Proceedings*. Hobart.

Taylor, D. 1973. "Enter the Cautious Mr. Cosgrave." *The Times* (London), March 3, p. 14.

Taylor, P. J. 1973. "Some Implications of the Spatial Organisation of Elections." *Transactions, Institute of British Geographers* 60: 121–36.

——, and G. Gudgin. 1977. "Antipodean Demises of Labour." In *People, Places and Votes*, edited by R. J. Johnston, pp. 111–20. Armidale: University of New England.

——, and R. J. Johnston. 1979. *Geography of Elections*. London: Penguin.

——. 1978. "Population Distribution and Political Power in the European Parliament." *Regional Studies* 12: 61–68.

Times, The. 1973a. "Fianna Fail Concedes Defeat in Eire." *The Times* (London), March 2, p. 1.

Times, The. 1973b. "Mr. Cosgrave Comes to the Fore." *The Times* (London), March 3, p. 15.

Tufte, E. R. 1978. *Political Control of the Economy*. Princeton: Princeton University Press.

——. 1973. "The Relationship Between Seats and Votes in Two-Party Systems." *American Political Science Review* 67: 540–54.

Unkelbach, H. 1956. *Grundlagen der Wahlsystematik: Stabilitätsbedingungen der parlamentarischen Demokratie*. Göttingen: Vandenhoeck und Ruprecht.

Uslaner, R. M. 1983. "The Lord Helps Those Who Help their Constituents: Redeeming Promises in the Promised Land." Paper presented at the Annual Meeting of the Midwest Political Science Association, Chicago, April 20–23.

Weaver, L. 1984. "The Rise, Decline and Resurrection of Proportional Representation in Local Governments in the United States." In *Electoral Laws and Their Political Consequences*, edited by B. Grofman and A. Lijphart. New York: Agathon Press.

——. 1980a. *Majority Preferential Voting and Minority Representation: Some Optional Features of Local Electoral Systems in Michigan*. East Lansing: Social Science Research Bureau, Michigan State University.

——. 1980b. "How Unrepresentative Should Representative Government Be Allowed to Be?" Paper presented at the Annual Meeting of the American Political Science Association, Washington, D.C., August 28–31.

Weill-Raynal, E. 1973. "La réforme électorale: Enjeu des prochaines élections?" *Revue Politique et Parlementaire* 75: 6–22.

——. 1966. "La représentation nationale proportionnelle avec scrutin individuel." *Revue Politique et Parlementaire* 68: 23–29.

Weiner, M., and E. Ozbudun. 1984. *Competitive Elections in Developing Countries*. Washington, D.C.: American Enterprise Institute.

Wildenmann, R., W. Kaltefleiter, and U. Schleth. 1965. "Auswirkungen von Wahlsystemen auf das Parteien- und Regierungssystem der Bundesrepublik." In *Zur Soziologie der Wahl*, edited by E. K. Scheuch and R. Wildenmann, pp. 74–112. Cologne: Westdeutscher Verlag.

Wright, J. F. H. 1980. *Mirror of the Nation's Mind: Australia's Electoral Experiments.* Sydney: Hale and Iremonger.

Young, R. E. 1965. *The Place System in Texas Elections.* Austin: University of Texas Press.

Zentralarchiv für Empirische Sozialforschung. 1981. *Wahlstudie 1980.* Cologne.

——. 1979. *Politik in der Bundesrepublik, August 1969.* Cologne.

Zimmerman, J. F. 1982. "Proportional Representation in the Republic of Ireland." Paper presented at the Annual Meeting of the American Political Science Association, Denver, September 2–5.

——. 1972. *The Federated City: Community Control in Large Cities.* New York: St. Martin's Press.

——. 1971. "Electoral Reform Needed to End Political Alienation." *National Civic Review* 60: 6–11, 21.

——. 1969. "Designing an Electoral System for a Consolidated Government." Speech to the Charlotte-Mecklenburg Charter Commission.

Index

A

additional-member system, 8–10, 37, 43–44, 64, 153–77, 207–8, 241 (*see also* Germany)
AL (*see* at-large systems)
Allende, Salvador, 105
alternative vote, 4–5, 9, 10, 63–64, 74, 91, 93, 128–31, 139, 147–51, 225–26 (*see also* Australia)
Andrae, Carl George, 148
anti-system parties, 10, 182–89
approval voting, 5, 151
Aristotle, 25
at-large systems, 100–1, 192–93, 194–95, 202–3, 205 (*see also* plurality system)
Australia: alternative vote in, 4, 9, 10, 42, 63–64, 74, 91, 93, 128–31; STV in, 8, 9, 117, 128, 131–34, 148 (*see also* alternative vote)
Austria: double-ballot system in, 181–82; government stability in, 45, 79, 105, 171; PR in, 75, 78, 98, 217; two-party system in, 37, 79, 98, 208
AV (*see* alternative vote)

B

Balinski, M.L., 66–67
Bangemann, Martin, 241
Beard, Charles A., 16
Belgium: cabinet formation in, 32, 33, 57, 105; double-ballot system in, 181, 184–85; and European Parliament, 237, 238; PR in, 47, 218, 225
Berlin, 157
Blum, Léon, 23–24
Bocklet, Reinhold, 241
Brams, Steven J., 4, 5, 9, 10, 147–51, 175–77
Butler, David E., 9, 12, 225–29

C

Cambridge, Mass., 148, 197–98, 201
Canada: additional-member model for, 9–10, 165–74; electoral system debate in, 11, 166; federalism in, 109, 243; plurality system in, 42, 74, 96, 105, 145, 208
Capitant, René, 22
Chandler, J.A., 67
Cincinnati, 121, 123
Clark, C. Joseph, 172
Condorcet candidates, 33–34, 106, 147, 150–51 (*see also* paradox of voting)
Considérant, Victor, 15
Craxi, Bettino, 27, 28
cube law, 61, 97, 227
cumulative vote, 5, 10, 192, 225; defined, 116, 205; evaluation of, 116, 198–99, 201–04; in Illinois, 11, 116, 195, 198–99, 201–2, 204, 208
Curtice, J., 61

H

J

I

K

About the Editors and the Contributors

STEVEN J. BRAMS is Professor of Politics at New York University. His most recent books are *Approval Voting,* coauthored with Peter C. Fishburn, *Superior Beings: If They Exist, How Would we Know?,* and *Biblical Games: A Strategic Analysis of Stories in the Old Testament.*

DAVID E. BUTLER has been a Fellow of Nuffield College, Oxford, from 1951 on. He has been author or coauthor of each of the Nuffield election studies since then. Among his many books are *Political Change in Britain,* coauthored with Donald Stokes, *British Political Facts 1900-79,* and *The Canberra Model.*

MAURICE DUVERGER is Professor of Political Science at the Sorbonne, University of Paris I. He is the author of *Political Parties: Their Organization and Activity in the Modern State,* first published in French in 1951 and first published in English translation in 1954. He has also written many other books and articles in comparative public law and comparative politics.

PETER C. FISHBURN is a member of the Mathematics and Statistics Research Center of Bell Laboratories at Murray Hill, New Jersey. He is the author of several books in the areas of decision theory and mathematics, including *The Theory of Social Choice* and *Approval Voting,* coauthored with Steven J. Brams, and publishes widely in technical journals.

DOMENICO FISICHELLA is Professor of Political Science at the University of Rome. Among his many publications, the most recent books are *La rappresentanza politica, Elezioni e democrazia, Politica e mutamento sociale,* and *Analisi del totalitarismo.*

BERNARD GROFMAN is Professor of Political Science and Social Psychology at the University of California, Irvine. His main research concerns mathematical models of collective decision making. He has written numerous articles on subjects like jury decision making, voter turnout, the political consequences of electoral laws, and law and social-science issues.

GEORGE H. HALLETT, JR., is a Research Associate for the New York Citizens Union Foundation and the Civic Charter Review Coalition. Most of his career has been deeply involved in the study and improvement of election methods. He organized the first of the New York City community school board elections by proportional representation. He wrote the classic *Proportional Representation* with Clarence G. Hoag in 1926.

FERDINAND A. HERMENS is Professor of Political Science, Emeritus, at the University of Cologne, West Germany, and Research Professor at American University in Washington, D.C. He is the author of many books and articles, including the classic *Democracy or Anarchy? A Study of Proportional Representation,* first published in 1941, *Demokratie und Kapitalismus,* and *The Representative Republic.*

WILLIAM P. IRVINE is Professor of Political Science at Queen's University in Kingston, Ontario, Canada. His research interests are on parties and elections in Canada, and, in particular, on reform of the Canadian electoral system at the federal level. His publications include *Does Canada Need a New Electoral System?*

R. J. JOHNSTON is Professor of Geography at the University of Sheffield. His main interests are in electoral, political, and urban studies, and he is the author of several books in these areas, including *Political, Electoral and Spatial Systems*, *Geography of Elections*, coauthored with Peter J. Taylor, and *City and Society*.

MAX KAASE is Professor of Political Science and Comparative Social Research at the University of Mannheim, West Germany. His interests include democratic theory, electoral sociology, mass communications, and methodology. He is the coauthor, with Samuel H. Barnes and others, of the large empirical cross-national study *Political Action*.

RICHARD S. KATZ is Associate Professor of Political Science at the Johns Hopkins University. His main work has focused on elections and electoral behavior in Europe and the United States, on which he has published numerous articles. He is the author of *A Theory of Parties and Electoral Systems* and coauthor of *America Votes*.

ENID LAKEMAN was the Director of the Electoral Reform Society of Great Britain and Ireland from 1960 until her retirement in 1979, and now serves as Editorial Consultant to the Society. She played a major part in the defeat by referendum of the Irish government's two attempts to introduce the British electoral system in 1959 and 1968. Her many publications include *Power to Elect*, *How Democracies Vote*, and *Nine Democracies*.

AREND LIJPHART is Professor of Political Science at the University of California, San Diego. His field of specialization is comparative politics, especially the comparative study of democratic regimes and practices. He has written *Democracies*, *Democracy in Plural Societies*, and other books and articles.

DIETER NOHLEN is Professor of Political Science at the University of Heidelberg, West Germany. His research interests have focused on comparative political analysis and development studies. He is the author, editor, and coeditor of many books, including *Die Wahl der Parlamente*, *Wahlen in Deutschland*, *Wahlsysteme der Welt*, *Handbuch der Dritten Welt*, and *Pipers Wörterbuch zur Politik*.

KARLHEINZ REIF is Lecturer of Political Science and Research Director of "European Electoral Studies" at the University of Mannheim, West Germany. He is the author of *Party Government in France* and of articles on European elections, European integration, and French politics, editor of *Ten European Elections*, and coeditor of *Activists, Delegates, Middle-Level Elites of European Political Parties*.

WILLIAM H. RIKER is Wilson Professor of Political Science at the University of Rochester. His books include *Liberalism Against Populism, An Introduction to Positive Political Theory,* coauthored with Peter Ordeshook, *The Theory of Political Coalitions, Federalism,* and *Democracy in the United States.* His current work concerns a formal theory of heresthetic (political manipulation) and rhetoric.

RICHARD ROSE is Director of the Centre for the Study of Public Policy at the University of Strathclyde, Glasgow. Since 1959 he has been writing about parties, elections, and voting behavior in Europe and the United States. Among the thirty books he has authored or edited are *Electoral Behavior: A Comparative Handbook, The International Almanac of Electoral History* (with Thomas T. Mackie), and *Do Parties Make a Difference?*

REIN TAAGEPERA is Professor of Social and Political Science at the University of California, Irvine. He has published articles on subjects like the size regularities of national legislatures, the cube law, the measurement of the proportionality of representation, and the effective number of parties in party systems. He is the coauthor of *The Baltic States.*

PETER J. TAYLOR is Senior Lecturer in the Department of Geography at the University of Newcastle upon Tyne. His field of specialization is political geography with special reference to electoral studies and the role of the state in the world economy. His many publications include *Geography of Elections,* coauthored with R. J. Johnston, and *Seats, Votes and the Spatial Organization of Elections,* coauthored with G. Gudgin. He is the editor of *Political Geography Quarterly.*

LEON WEAVER is a Professor in the School of Criminal Justice, College of Social Science, Michigan State University. He is a political scientist, specializing in security systems, personnel administration, and election systems and behavior. He was a member of the Freedom House mission to observe the elections in Zimbabwe, and he has written *Nonpartisan Elections in Local Government* and other books and articles.

J.F.H. (JACK) WRIGHT is President of the Proportional Representation Society of Australia. His professional work has been in the physical sciences, but he has been involved in the study of electoral methods for many years. He is the author of *Mirror of the Nation's Mind: Australia's Electoral Experiments* and other studies of electoral procedures.